TABLE OF CONTENTS

SPRING 2021
VOLUME 1, NUMBER 3

EDITOR
LEON WIESELTIER

MANAGING EDITOR
CELESTE MARCUS

———

PUBLISHER
BILL REICHBLUM

———

JOURNAL DESIGN
WILLIAM VAN RODEN

WEB DESIGN
HOT BRAIN

———

Liberties is a publication of the
Liberties Journal Foundation,
a nonpartisan 501(c)(3) organization based in Washington, D.C.
devoted to educating the general
public about the history, current
trends, and possibilities of culture
and politics. The Foundation
seeks to inform today's cultural
and political leaders, deepen
the understanding of citizens,
and inspire the next generation
to participate in the democratic
process and public service.

Engage
To learn more please go to
libertiesjournal.com

Subscribe
To subscribe or with any questions
about your subscription, please go to
libertiesjournal.com

ISBN 978-1-7357187-2-9
ISSN 2692-3904

———

EDITORIAL OFFICES
1604 New Hampshire Avenue NW
Washington, DC 20009

———

FOUNDATION BOARD
ALFRED H. MOSES, *Chair*
PETER BASS
BILL REICHBLUM

DIGITAL
@READLIBERTIES
LIBERTIESJOURNAL.COM

Liberties

GILLES KEPEL

The Murder
of Samuel Paty

I

It was Friday, October 16, 2020, the last day of school before
the All Saints' Day break at the Bois-d'Aulne middle school in
Conflans-Sainte-Honorine on the outskirts of Paris. In front of
the school, a man named Abdullakh Abouzeidovich Anzorov
decapitated Samuel Paty, a professor of history, geography, and
civics. The knife-wielding executioner was an eighteen-year-
old Chechen born in Moscow who had been granted political
refugee status with his family in France. In the minutes following the brutal act, the killer posted on his Twitter account
a photo of the victim's severed and bloodied head on the
pavement, along with this prepared comment:

In the name of Allah, the Most Merciful, the Most Merciful. From Abdullah, the Servant of Allah, to Marcon (sic), the leader of the infidels, I executed one of your dogs from hell who dared to belittle Muhammad (Sal'am); calm those like him before you are severely punished.

The teacher had already been the subject of an online harassment campaign that was begun on October 7 by Brahim Chnina, the father of a girl in one of his classes. The reason was that Samuel Paty had shown the students in his civics class a cartoon of the Prophet, depicted naked, that appeared in the satirical weekly *Charlie Hebdo*. It was a pedagogical exercise designed to stimulate reflections on freedom of expression and blasphemy. Paty had been careful to excuse anyone likely to be offended by the picture on religious grounds from the classroom. The father, however, accused him of singling out Muslims and ejecting them. With such an interpretation, clearly designed to be prejudicial, he wanted to prove that they had been purposely discriminated against. It turned out later that his daughter had not even been in class that day.

Chnina senior, born in Oran, Algeria, drawing in-work welfare and child subsidy payments for his six daughters, had a following on the Islamist web as an organizer of pilgrimages to Mecca and charitable activities connected to mosques. His half-sister had joined ISIS in Syria in 2014 and at the time was still detained in the Al-Hol camp in northeastern Syria at Rojava, a territory controlled by Kurdish forces, from which he had tried to repatriate her. His several hundred social media friends included many well-known activists of the Muslim Brotherhood and Islamo-leftist movements who lost no time sharing his message. In his first video on Facebook, posted on October 7, Chnina urged his Internet audience to mobilize — to ensure that, as he put it, "this scoundrel does not stay in public education." He also advised them to protest if they became aware of similar cases. The video was rebroadcast on the website of the Pantin Mosque, located in a large *banlieue* in Paris, to its nearly 100,000 subscribers, on the orders of its president, M'hammed Henniche. It went viral as far as Algeria and the rest of the Maghreb.

But this was just the beginning. Henniche, himself of Algerian origin, the son of a senior gendarmerie officer in Algeria and an erstwhile student at a suburban Parisian university, controlled the umbrella group for this mosque that had been founded in 2013. In 2001, in the Seine-Saint Denis department north of Paris, he had established the Islamic political lobby UAM 93 (Union of Muslim Associations, the numeral 93 being the postal code for Seine-Saint Denis), which claimed to be the first of its kind. Having claimed that the area's population consisted mostly of his coreligionists, he hit on the idea of creating a political pressure group modeled on CRIF, the Representative Council of Jewish Institutions of France. He used it to "monetize" Muslim votes in elections by pressuring candidates to take positions favorable to various Islamic causes in return for the group's support. It gave him control or influence over the issuance of building permits to mosques, the granting of subsidies to "cultural" or charitable associations endorsed by his group, the opening of Islamic charter schools, and more. The group even staged an annual UAM 93 *iftar* to break the fast of Ramadan, in imitation of the annual CRIF dinner. Local politicians rushed to it as if to some kind of *halal* popularity contest. UAM had an opportunistic attitude towards right and left, socialist, centrist, or communist ideologies. Patterned on the way Israel's Orthodox Jewish religious parties horse-traded their votes in the Knesset in return for subsidies to their yeshivas, Henniche could boast of making or unmaking mayors, department councilors, or members of Parliament in the "most Muslim department in France."

In October 2020, the Pantin Mosque occupied temporary quarters in a former sports hall that could accommodate up to 1,300 people. The cornerstone for a permanent building had been laid on Saturday, February 29, 2020, just prior to the municipal elections of March 15, in which the incumbent Socialist mayor Bertrand Kern was reelected during the first round. Close to Henniche, he had signed off on a long-term leasehold for the mosque as early as 2013, conditioned on its being open to all ethnic components of the local Muslim population. Hence the Friday imam, Ibrahim Doucouré, also known as Ibrahim Abou Talha, was of Malian origin, and had been educated in Dammaj, in northern Yemen, an area now occupied by Houthi rebels. This was where the principal local Salafist ideologue, Muqbil al Wadi'i, a lapsed Zaidi (local Shiite), had established his seminary, Dar al-Hadith, after he had joined the most virulent current of Wahhabism in neighboring Saudi Arabia in the 1990s. In Yemen, he preached an ultra-rigorist doctrine with a new convert's zeal, attracting many foreigners, including French-speaking converts. The rebel Houthi movement in fact was created in reaction to Muqbil's brand of fanatical proselytism. In 2015, when the rebels took over the area and then the capital at Sanaa, they destroyed the seminary's buildings and hunted down its students. Many of Muqbil's French-speaking disciples today are refugees in Birmingham, the nerve center of the main Islamist power networks in the United Kingdom. It also spawned a group of activists who edit the "Islamologists of France" website, on which they regularly pillory French academics in this field when they take a critical approach to their subject. Thus, on

9

October 9, 2020, two days after the Paty affair burst into the headlines, the site inveighed against two alleged academic "Islamophobes" as "ideologues of the new fascism" in the service of France's department of education, which was described on the website as "a secular Gestapo."

Another one of UAM 93's preoccupations was schools. On August 27, 2018, Hassen Farsadou, Henniche's heir-apparent in the Islamist lobby, which was now very active in Pantin, had made headlines of his own with a post on his Facebook page. It was a cut-and-pasted message from Davut Pasha, an Alsatian convert to Islam in Erdogan's Islamic AKP party in Turkey. Based since 2019 in the vicinity of Ankara, he acted as the chief drumbeater for Erdogan and his party's networks in the French-speaking Islamosphere:

> In 2004, the secularists removed the hijab from the school = you left your children in them.

> Between 2004 and 2015, the secularists launched a vendetta against bandanas, long skirts, school outings = you continued to leave your children to them.

> In 2015, secularists put eight-year-olds in front of prosecutors and implemented the ABCD [of equality, as opposed to gender stereotypes] = you continued to let them have your children.

> In 2018, the books to teach them masturbation are ready = you will continue to leave your children with them.

> Are you waiting for the school outings in Gay Pride to get your act together?

After his conversion, Davut Pasha, born David Bizet, had risen to become a high-ranking member of the European networks of Milli Görüş, or National Vision, a religious-political movement and the leading Turkish diaspora organization in Europe, and a key element of the Brotherist-Islamist network from which Erdogan issued. It is highly influential in Strasbourg's Turkish Eyüp Sultan mosque. Davut Pasha, who ran unsuccessfully in the municipal elections in Mulhouse in 2014 and in the parliamentary elections in 2017, can lay claim to having invented the "Islamic revisionist history of France," according to which the Muslim invasion of Provence from Andalusia, and the many subsequent raids between the eighth and tenth centuries, were the cornerstone of the modern French state, one allegedly hidden by Christian "falsification." He even claimed to have excavated its supposed remains, especially at Narbonne, the seat of a short-lived emirate. A video posted on many platforms under the title *When the Islamic State Was in France* illustrated this revisionism as early as 2015, when ISIS was at its peak. It was an attempt at fitting the quest for re-Islamizing France into the *longue durée* of a grand historical saga. Davut Pasha defines himself as "caliphalist." He regards Erdogan as the ideal contemporary incarnation of the Commander of the Faithful, exhorting him to invade Syria and Libya and thereby restore the Ottoman Empire within its erstwhile most extensive perimeter.

Farsadou, who, with the support of his mentor, provided a somewhat muddled justification for the posting of Davut Pasha's message, also presides over the Muslim association called Hope of French Youth based in the town of Aulnay-sous-Bois, also located in postal code 93. It sponsors a private charter school named after Philippe Grenier, a nineteenth-century physician who converted to Islam. In 1896, Grenier was elected the first Muslim member of the National Assembly, serving in that capacity until 1898. His career is ritually highlighted by the Islamist movement as prefiguring the inevitable conversion of the French, including the political elite, to Islam. The school opened its doors for the first time in premises rented from the municipality's right-wing and center-right local majority, headed by Bruno Beschizza, a hardline former police union official. Farsadou and Henniche had campaigned for him in the municipal election in 2014, helping him to defeat the socialist incumbent Gérard Ségura. UAM 93 had sanctioned the latter for reneging on his town's commitments to rent school premises to them.

This mixing of departmental policy and Islamist lobbying came to a halt, at least temporarily, on October 19, 2020, when the prefect of Seine-Saint-Denis department, Georges-François Leclerc, decreed a six-month closure of the Pantin mosque. The decree implemented a request by the Minister of the Interior, in reaction to Henniche's spreading Chnina's post about Samuel Paty. The Salafist imam Abu Talha, who had enrolled some of his children in an underground Islamist school in Bobigny that was closed on October 8 by the police, announced a few weeks later that he was "stepping back from [his] "activities" while "rejecting the complaints articulated in the prefectural decree." The decision was upheld three days later by the Administrative Court at a hearing attended by Leclerc. The Council of State gave its imprimatur for the decision. On November 25, 2020, Leclerc issued this statement: "The words of the leaders of the Great Pantin Mosque and the ideas or theories disseminated within it constitute a provocation linked to the risk of inciting acts of terrorism, violence, hatred or discrimination and are of a nature to justify closing the place of worship."

On the defensive in the face of an outcry, Henniche removed the Chnina video and deplored the teacher's beheading. He pointed out to the press that he had not relayed a second video that had been posted the following day. The previous evening the student's father had tried to stoke the Islamist mobilization and focus it on Samuel Paty by posting two statements in succession. They called for "contacting the CCIF" and doxing the "professor's address and name to tell him STOP." The CCIF, or the Collective Against Islamophobia in France, was founded in 2003. Its aim was to weld Muslims into a community solely defined by the discrimination to which its members would be subjected because of their religion — in a word, Islamophobia. This notion, characterized in CCIF propaganda campaigns as a "crime," is strangely based on the Islamist understanding of anti-Semitism. The Islamist movement considers anti-Semitism a strategy according to which Jews cleverly play the victim card to fend off any criticism of Israel and its policies. In one respect, though, the two cases differ: anti-Semitism advocates hatred of individuals, whereas "Islamophobia" — an English word that was manufactured in the wake of the Rushdie affair in the United Kingdom — works by stigmatizing and prohibiting any criticism of Islamic dogma — particularly its Brotherist, Salafist, and even jihadist interpretations.

The CCIF raised the victimization strategy to an art form in putting French society on the defensive whenever jihadist crimes or attacks were committed. A case in point was the attack in Nice on July 14, 2016, Bastille Day, when an Islamist terrorist killed eighty-six people by plowing into the celebrating crowd on the seaside Promenade des Anglais with a truck. The CCIF promptly mounted an intense campaign denouncing the "discrimination" suffered by Muslim women

13

for wearing a burkini on the beaches of the Riviera within a stone's throw of the killing committed a few weeks earlier. The aim clearly was to divert attention from the massacre. After the murder of Samuel Paty, CCIF similarly weaponized the publicity generated by the incident at the school: in order to arouse a victimization reflex in the Muslim community, it spun what happened in the classroom as an Islamophobic act.

It was aided in this effort by the political context, which was dominated by news of several major trials incriminating jihadism that were about to begin. These trials promised to expose how the ideology related to, and had benefited from, a much larger movement. The court cases included those pertaining to the *Charlie Hebdo* massacres, the killings at the Jewish HyperCacher supermarket, and the murders of two police officers of West Indian and Maghrebian origin, all on January 7-9, 2015. Two other courts would have Algerian nationals in the dock. In one, a student named Sid Ahmed Ghlam would go on trial for the murder of a young woman and an abortive plan instigated by ISIS to attack churches in Villejuif in April 2015. In the other, a former journalist, Farid Ikken, was charged with the attempted murder with a hammer of a policeman outside Notre Dame Cathedral in Paris in 2017. In addition, the trial of the terrorist in the abortive attack on the Thalys Brussels-Paris train in August, 2015 was scheduled to begin on November 16: it would see the Moroccan jihadist Ayoub al-Khazzani prosecuted for planning to assassinate passengers with an AK-47. The orders for this operation had come from the main actor behind the November 2015 attacks, the Belgian-Moroccan ISIS operative Abdelhamid Abaaoud. It was against this background that the Ministry of the Interior moved to dissolve CCIF by November 19. The association preempted the ministry's move by announcing on October 27 that it was disbanding and redeploying its activities abroad.

On October 8, the señior Chnina, accompanied by the veteran Islamist agitator Abdelhakim Sefrioui, met with his daughter's school principal to lodge a complaint against Samuel Paty for "spreading child pornography." The libel would earn the latter a summons to the police station. This meeting between a school headmistress and a well-known activist recalls one that took place when the issue of wearing the *hijab* in a public school first erupted in September, 1989 at the Gabriel-Havez middle school in Creil, another small town on the outskirts of Paris. There, too, the school's headmaster, Ernest Chénière, had been paid a visit by a delegation from the Union of Islamic Organizations of France, an association with Brotherist leanings, which advocated for the students in question and their parents. This campaign subsequently brought UOIF considerable fame in the French Islamist movement.

Sefrioui, a sixty-year-old born in Morocco, had staged multiple spectacular provocations starting in the 1980s. His goal, according to Tareq Oubrou, the imam of Bordeaux, also originally from the Alawite kingdom, was "fortifying the most fragile minds by systematically making Muslims victims of the Republic. These victimology theses managed to convince the most reckless who, as foreseeable, took action." In particular, Sefrioui created the Sheikh Yassine collective, named after the founder of Hamas killed in 2004 by Israel. He campaigned for Dieudonné, the anti-Semitic comedian and pro-Iranian regime activist, in his presidential run in 2007, as well as for the conspiracy theorist Alain Soral, and he harassed Hassen Chalghoumi, the imam of Drancy — another city in 93 — for his closeness to Jewish institutions. He also had agitprop experience in protests relating to schools on his resume: he had led the revolt against the administration of Saint-Ouen High School when it tried to prohibit the wearing of *jilbeb*, a garment with which Salafi women must cover themselves (a case also cited by Davut Pasha and Farsadou).

After the meeting on October 8 with the headmistress, Sefrioui taped an interview in the wooded environs of this suburban school, in which he claimed membership in the Council of Imams of France, an association founded in 1992. Its secretary-general, Dhaou Meskine, a preacher of Tunisian origin himself and close to the Brotherist movement, denied that Sefrioui was authorized to speak on the Council's behalf. He cited "differences over methods" and indicated he had ceased all contact with him ages ago. Sefrioui further announced that he had insisted to the headmistress on the need for "the exclusion of this scoundrel," meaning Samuel Paty. He threatened a mass protest outside the school to make his demand stick. He had already protested the humiliation of "Muslim students," which he described as a systematic policy in place "for five years." The involvement of this nationally known Islamic online agitator — with an "S" card on file, designating him as a serious threat to national security — escalated the incident to a higher level than the student's father alone could have achieved. It is true that Chnina was active on the Islamist web, but he had a less extensive following. On October 12, Sefrioui raised the heat even more when he broadcast a video of himself in front of the school, in which Chnina's daughter gave her version of events. Her story did not hold up under scrutiny: she displayed no first-hand knowledge of the events that she described.

II

The murder of Samuel Paty should be properly understood as an expression of what might be called atmospheric jihadism. Such terrorism dispenses with the murderer's prior membership in an al-Qaeda-type pyramidal organization or with affiliation with a network-based structure such as ISIS. It is galvanized instead by the spread of mobilization messages on social media: they trigger the crime. Atmospheric jihadism crystallizes in the encounter of a demand for action spread online by "entrepreneurs of rage" — in Bernard Rougier's phrase — and a terrorist offer in response to it. The connections no longer need to be formalized, notwithstanding that in Paty's case the police investigation revealed telephone contacts between the student's father and Abdullakh Anzorov. The parent posted the teacher's contact information on his Facebook page and the assassin found it. Reporting in *Le Monde* showed that the young Chechen had been combing through social networks since September 25, searching for someone who merited punishment for disrespecting Islam.

As it happened, on that date a certain Zaheer Hassan Mahmood, another refugee, this time from Pakistan, entered the picture. He came from a family sympathetic to a Pakistani radical Islamist organization back home, and was collecting public assistance after having falsely claimed to be an "unaccompanied minor" upon his arrival in France. He spoke no French and only broken English. He had been incensed by what he saw on the cover of *Charlie Hebdo* on the first day of the trial of the perpetrators of the massacre of the magazine's staff. Below the headline "All that for this," he saw, re-published, some of the offensive drawings that had set the attack in motion in 2015. Mahmood obtained a meat cleaver shaped like the cutlasses brandished in viral videos on social media by Urdu- language protesters in Karachi and Lahore who had marched to demand the beheading of the *Charlie Hebdo* cartoonists. Of low intellect and means, Mahmood nevertheless had managed to go online and find the address where the attack on the weekly's office had taken place (the editors had moved since then to a secret location). Having made his way to the building, he randomly singled out two people working in a film production company on the premises, neither with any connection to the case. He grievously injured them by blows to the head, without killing, much less decapitating, them. With no escape plan, stunned by his own act, he was easily and quickly apprehended. Subsequent investigation into his Parisian surroundings, where he lived in a crack house while awaiting an order expelling him from French territory, failed to uncover any accomplices or network affiliations.

Abdullakh Abouzeidovich Anzorov, Paty's killer, turned out to have more elaborate jihadist connections. The testimonies taken in his circle indicated that he had gravitated to a radical Salafist vision. He had openly proclaimed it on his Facebook page and Twitter account at least six months, if not a year, before the crime. He evinced a horror of all promiscuity with the other sex; he hated atheists, Christians, and "deviant" Muslims, such as Sufi mystics or Saudi Crown Prince Mohammed Bin Salman; he took an interest in international Islamist issues. He admired the Taliban and he worshipped Erdogan. The latter was swathed in a nimbus of neo-caliphate glory after recently ordering Istanbul's Hagia Sophia to be converted into a mosque. Moreover, in the Chechen's native Caucasus, Erdogan had also just sided with Azerbaijan in its war against Christian Armenia.

Anzorov was also plugged into the French online Islamist milieu. On October 7, on the day that Chnina posted his first video, Anzorov voiced his support for Idriss Sihamedi, the founder and president of BarakaCity, an Islamist NGO in France, who had been indicted for cyberstalking and threatening the former *Charlie* journalist Zineb El Rhazoui. The NGO would be dissolved by the Council of Ministers on October 28. Its demise was affirmed by the Council of State on November 25, on the grounds that "the words of its president may be attributed to it and constitute discourses fomenting discrimination, hatred or violence sufficient to justify dissolution." Anzorov kept silent on the early developments of the Conflans affair, probably because he wanted to keep his murderous plot away from police surfing the web, and deleted his posts starting on October 11. Yet he and Chnina were said to have exchanged phone calls, their substance still shrouded in mystery. He also had online contacts with two jihadists in the Idlib zone in Syria. Between the moment he cut off Samuel Paty's head and when the police shot him dead, he messaged one of them in Russian.

He seems to have been spurred into action by Zaheer Mahmood's attack. At first, he cyberstalked young people suspected of mocking the Prophet or Islam on social media. In all probability, this is when he stumbled on the accusations leveled against his future victim. He nurtured his own plan to "avenge the Prophet," drawing on the means with which his specific cultural tradition had equipped him. In the monstrous execution of his crime, two actions were particularly telling: first, his bribing, with three hundred euros, of some of the middle school's students to identify their teacher, so that he could be sure of his victim; second, the terrifyingly professional way in which he carried out the beheading, and, without missing a beat, messaging the Russian-speaking jihadist in Idlib. The first act links the murderer more to the criminal underworld than to standard jihadist practice; the second, to a rite of passage by Chechen teenagers for whom cutting off a sheep's head opens the door to manhood (as opposed to slaughtering it the way Muslims generally do). It explains how someone like Anzorov could perform the counterintuitive motions inflicted in this particular kind of savagery. This skill cannot be acquired only by watching the many beheading videos that ISIS had been putting online since 2014. At most, these might have proved addictive, or may even have trivialized this killing method in the collective Islamist consciousness. (A Tunisian jihadist named Brahim Issaoui, who struck in Nice thirteen days later, failed in his attempt to behead his victims.)

The Chechen population in France, estimated at nearly 50,000, arrived mainly as political refugees after the war of 1994-1996 and especially after the war of 1999-2009. Both of those bloody conflicts had pitted local separatists, whose ranks jihadists had gradually come to dominate, against Russian troops. Despite its relatively small size compared to other segments of the Muslim immigrant population, the French Chechen community made headlines. Some were frequently employed in "security" and known for extreme violence. Others controlled narcotics trafficking (and security for the properties of Russian oligarchs) on the French Riviera, one of their major stomping grounds. Some Chechen "protectors" took the drug business over by preying on the traditional Maghreb drug-trafficking channels, a phenomenon that gradually spread across France.

In the week of June 16, 2020, for example, this takeover spiraled into four days of spectacular clashes in Dijon, the

Burgundian metropolis. It began with a raid on Moroccans in the context of a conflict of honor. It brought together hundreds of Chechen thugs mobilized on social media from all over France and neighboring countries. In their muscle cars, they patrolled an entire working-class neighborhood, while the police kept its distance. The press was dumbfounded. The frenzy of violence came as a major shock to most of Dijon's citizenry, who were exposed for the first time to these mores and habits of some of the people in their midst. The explosion happened just four months before the beheading of Samuel Paty in Conflans-Sainte-Honorine. Mediation between these two Sunni communities that totally shut out the French state authorities in charge of public order finally took place at the local "Fraternity" mosque. It was provided by its imam Mohammed Ateb, the regional representative of the Brotherist UOIF, in concert with his Chechen counterpart from Dole, a city in the nearby Jura department. The reconciliation was sealed against the backdrop of the Eid-el-Kebir holiday by the Chechens offering the Moroccans three sheep, transactional gifts immediately put to the sword in sacrifices of atonement.

Abdullakh Anzorov, disqualified by a record of delinquency from working as a security guard like his father, was barely of age when he committed his crime. One of his countrymen, Khamzat Azimov, under "radicalization" watch since 2016, had previously carried out a jihadist knife attack in the Opera district in Paris on May 12, 2018. He killed a passerby, only to be shot dead by police. ISIS, which still had a spokesman then, claimed "credit" for his act, despite the absence of any affiliation. In any case, the Chechen jihad, less notorious than its Afghan parallel, has an equivalent claim to fame in Islamist hagiography: in the opening pages of *Knights Under the Banner of the Prophet*, the manifesto that he published online around 1997, Ayman al-Zawahiri, Bin Laden's successor as the head of what was left of al-Qaeda in 2020, had put the Taliban and these fighters in the Caucasus on the same plane, arguing that both had established the first two "caliphates" on liberated territory, which would eventually extend to the entire planet.

Before he was shot, Anzorov sent his last message to someone in a Chechen brigade stationed in Idlib under the protection of Turkish forces. The Chechens fighting in the Syrian jihad were notorious for their violence. In Russian folklore, Chechens are known for their fierce secular resistance to St. Petersburg's troops. From that epoch came the dark legend of the "Chechen villain crawling on the riverbank, sharpening his knife," as depicted in a poem by Lermontov that was turned into a famous lullaby. The bogeyman of the *tchétchènskie golovorezy* (Chechen head cutters) runs through the modern history of Russia ever since the Tsarist wars, as described by Tolstoy in his novella *Hadji Murad* (which also celebrates the chivalrous character of the eponymous hero). A steady drumbeat of beheadings of Moscow's soldiers also marked Putin's wars. These unspeakable images were posted in profusion on social media to terrorize the latest Russian adversary.

After the assassination of the teacher at the school in Bois-d'Aulne, France was in shock. Even Jean-Luc Mélenchon, the leader of the leftist La France Insoumise (France Unbowed) and a fierce critic of Emmanuel Macron, asserted that there was a "Chechen problem." It earned him accusations of stereotyping from his political opponents — despite his having taken part in the "demonstration against Islamophobia" on November 10, 2019 in the heart of Paris, organized by the CCIF. Its ex-director, Marwan Muhammad, had galvanized the crowd at the event on the Avenue de la République with shouts of *Allahu Akbar*. Mélenchon perfectly exemplifies the problem for the French left: he must support both his MPs from Seine-Saint-Denis who need the Islamic votes mobilized by UAM 93 and an electoral base in which teachers such as their colleague in the Bois-d'Aulne middle school figure heavily. He must find a way to reconcile Islamism and leftism in his movement and in his opposition to Macron.

The murder of Samuel Paty buttressed the vision developed by the President of the French Republic in a speech two weeks earlier at Les Mureaux, a commune in the same department of Yvelines. In it, Macron advocated a legislative overhaul to better combat "Islamist separatism." It was in in the nearby village of Magnanville, on June 13, 2016, that a policeman and his wife were stabbed to death in front of their young child at their home. The crime had been committed by Larossi Abballa, a jihadist of Moroccan origin. Recently released from prison, he was linked to and communicated online with Rachid Kassim, an ex-rapper and social educator born in Oran, Algeria, and formerly based in central France at Roanne, who at this time was running ISIS "external operations" from Raqqa, the erstwhile capital of the "caliphate" in Syria.

Aside from the similarity between the two murders, even down to the murder weapon, the modus operandi had changed from June 2016 to October 2020. The first killing had been amplified by Larossi Abballa's calling on his "Muslim brothers" to kill a French academic (more specifically, the author of this essay) and some journalists whose names he exposed to public condemnation on Facebook Live before he, too, was shot dead. With the assassination of Samuel Paty in Conflans, as I noted earlier, the network-based jihad that culminated in ISIS gave way to an atmospheric jihadism, for which it provided a model. To prepare a case against the perpetrators of the attacks

23

of the previous era, which the public discovered only after they were carried out, required lengthy clandestine operations of the police. Such had been the case with the slaughters of January 2015 — whose trial was unfolding in the fall of 2020 and providing the backdrop for the crimes committed first by Zaheer Mahmood, then Abdullakh Anzorov, and then Brahim Issaoui. But today jihadist crimes are preceded by an explicit and public "cultural disavowal" engineered by "entrepreneurs of rage": they are not prepared in secret, they have already been advocated on social media. This is how a teacher came to be singled out for Internet users as a scapegoat to rage against — and for one of them to assassinate.

This change means that the struggle of the secular French Republic must not be limited to after-the-fact criminal justice. It must instead fight an ethical battle against an ideology which rends the very fabric of French society by distinguishing between "believers" (*mou'minin*) and "nonbelievers" (*kouffar*), between "Salafist" (*salafi*) and "infidel" (*mouchrik*), "apostate" (*mourtadd*), "hypocrite" (*mounafiq*), and "deviant" (*mounharif*). These rigid categories are anathemas of exclusion: they propound a doctrinaire separatism that dehumanizes the designated enemy and forbids making a society with him until he submits to the faith or is put to death. This desire to secede from the surrounding citizenry was the founding impulse of Salafism. Nowadays, five decades after the upheaval of values from nationalism to Islamism, precipitated in the Muslim world by the October 1973 war, this agenda has been taken up by a spectrum of militants ranging from Brotherism to jihadism.

Known in the West as the Yom Kippur War, since it was launched on that Jewish holiday to maximize the effect of surprise on the Israeli enemy, it was referred to in the Muslim World as the Ramadan War, since it coincided with the month of fasting; and in order for Muslim soldiers to be fed in combat, the *ulema* pronounced it a holy war — a jihad, which abrogates daytime fast. This theological elevation of the war reinforced the feeling that it was a Saudi and Islamic victory — as the army of the Jewish state had to end its counter-offensive on the order of Western powers who could not withstand the oil embargo decreed at the initiative of King Faysal of Saudi Arabia. From those days came the tilt toward a general Islamization of politics, leading to the use of concepts drawn from the Scriptures to decipher events or engage in action. For instance, what Macron called "separatism" matches what Islamists and jihadists call in Koranic parlance *al-wala wal-ba-ra'a'*, "alliance and rupture." In the Salafized patois of the "conquered territories of Islamism," to use the title of Bernard Rougier's recent book, it is rendered as "allegiance and disavowal." It is all about implementing an exclusive and total submission to dogma in its strictest and literal definition, as defined by the self-styled "orthodox." It means "allying" only with those who share this ideology and breaking with the rest by "disavowing" them.

The speech in which Emmanuel Macron spoke about "Islamist separatism" caused an uproar in France's political Islamist movement and in the Muslim world. This happened despite the crime perpetrated in Conflans less than two weeks later, which corroborated Macron's analysis. Macron's opponents and detractors used the tactic of shifting the burden of proof back on the French president by accusing him of Islamophobia — of discrimination against all Muslims, while the "separatists" promoted themselves as their representatives par excellence. This move was facilitated by a linguistic peculiarity: the term "Islamist" as such does not exist in the Arabic or Turkish languages, nor is it generally known there.

The Murder of Samuel Paty

It was originally coined in the 1980s by European scholars of contemporary Islam to describe "political Islam movements" that originated in the aforementioned shift in the wake of the Yom Kippur/Ramadan war in 1973. Its literal translation in Arabic, *Islamawi*, is understood only by a few intellectuals who manage to distance themselves from the prevalent religious dogma. And so it was that the expression used by Macron came to be falsely rendered as "Islamic terrorism" in the Muslim world, easily letting it be construed by those who had a political interest in such a misunderstanding as an aggression against all of the Prophet's followers.

In this charged context, the last week of October in 2020 saw the tensions and the commingling of French and international issues reach a climax. In the forefront was Erdogan's Turkey. It set the tempo for the pan-Islamic campaign against Macron, to bolster its own president's neo-caliphal stature after he had rededicated Hagia Sophia as a mosque. Noticeably absent were leaders of the Muslim world, even those participating in the Abraham Accords and opposed to the Brotherist-Shiite axis. They might have been capable of swimming against the tide, but they held back out of fear of being tagged as Islamophobes.

Thursday, October 29, 2020, marked the Feast of Mouloud, as the Prophet's nativity is known in the Maghrebian dialects (*al-mawlid an-nabawi,* in classical Arabic). Its date is calculated by the Hegirian (lunar) calendar, and thus each year occurs ten days earlier than the previous year. As a symbolic date, it plays a key role in the spirituality of the Muslim masses in North Africa. They revere the figure of the Prophet in particular because it lets them feel charismatically and vibrantly close to him — unlike the scriptural Islam of the scholars (and that of the Salafists, now in digitized form). At 8:29 a.m. on that day, Brahim Issaoui, twenty-one years old, an illegal Tunisian immigrant who had just set foot on French soil after crossing the nearby Italian border, killed three people inside the Basilica of Notre-Dame de l'Assomption in Nice.

This neo-Gothic building's portal opens onto the city's major thoroughfare, Avenue Jean-Médecin, now a pedestrian mall with a streetcar line. Its apses back onto a public garden filled mainly with mothers garbed in *jilbeb* and their children tagging along. Beyond this garden lies Nice's "Islamic quarter" of Notre-Dame, which ironically takes its name from the Basilica. Two blocks further, on the ground floor of 12 rue de Suisse, the first mosque opened in the heart of Nice has operated for the past twenty years. In January 2019, the city, which owns the building, issued a notice of non-renewal of the mosque's lease to the imam of the Chechen community and the president of the management association. This place of worship, too cramped for the crowd of worshippers who spilled over into the street at prayers, was no stranger to controversy. In 2011, Nissa Rebella, the rightist group in Nice, whose leader regularly runs in the municipal elections on the National Front ticket, had plastered placards bearing the words "of the Stoning," "of the Burqa," and "of the Muslim Brotherhood" over existing street signs. In 2013, he sued the municipality for undercharging rent on the mosque's lease. In 2020, the prayer hall closed, only to relocate nearby, according to a sign on the door. But the main Salafist stores selling Arabic and French books promoting "allegiance and disavowal," as well as diverse "Islamic outfits," and other attire, remain in the area. They equip the movement's followers with the paraphernalia for

27

The Murder of Samuel Paty

flaunting their distinctive identity around the neighborhood. (Alpes-Maritimes, of which Nice is the capital, ranked second among French departments in the number of departures to the ISIS "caliphate" in Syria between 2014 and 2017.)

The Basilica of Notre-Dame is located a few hundred meters from the main train station, where surveillance cameras captured Brahim Issaoui changing clothes before making his way to the scene of his crime. He was "de-silhouetting," a common practice in the lead-up to a crime but usually not done in public view. He had slept the night before in a stairwell on a piece of cardboard, which he had shown his mother, at home in Tunisia in the Sfax suburbs, via cell phone video, also telling her that he had made a contact in Nice. Soon afterward he rampaged through the church, slitting the throat of a sixty-year old woman, then striking at the sacristan's throat, before slashing a young Brazilian mother. All three died of their wounds. Intercepted by the municipal police, Issaoui was shot and wounded while chanting *"Allahu Akbar"* in a trance before being transported unconscious to the hospital.

An Italian Red Cross certificate found on him indicated that Issaoui had landed at Lampedusa on September 20 on a boat in distress filled with North African migrants, who had to be rescued by an Italian ship. After a two-week Covid19 quarantine on board, an NGO's boat took him to the mainland, depositing him in the port of Bari, in southeastern Italy. There, on October 9, he was put in a screening center with eight hundred other illegals. Under order to leave Italian territory, he was released from the center due to a lack of space. Here the trail goes cold. There is every reason to believe that, like most Tunisian illegals, he took the train to the border town of Vintimille, sneaked into France, made his way to Menton, and from there proceeded to Nice.

Little is known of his personal history. He came from a poor family of eleven children, from a village on the outskirts of Kairouan, the Tunisian city that is an Islamic metropolis and the site of its most prestigious and ancient mosque. The family emigrated to an underprivileged suburb of Sfax, the economic capital on the country's southern coast, where the local Diwan Radio podcast reported on the crime in Nice the day after it was committed. The signs that this is a rough and blighted neighborhood abound: young people in tracksuits emblazoned with counterfeit logos hanging out aimlessly amid unfinished construction projects; the killer's parents, brothers, sisters, and friends expressing themselves in a thick working-class dialect with rudimentary vocabulary. From them it emerged that Brahim Issaoui, like everyone else, eked out a living in the gray economy, in his case by occasionally repairing mopeds. He later increased his income by smuggling fuel from neighboring Libya and offering it for sale in glass bottles at roadsides throughout the country's south.

His family and friends described him as a young man who conscientiously attended the mosque and also had a taste for hashish and alcohol, testifying to the kind of cultural and moral schizophrenia often found in such working-class environments. If his father approved of his leaving for France to escape the misery, his mother worried because he did not "know French." Nice is in fact France's "most Tunisian" city, with immigrants from that country constituting the majority among the population of Maghreb nationals. Apart from a claim on the day of the murder that was quickly dismissed as bogus, no jihadist network claimed "credit" for what Issaoui did. Whatever the complicities or the motivations for this act, the Nice attack is one more instance of atmospheric jihadism in Europe after the abandonment of militants by ISIS and its network. This was confirmed when the police announced in mid-November that they had found a photo of Abdullakh Anzorov on Brahim Issaoui's phone.

But what to make of this triple murder committed by an individual who had spent just a few hours in France? Clearly he could not have been exposed to any "Islamophobic discrimination" in France sufficient to set him off on a murder spree. It conjures up instead a worrisome link between the dynamics emerging from North Africa — poverty brought to a head by the Covid-19 pandemic and the collapse of the price of oil, the dereliction of the political order, clandestine emigration, the force of an Islamist ideology radicalized by the Salafist doctrine of "allegiance and disavowal" — and those now busily roiling the social and cultural cohesion of Europe.

III

On September 10, 2020, in Cairo, the Arab League condemned Turkey's occupation of parts of western Libya, Syria, and Northern Iraq, claiming that it evoked the dark hours of the Ottoman colonization of Arab lands prior to 1918. That solemn declaration somewhat tamped down the zeal of the Brotherist-Shiite axis in the Middle East that had been excited by the Turkish president's bellicose policies. In this situation, Erdogan sought to break his isolation by taking his own turn as an "entrepreneur of rage." He proceeded to stoke his anti-French campaign, with which he had initially inflamed part of the Muslim world by coming out against *Charlie Hebdo's* republication of the cartoons on September 3. He now followed up with broadsides against Macron's denunciation of "Islamist separatism" in his speech in Les Mureaux and in his tribute to Samuel Paty on October 21 in the courtyard of the Sorbonne, where the president declared that France would never repudiate the caricatures.

Erdogan's self-interested pivot, his renewed campaign against France, was aided by the collapse of Islamic studies in France, which had been reinforced by a cast of senior bureaucrats convinced that, to quote Olivier Roy's aphorism, "knowing Arabic is of no use in understanding what is happening in the *banlieues*." (To which I would add: or anywhere else.) France's representatives were not up to the task of explaining to the Muslim world what Macron's envisaged measures actually meant. They stymied the production of any translation of the presidential words into this "useless" language. None materialized until Macron bravely decided to express himself on Al Jazeera with a quality dubbing in Arabic. But by that time the allegations of Islamophobia had been revved up. Invoking universal principles, a phalanx of critics, ranging from Iran's Supreme Leader to the *Financial Times*, had won over international opinion to the view the real problem in France is the hatred of Muslims.

Yet this consensus of ignorance between the executive and a few asinine academics overshadowed the fundamental problem: as I have noted, the term "Islamist" — which in French connotes political Islam, and particularly the Muslim Brotherhood culturally permeated with a radicalized Salafism — has no functional equivalent in Arabic. The word that comes closest, *Islamawi*, proved to be useless in the crisis, since it is devoid of shades of meaning that would matter to Muslims. And the notion of "separatism" — for which Arabic actually does have meaningful equivalents, ranging from *fitna* (sedition, especially of a denominational nature, usually in the phrase *fitna ta'ifiyya*) to *bara'a* (rupture with, or disavowal of, nonbelievers) on which Salafist ideology assiduously bases itself — requires a significant effort of explanation to make the link between the two lingusitic registers. This was why Macron's criticism of "Islamist separatism" was widely portrayed as a questioning of Muslims generally ("Islamist" being rendered simply and inaccurately by *Islami*, or "Islamic"). This distortion was originated by political and propagandistic organizations and associations in France, such as the "humanitarians" of BarakaCity and the CCIF beating the drums of "French Islamophobia."

After Macron's speech, and in the aftermath of the murder of Samuel Paty, the Anglo-Saxon press, always anxious about being on the wrong side of identity and inclusion, and always eager to denounce French-style secularism, were quick to chime in. They ignored the momentous fact that the French approach to religious freedom implied also freedom from religion — the emancipation of the individual from clerical domination, which is not a small problem, as honest members of devout religious communities will attest. Instead, in the name of certain Protestant or Jewish perspectives, they accused Macron and his predecessors of acting in the nefarious traditions of the anti-Huguenot dragonnades of Louis XIV or Pétain's anti-Semitism. According to this view, the freedom to blaspheme, one of the fundamental accomplishments of the Enlightenment and a central feature of any open society, amounted only to the heartless and hegemonic injunction to "spit on the religion of the weak." This stupidity is now professed by our Islamo-leftists, post-colonials, and intersectionals, who hold the high ground in the universities and interdict any critical approach to Islam — which, like Christianity, Judaism, and Hinduism, and for that matter atheism, agnosticism, and freemasonry, is a faith in which one can distinguish denominations and persuasions, many different schools of theology and currents of practice, various forms and styles of piety, including the spirit of confrontation and intolerance as well as the spirit of integration and respect.

The general ignorance of Arabic languages and cultures, of the diversity of idioms and traditions in Muslim lands and communities, has led to a colossal irony: some on the left have invented an image of Islam with a structure identical to the image propagated by the extreme right, only it is inverted. Where the latter demonize all Muslims and their religion as an ontologically negative religious entity, the former are content to turn such generalizations into a positivity as lenient as it is essentialist. They would be well advised to ponder what happened to their Turkish counterparts, who, at the start of this century, made a hero of Erdogan by crediting him with democratic virtues and cultural authenticity in facing down the "secular fascist" heirs of Ataturk. These partisans ended up rotting in his prisons, suppressed and tortured like Communist fellow travelers of yore — useful idiots whom the Stalinist regime thanked for their willful blindness by locking them up in the Gulag.

The sensational trial of the murderers of January 7-9, 2015 should have started to heal the deep wounds that they inflicted on French society. It should have been a kind of Nuremberg tribunal for this ideology and its crimes. Unfortunately, it ended up being eclipsed first by the Covid-19 outbreak and the ensuing lockdown, and then by the campaign against "French Islamophobia." The objective of that campaign was to prevent anybody from shining a light on the continuum between the radical Islamist "entrepreneurs of rage" and the jihadist assassins acting on their ideas. This strategy of diversion was similar to the one that the Collective Against Islamophobia in France successfully employed in the summer of 2016 to becloud the Bastille Day massacre in Nice, when they preferred instead to focus on the hostile "Islamophobic" reactions provoked by burkini-clad bathers on the beach above which the slaughter had taken place.

All this tumult, all this violence, was provoked by the cartoons of the Prophet that *Charlie Hebdo* republished at the opening of the trial. And so it is important to add a further reflection. Criticism is not censorship: it is a social and intellectual duty. Once we recognize that there exists a right to blaspheme, nothing prevents us from making an ethical judgment about a drawing. The freedom to publish it, which must be fiercely defended, does not amount to an endorsement of its content. Nor does it prohibit us from criticizing it — no matter the solidarity expressed with the *Charlie Hebdo* staff that was decimated by the jihadist killers in 2015, and with the victims of those who followed them in 2020.

A day after the cartoons that became an excuse for murder originally appeared in the September 19, 2012 issue of *Charlie Hebdo*, I went on French public radio. In a discussion with the journal's lawyer, I expressed my revulsion at this mediocre sketch, and our exchange went downhill from there. Although the journal's cover title "Muhammad: A Star Is Born" referred to the Prophet, I saw its cartoon less as blasphemy and more as an attack on human dignity in the form of a degrading depiction of believers of whatever kind, whose faith the atheist in me respects even if he cannot share it. Eight years and dozens of deaths later, I take back nothing from my view at the time. Jihadist terrorism and its breeding ground of Islamist separatism pose a serious and wrenchingly complicated problem for our societies that neither foolishness nor ignorance will contribute to solving. We have been called upon to be firm about many things.

INGRID ROWLAND

The Unsettled Dust

SICILIANS AND GREEKS

To celebrate the hundredth anniversary of the birth of the Sicilian writer Leonardo Sciascia, the Italian newspaper *La Repubblica* is reissuing his books, one a week for twenty weeks. In theory, I have read most of them: when I first lived in Italy, I used to buy them at the newsstand in Rome's Termini station just before boarding a train to Siena or Florence, back when trips that now take an hour and a half took a good four hours and the conductors would announce our arrival in person, out loud, their Tuscan accent pleasantly interrupting Sciascia's Sicilian reveries. At that stage of my life, I had never been to Sicily. My Italian was little better than restaurant Italian. It didn't matter: Sciascia's ability to evoke an atmosphere and a psychology penetrated all the clouds of unknowing, so that the ugly hotel and corrupt politicians of *Todo Modo* and the Maltese forger of *The Council of Egypt* took up permanent lodging in my memories among other fantastic imagined people and places.

Reading the books again, after years in Italy, is almost like reading them afresh. Most of all, perhaps, Sciascia's present has become a historical past; for readers in their twenties today, the tangible realities of life in the 1960s and 1970s are no longer accessible experiences, not only the long-altered political and economic situations but also the tiny details of existence: telephones that took special grooved tokens, the smell of tobacco and sweat on a crowded bus, the formality, and the modesty, of everyday dress. And with a knowledge of Sicily, I can see now how Sciascia's urge to tell a certain kind of story has emerged from the same sere, eroded volcanic landscape as the works of Luigi Pirandello and Andrea Camilleri, a terrain where implacable nature has contended in combat stupendous with deep-rooted culture: the region around Agrigento, once the great Greek city of Akragas, its splendid panorama now blighted by cheap, shoddy high-rises, yet still one of the most beautiful, mysterious places on earth. Now it is easier to catch the barrage of sly, oblique comments Sciascia makes as an author. They passed me by on first reading, and not only because my Italian was so raw; only older people have the restraint to express their insights with such world-weary economy. I missed Sciascia's caustic wit back then not only because I grew up in another country, but also because I was young, or distracted by the fact of riding on a train: interrupted by the ticket collector, or by the luminous view out the window of twilight in the heart of Tuscany.

The best books need to be read in a variety of ways, and reward reading more than once: both in a rush of adrenaline and slowly, closely; as a young person and as an older person; when times are hard and when times are hard again, perhaps under different conditions of hardship, perhaps hewing to the same old unchanging patterns. When my professors in graduate school decided to challenge me by giving me four months to study for my doctoral exams rather than the usual year, I had to read one Greek tragedy a day for a month and add in a second tragedy a couple of times a week. (I reserved the double-headers for Euripides' crazy melodramas.) I split another month between all the comedies of Aristophanes and Thucydides' history of the war between Athens and Sparta, reading so fast that I began to dream in ancient Greek, and the little words, called particles, that signal the nuances of an ancient Greek sentence took on the vividness of living language. I had been to Athens and Sparta when I read Thucydides in Rome for my exams, in a state of abject panic and manic illumination, not quite aware yet of the extent to which his history finds its real dramatic center in Sicily, in Syracuse, a place as lush as Agrigento is pitiless. One of Sciascia's Agrigentine characters declares that people from the province of Syracuse are stupid, implying that life is too easy in that southeastern corner of Sicily. But fertility brings its own perils, as Syracuse has discovered time and again: perils like an Athenian fleet appearing on the horizon with plans to invade you before moving on to conquer Carthage, back in the days (415 BCE) when the Athenian fleet was the most powerful in the Mediterranean world. Two years after that glittering epiphany, however, Thucydides shows us the remnants of the Athenian army (the ships of the fleet have all been captured, sunk, or incinerated) as they beat a miserable retreat through the farmlands and gullies to the west of Syracuse. When the stragglers come to the river Assinaros, they are so exhausted and so thirsty that they swarm into the water to drink and there they are cut down *en masse* by the Syracusan cavalry, greedily gulping down the river's water even when it turns red with their blood and muddy from the churning of horses' hooves. Thucydides had long since suggested that the war between Athens and Sparta had become one great atrocity, but this scene is the most atrocious of them all. The survivors of the slaughter were thrown into the quarries of Syracuse, in the shadow of the theatre where Athenian tragedies played, then and now, and prisoners who could quote the latest play of Euripides were allegedly released. Almost exactly two hundred years later, a very smart Syracusan, Archimedes, would be struck down in his home by an invading Roman soldier after holding off the Roman fleet for two years with the world's most ingenious array of catapults, another utter foolishness of war.

One of the great joys of rereading any book at a later stage of life is the freedom to draw one's own conclusions. It is easier to read freely when fortified by the twin bastions of age and familiarity, two immemorial guarantees of authority. (One of the professors who eventually sat on my Ph.D. committee complained that as a graduate student I wrote like someone looking back on a long life in the classics, but I was only twenty-three.) But the only way any of us reads at all is by starting from nothing, and sometimes the absence of preconceptions about what we read can be as liberating as long intimacy. Insight, after all, is unpredictable. Anwar el-Sadat discovered his mission as a statesman with the help of an article he read in a prison copy of *Reader's Digest* (see Jehan Sadat, *A Woman of Egypt*, p. 86).

Last semester, confronted with Thucydides for the first time, one of my students asked why the ancient Greeks were so violent. That same question has led to one of the most powerful recent retellings of a Greek tragedy: Yaël Farber's *Molora*, which appeared in 20007, takes the *Oresteia* of Aeschylus, transposes its action from Bronze Age Greece to South Africa during the years of the Truth and Reconciliation Commission, and has a chorus of Xhosa women preempt the trilogy's climactic act of vengeance, Orestes' murder of his mother Clytemnestra (but not until Orestes has done a spectacular sword dance around a bonfire). The same motive lies behind Plato's decision to expel the epic and dramatic poets from his ideal Republic, for by showing the gods and heroes as violent and base, these writers have set a bad example for the young. His discussion has often been condemned as censorship endorsed by a hidebound conservative, though it is hard to see what is conservative about an ideal state that abolishes the family and grants equal rights to women. It may be more useful to read these sections of the *Republic* as an account of Plato's own struggles with deciding what and how to write. As a young man, he had composed tragedies, but the political turmoil that engulfed Athens at the end of the war with Sparta drove him to abandon traditional literature. Instead, he invented an entirely new kind of drama: the philosophical dialogue.

As for the expulsion of the poets, I came over to Plato's side after hearing a lecture some years ago by a distinguished classicist. He began by conjuring up the climactic scene on which the *Iliad* hinges: in what is in effect a journey through hell, King Priam of Troy has crept by night across the battle lines to beg the Greek hero Achilles to give up the body of his slain son, Hector, which Achilles has been dragging behind his chariot, an act that even the violent Greeks found repugnant. For a moment Achilles sees his own father mirrored in the elderly king, and agrees to release Hector—but warns Priam to withdraw quickly because he might change his mind at any moment. "This," proclaimed the venerable scholar, "is what it means to be a man." Women, it was easy to surmise, were incapable of rising to similar heights of manhood in his view, that is, to attain the twinge of empathy that shot through the shaggy breast of that capricious brute Achilles, and induced him, finally, to leave off mutilating the corpse he had been playing with for days. All I could think of in that instant was Plato imitating my undergraduate classics professor, Harry Carroll, who once shook his finger at a favorite student who had used the word "pissed" in his presence and repeated, "Out, out, out, out, out," until the student had backed out the door of Harry's office.

Like Farber's *Molora*, Plato's *Republic* suggests that we might hold ourselves, not just men, to a higher standard of existence than Achilles' temporary exchange of compassion for slaughter, and he does so by wielding the mighty weapon of humor. In the third book of the *Republic*, Socrates and Plato's sardonic brother Adeimantus sling an impressive series of poetic quotations at each other, each one beautiful of form and pernicious in its implications for the basic character of gods and mortals. As the crescendo rises, we readers end up being swept along with the two of them into agreeing that Homer's best — or, better, the atavistic "this is a man" reading of Homer's best — is simply not a worthy model to live by. Socrates and Adeimantus are men who nurture other aspirations than snatching women, sacking cities, and skewering each other with spears (though they both did distinguished military service for Athens), and they prefer gods who behave in ways

40

more evidently in harmony with the order of the universe than the capricious deities of Homer. Achilles may have sung "the glories of men" to the percussive rhythm of his lyre, but he was mean and slightly slow-witted, and so are the Homeric gods.

Interestingly, the poetic citations that Socrates and Adeimantus throw at each other often differ from the texts we have now. Did Plato and his contemporaries read slightly different versions of Aeschylus and Homer than we do today, or did the philosopher enjoy catching, and immortalizing, his teacher and his big brother showing off their prodigious memories while slyly noting that memories are fallible? It is tempting to imagine Plato reveling in his elders' senior moments and Freudian slips as he shares their glee at sending up that dreadful old Homeric model of "what it means to be a man." All three of them knew perfectly well that the *Iliad* ends not with Achilles's fleeting change of heart, but with a funeral: with the women cleaning up the mess the men have made, and weeping at all the useless carnage.

Asking the ancient questions about who we are, and discovering new answers, are just some of the reasons that everyone, anyone, should be able to read the classic writers, Greek, Latin, Chinese, Babylonian, and read them again and again. For all its cruelties and its limits, neither Plato nor I would ever renounce the reading of Homer's *Iliad*, a poem that emerged in its magnificent coherence around 750 BCE, as the relics of the collapsed Bronze Age pulled together to forge another culture of international resonance. As a human being, Achilles is a mass of brutal confusion, but Homer, by contrast, is a storyteller of masterful discipline and ingenuity: he restricts the subject matter of the *Iliad* to Achilles' brief temper tantrum toward the end of the ten-year Trojan War, and yet manages to tuck the whole history of that conflict in between the lines. We can easily grow beyond Achilles as an exemplar of "what it is to be a man"; it is much more difficult to grow beyond Homer as an exemplar of what it is to be a poet.

This freedom, this curiosity, this search for wisdom wherever it might be found, does not have to imply the moral or political endorsement of the societies that produced these works of literature — writers themselves are often the most trenchant critics of their own societies. Homer provided the model for Greek education in Plato's childhood, and Plato, as an adult, overthrew that model, along with much of the rest of the Athenian social structure as he knew it. From the standpoint of justice, all societies have been to some degree culpable, there is evil everywhere, and all cultures have shown prejudice and ignorance and intolerance (including the cultures of the oppressed). Should we, then, study nothing and rely only on our wonderful selves? Both Homer and Plato may have known slavery first-hand: *homeros* in Greek means "hostage," and Plato, in his thirties, was sold on the slave market by a treacherous Syracusan sea captain. His purchaser knew who he was and set him free immediately, but he never forgot the experience. It may be one of the reasons that neither he nor Homer could imagine a human society free from slavery or war.

When Socrates and Adeimantus decide to expel the poets from their Republic, they do so from intimate knowledge, and they are fantasizing. But when the communications office of my university insisted in a recent mass email that education went beyond "dusty archives," they were using an empty cliché, like "dead white males" to refer to immortal authors whose skin was mostly Mediterranean brown, and, in such cases as the Roman playwright Terence and St. Augustine, may have been considerably darker than that. There are few experiences more intoxicating than being in a place like the Vatican Library amid relics of millennia of human endeavor. The dust has *not* settled on those old tomes. They are as volatile and subversive now as ever — which is exactly why certain kinds of putative "educators" want to keep them out of your hands.

We should be able to read, and reread, whatever helps us wind our way through the labyrinth of life. Thucydides helps me through humanity's worst precisely because he endured the worst: plague, exile, war, the degeneration of democracy into tyranny. Plato, who saw these same terrible things in his own life, and many more, including treachery and slavery, provides unflagging hope that we can do better. And he hands the ultimate spiritual revelation of his intoxicating dialogue, the *Symposium*, to a woman, the priestess Diotima. Despite the fact that generations of self-absorbed men have continued to misread Plato in search of "what is it to be a man," more careful reading will reveal a visionary of a far more lofty order.

THE NAZGÛL

I first read J.R.R. Tolkien's *The Lord of the Rings* as a thirteen-year-old. It was an unsettling tale for a teenager: unlike fairy-tale heroes, Frodo Baggins returns from his quest physically and psychically damaged, and the world he has struggled to save is no longer the same world at all. Tyranny has degraded its wild lands, erected monstrous buildings, and eroded the souls of every kind of living thing: birds, horses, spiders, trees, knights, kings, gossipy neighbors. For a young person, the end of the books presented a troubling anti-climax, but there was no way to stop reading before that puzzling end — the suspense was too unbearable.

Thirteen-year-olds are unlikely to bother with literary analysis, but they are certainly susceptible to a well-structured plot. Tolkien's epic tale begins in the exact antithesis to an epic setting: a placid village in the comfortably named Middle Earth, a fantasy version of the classic English countryside, green, prosperous, isolated from any forces more complex than the occasional tensions of village life and the round of the seasons, inhabited, as the English countryside always has been, by fantastic little people of human form but not quite human customs. In the 1930's Tolkien invented his own set of little people for his three young sons: hobbits were child-sized individuals who walked about on large furry feet and lived in burrowlike houses, conservative in their ways and scrupulously tidy in their lace-curtained housekeeping. He enshrined them first in a charming book about a more adventurous member of the breed, *The Hobbit*, which appeared in 1937 and was immediately regarded as a classic.

The hobbits in *The Lord of the Rings*, the much longer narrative that he published in three volumes in 1955, became more complex as its target audience, the Tolkien boys, grew into adult readers. These hobbits are revealed as naïve isolationists in a much larger real world, and they ignore the forces beyond their borders at their own peril. Tolkien may have been writing in the mid-twentieth century, but, given the opportunity, his hobbits in their pastoral Shire would have voted eagerly for the equivalent of Brexit, with the same devastating results. As a South African who moved to England in childhood, Tolkien knew that the world was vast and that he was different from most of his neighbors.

The hobbit stories address a child's contradictory longings for stability and adventure, like the children in the Narnia series by Tolkien's friend C.S. Lewis, who can climb through a wardrobe and become kings and queens on the other side. There is something eminently twentieth-century about the idea of launching an epic tale from the midst of middle-class comfort. Most heroic sagas begin in the midst of hardship: Virgil's *Aeneid* with a shipwreck, Homer's *Iliad* with a battlefield, Dante's *Divine Comedy* in a darkened forest. Both Tolkien and Lewis are clearly inspired by the *Odyssey*, an epic that is driven by a similar longing for home, and reveals, like the *Lord of the Rings*, that home will require a good scouring before it truly becomes home again. Yet after it has been well and truly scoured, home will still be forever different from what it was, and the hero will leave again for yet another quest. The *Odyssey* provides its own trenchant critique of the *Iliad's* version of "being a man." Jean Cocteau's twentieth-century Orpheus walks through a bourgeois bedroom mirror into the netherworld.

What I remember most about that adolescent reading of *The Lord of the Rings* is a feeling of dread that quickly turned into abject terror. Like that first dying rat in Camus' *The Plague*, the initial seed of foreboding is planted by an apparition that, as the hobbits put it, seems "queer" rather than openly menacing. In chapter three of *The Fellowship of the Ring*, the first volume in the series, Frodo Baggins and his friends have taken to the road when they realize that they are being followed:

> Round the corner came a black horse, no hobbit-pony
> but a full-sized horse; and on it sat a large man, who
> seemed to crouch in the saddle, wrapped in a great
> black cloak and hood, so that only his boots in the
> high stirrups showed below; his face was shadowed
> and invisible.

When it reached the tree and was level with Frodo the horse stopped. The riding figure sat quite still with its head bowed, as if listening. From inside the hood came a noise as of someone sniffing to catch an elusive scent; the head turned from side to side of the road.

The hidden face, the doglike sniffing, the odd posture, and the swaying motion already give the Black Rider an unearthly aura. Shrewdly, however, Tolkien fleshes out that intimation of wickedness without rushing the pace of his ample narrative. We assemble information about the Rider from brief glimpses, sometimes when he appears in person, sometimes, to great effect, when we only hear of him by rumor. We learn at second hand that he has been searching for "Baggins," and that he has a foul temper: "He seemed mighty put out, when I told him Mr. Baggins had left his home for good. Hissed at me, he did. It gave me quite a shudder." The Black Rider is almost animal at times, sniffing like a bloodhound, hissing like a snake. In his second appearance, he stoops down and crawls on all fours:

The sound of hoofs stopped. As Frodo watched, he saw something dark pass across the lighter space between two trees, and then halt. It looked like the black shade of a horse led by a smaller black shadow. The black shadow stood close to the place where they had left the path, and it swayed from side to side. Frodo thought he heard the sound of snuffling. The shadow bent to the ground and began to crawl towards them.

At the sound of voices, the shadowy horseman retreats again, but by this time we know he will be back — as Chekhov warned, that one must never place a loaded rifle on stage if it isn't going to go off. Tolkien places his loaded rifle early, and returns to his Black Rider, to increasingly terrifying effect, throughout the course of his epic tale. Soon that literary loaded rifle turns out to be a whole arsenal: that first, evil-tempered "he" is quickly revealed as a "they" when a Black Rider appears dramatically on an isolated crag, and lets forth an eerie scream — answered in kind by another scream. The dark horses start out as earthbound creatures, and then take to the skies. Bit by terrifying bit, the Black Riders shed their earthbound qualities of snake and bloodhound to resemble, more and more vividly, the Four Horsemen of the Apocalypse (Conquest, War, Famine and Plague) — but there are nine of them, who serve the Prince of Darkness (under the reptilian name Sauron) as loyally as the four horsemen in the *Book of Revelation*.

In Tolkien's world, the Black Riders are finally identified as "ringwraiths" or Nazgûl, once noble knights who have sold their souls for the sake of power and have existed ever after in a border zone between life and death. They have bodies, but those bodies are utterly invisible; their lust for dominion has literally turned them into servile nobodies. When I was thirteen, the stealthy irruption of these frightening half-men into the apparent peace of the hobbits' comfortable Shire scared me as much as the prospect of a California earthquake in my placid Corona del Mar, and no rereading of *The Lord of the Rings* has ever matched the sheer thrill of that primal terror. The Black Riders are one of Tolkien's most enduring creations. Their power of suggestion has been so great that an ant, a crustacean, and a wasp all bear Nazgul as part of their scientific names, and at least one respectable American historian's panoply of extracurricular talents includes a Nazgûl scream that she perfected in adolescence.

I was not perfecting my Nazgûl scream; I was looking skyward for flying horses. When I first read *The Lord of the Rings* in Southern California in the mid-1960's, my own skies were filled with amphibious helicopters, bound for Vietnam from the El Toro Marine Air Station, and undoubtedly my own imaginary picture of the Nazgûl was conceived in their image. When Frodo complains about having a Black Rider upset his peaceful travels within "my own Shire," Gildor the elf retorts that the Shire is not his at all, and furthermore, "The wide world is all about you; you can fence yourselves in: but you cannot forever fence it out." The Marine helicopters that chopped their way westward from El Toro reminded everyone in their path that the wide world reached deep into our sleepy beach town, and it was that same idea of connection with the outside world and the immanence of its tribulations that made the Nazgûl so scary for an adolescent. For most readers of the *Lord of the Rings*, the Black Riders lodge in the imagination in their final airborne form, screaming back and forth as their steeds flap leathery wings; it is hard to remember how slowly and cleverly Tolkien builds up this dread vision across hundreds of pages before he completes it.

Thirty years after that first reading, I began to wonder whether the scream of the Nazgûl might really be the scream of the V-2 rockets that rained down on Britain in 1944-1945. Tolkien himself rejected any simple connections between his work and the Second World War. In his foreword to the second edition of *The Lord of the Rings*, he protested that his "prime motive was the desire of a tale-teller to try his hand at a really long story that would hold the attention of readers, amuse them, delight them, and at times maybe excite them or deeply move them." But the screaming rockets of Wernher von Braun must have crossed his mind, for in the same foreword he describes his process of composition: "It was during 1944 that, leaving the loose ends and perplexities of war which it was my task to conduct, or at least to report, I forced myself to tackle the journey of Frodo to Mordor [that is, his hobbit hero's confrontation with absolute evil, with all nine Nazgûl zipping about in full regalia, mounted on pterodactyls]. These chapters…were written and sent out as a serial to my son, Christopher, then in South Africa with the RAF." Still, he also warns that "an author cannot of course remain wholly unaffected by his experience, but the ways in which a story-germ uses the soil of experience are extremely complex, and attempts to define the process are at best guesses from evidence that is inadequate and ambiguous." Whatever sound the Nazgûl scream made inside Tolkien's head, it was no less effective inside mine at the age of thirteen, piercing through the staccato whap of the rotors of Boeing CH-46 Sea Knights.

I have reread *The Lord of the Rings* at least three times since that first immersion, and the Black Riders have never stirred up such vividly immediate fears as they did in my adolescent imagination. The fear they inspire now is a thoroughly adult fear, because the Nazgûl still move among us, creeping, snuffling, hissing, foul of temper and fouler of temperament. Today they tend to be dressed in suits rather than cloaks, with names like Mitch and Ted and Mike rather than Khamûl, with titles like The Senator from Kentucky and The Former Vice President rather than The Witch-King of Angmar, but their story is always the same, and sadly eternal:

They were once men. Great kings of men. Then Sauron
the deceiver gave to them nine rings of power. Blinded
by their greed, they took them without question. One
by one, they fell into darkness and now they're slaves

to His will. They are the Nazgûl, Ringwraiths. Neither living nor dead.

And unfortunately, our Nazgûl, unlike Tolkien's cloaked and crowned voids, show us the faces on which their iniquity has been written.

THE PRANCING PONY

One of the reasons that the first *Star Wars* film left my youthful self unimpressed was the obvious derivation of its bar on the edge of the galaxy from the bar in one of the most famous episodes of the original TV show *Star Trek*, "The Trouble with Tribbles." The futuristic furniture, the customers from all corners of the galaxy exhibiting every variety of body type and speaking every kind of language, these had already been done to brilliant and humorous effect, and the fact that they were done for a tiny screen in cheap materials in black-and-white had made no difference to me: the idea was the thing. *Star Wars*, of course, meant to restyle the intergalactic bar for eyes accustomed to color, wide screens, and digital special effects; in the eyes of a moviemaker, these matters of superficial form defined an absolute distinction where my censorious young self saw an act of plagiarism. I was too young then to recognize that in any case the intergalactic bar was only a recent manifestation of an immemorial archetype, the inn at the border between one place and another, the diversorium, the caravanserai, the frontier saloon. Douglas Adams' Restaurant at the End of the Universe is no different in its way from the tavern on the River Mincio where Verdi's Rigoletto meets the assassin Sparafucile to plot the death of the Duke of Mantua, who appears at the same inn in disguise to sing "*La donna è mobile*." Inns have always catered to different social strata as well as different geographies, and there is often something disreputable about them because they exist where the usual limits that define society turn flexible.

In both *The Hobbit* and *The Lord of the Rings*, that border saloon is a pub called the Prancing Pony, situated just over the human side of the border between the Shire of the hobbits and the world of men, in a village called Bree. The Prancing Pony caters to guests and animals who come in two different sizes: hobbit and human, pony and horse, and, on one memorable occasion, a hit squad of Nazgûl who end up stabbing pillows rather than Frodo and his friends. The Nazgûl, it seems, have not only surrendered their souls to greed, but also a good bit of their common sense. They are a singularly dimwitted lot — but then they had to be dimwits to sell off their principles in the first place. As Thucydides, Dante, and Machiavelli will happily remind us, people who choose to keep their souls and their principles also tend to keep their intelligence as well, albeit at the price of exile.

Tolkien and C.S. Lewis and a group of literary friends who called themselves the Inklings used to meet at an Oxford pub called the Eagle and Child, at the edge of town on the road from Oxford to Woodstock. Just beyond this establishment (wags call it the "Bird and Baby"), a little farther up the road out of Oxford, is the Catholic church of St. Aloysius, where Tolkien was a parishioner. Built by the Jesuits in 1875 to serve the city's Catholic community, St. Aloysius faces an explicitly anti-Catholic monument erected in 1843 to commemorate three bishops of the Church of England, all burned at the stake in Oxford during the reign of the Catholic queen Mary Tudor. Hugh Latimer and Nicholas Ridley died as heretics in 1555 in the city's Corn Market. A third, heretic, Thomas Cranmer,

Archbishop of Canterbury, watched their excruciating demise (Ridley took a long time to ignite) from a tower prison nearby and was burned himself the following year. As he mounted the scaffold, Latimer is said to have exhorted his friend, "Play the man, Master Ridley; we shall this day light such a candle, by God's grace, in England, as I trust shall never be put out." The Martyrs' Monument on the road out of Oxford rose as a local protest against the Anglo-Catholic Oxford Movement that had begun to flourish in the 1840's; in effect, it marked the border between town and country by affirming Oxford's Protestant identity, secured when Elizabeth I succeeded "Bloody Mary" in 1558, and resisting any attempts to heal the centuries-old hostilities between Catholic and Anglican.

But if the Martyrs' Monument and the church of St. Aloysius represented an ancient Oxonian religious conflict, Somerville College, a little farther out than the Catholics on the road to Woodstock, presented an entirely new challenge to Oxford when it was founded in 1879: the college admitted women, for the first time in the eight hundred years since the university was founded.

A few years ago, at a conference at this same Somerville College, a Danish friend and I went out to find some dinner. We walked the length of Somerville, passed St. Aloysius, passed the Martyrs Monument, and turned into the first pub we saw: none other than the Eagle and Child. We were thrilled to sit with our pints where the Inklings had once sat before us, there on the borderland between traditional Oxford and the wild unknown of Catholics, women, and countryside. He suddenly grinned and exclaimed, "We're in the Prancing Pony!" And of course we were. Physically, the Prancing Pony of Bree is said to be have been modeled on the Bell Inn of Moreton-on-Marsh, where Tolkien was also a regular, and the town of Bree is itself a thin disguise for the village of Brill, which stands on the border between Oxford and Buckinghamshire, but there is no doubt that the Eagle and Child (at least up to its present remodeling, now in progress), is, or has been, a classic Restaurant at the End of the Universe, where minds meet and ideas fly free on wings of conversation.

In ancient times, travelers arriving in Athens from the south passed by a verdant grove, dedicated to the hero Hekademos, before reaching the city walls. Eventually Plato took over responsibility for this property, and turned it into a school, his Academy, a Prancing Pony whose Inklings included, among many others, his nephew Speusippus; Dion, a Sicilian prince; two women students, Axiothea and Lastheneia, and a flashily-dressed, bejeweled beach boy from the north of Greece named Aristotle. No one could enter without knowing geometry, Plato's idea of what it meant to be — not a man, but human.

The Unsettled Dust

VLADIMIR KARA-MURZA

Putin's Poisons

Russia is a country of symbols. Major political shifts here are always accompanied by a change of outward trappings, as a graphic demonstration of a rupture with the old. In March 1917, as the Russian throne stood empty after the abdication of the last Czar, the crowned double-headed eagles — the symbols of the fallen empire — were being toppled all over the country: thrown down from the façades of government buildings, bridges, theaters, department stores, and spectacularly from the rostrum in the State Duma's hemicycle in Petrograd. The new currency printed by the provisional government featured the eagle without the crowns or the scepter — a rare collector's item as it only lasted a few months, until the eagle was eliminated altogether when the Bolsheviks seized power in a coup d'état later that year.

Trying desperately to cling to power as the country — and the world — was changing around them, a new generation of Communist leaders attempted another coup d'état in August 1991. It seemed bound to succeed — after all, the leaders of the coup, who tried to stem a democratic tide provoked both by the half-hearted reforms of the 1980s and by the deteriorating woes of the socialist economy, held all the levers of power. The self-proclaimed "emergency committee" included the USSR's vice president, prime minister, ministers of the interior and defense, and the chairman of the KGB — the top brass of the regime which had control of the party and state machinery, the propaganda apparatus, and all branches of the security forces, from the regular army to the secret police. And they had tanks, which they sent to occupy downtown Moscow.

What they failed to account for was a changed Russian society: people who had tasted a sampling of freedom, however imperfect, were not prepared to give it up. The Muscovites who went into the streets — initially in the thousands, then in the hundreds of thousands — were not armed with anything except their dignity and a determination to defend their freedom. They came and stood in front of the tanks, and the tanks stopped and turned away. A mighty totalitarian system that had held the world in fear for decades went down in three days, defeated peacefully by its own citizens. I was a ten-year-old boy in Moscow — too young to join my father at the barricades by the White House (the seat of the Russian parliament that became the center of resistance to the coup) but certainly old enough to grasp the lesson of what was happening: that however strong a dictatorship, when enough people are willing to stand up to it they will succeed. The tanks will stop and turn away.

The fall of the Soviet regime was followed, inevitably, by the overthrow of its symbols. On August 22, as the Russian republic's president, Boris Yeltsin, who had led the opposition to the coup, addressed a huge victory rally from the White House balcony, thousands of Muscovites went over to Lubyanka Square, the site of the KGB's headquarters, to tear down the monument to its founder, Felix Dzerzhinsky. The nineteen-foot bronze statue of the Soviet secret police chief hanging from a noose as a crane lifted it from its pedestal remains among the most enduring images of Russia's democratic revolution. That same evening, a memorial plaque honoring Yuri Andropov was dismantled from the façade of the KGB building. Andropov was someone who had epitomized both the domestic repression and the external aggressiveness of the Soviet system. As ambassador to Budapest, he was among those who oversaw the Soviet invasion of Hungary in 1956. As longtime chairman of the KGB, he made a priority of targeting political dissent, setting up a special directorate to fight "anti-Soviet activities" at home and expanding the gruesome practice of punitive psychiatry in which dissidents were confined to torturous conditions of forced psychiatric "treatment." A plaque honoring this man as a "distinguished statesman" was inconceivable in a democratic Russia.

In December 1999, President Yeltsin was preparing to hand over power to a former KGB operative by the name of Vladimir Putin — a relatively obscure apparatchik who had recently been appointed prime minister and enjoyed a meteoric political rise on the back of mysterious apartment bombings blamed on Chechen terrorists and a brutal military campaign in Chechnya that culminated in his newly formed party's victory in parliamentary elections. Much of the world media, pundits and foreign leaders everywhere, wondered who this Mr. Putin was and what they should expect from him, domestically and in the realm of foreign policy. For anyone willing to notice, however, the answer was already there. On December 20 — the anniversary of the founding of the Soviet secret police — Putin held a low-key ceremony on Lubyanka Square, attended by a few former colleagues and a handful of journalists, to unveil the restored memorial plaque to Andropov, the "distinguished statesman." It was the same one that had been dismantled in August 1991, carefully preserved and waiting for its moment.

In this country of symbols, Putin could not have chosen a more potent one to mark the start of a new political era. As if in confirmation of his intentions (if one were needed) he proceeded, in the first year of his presidency, to reinstate the Soviet-era national anthem once personally selected by Stalin. "A national anthem is a symbol," Boris Strugatsky, a celebrated Russian science fiction novelist, wrote in 2000. "What can be symbolized by a return to the former Communist Party anthem except a return to the former times? This is frightening... It seems we are destined for a new spiral of suffering: a rejection of democracy, a return to totalitarianism and great-power games, an inevitable failure — and then another *perestroika*, democratization, freedom, but in the context of a total economic collapse and an impending energy crisis. I would very much like to be wrong."

Alas, he wasn't. Symbols were followed by substance. On the fourth day after Putin's inauguration as president in May 2000 — in keeping with the Russian saying that "those who will offend us won't survive three days" — he dispatched armed operatives from the prosecutor-general's service and the tax police to raid the offices of Media Most, Russia's largest private media holding and the parent company of NTV, an influential television network. For years, NTV had been a staple in millions of Russian households, carrying critical news coverage, unfettered talk shows, and hard-hitting political satire — including the weekly program *Kukly* (Puppets) that did not shy away from deriding Russia's most powerful politicians. Former deputy prime minister Boris Nemtsov once recalled how President Yeltsin, during one of their meetings in the Kremlin, remarked that he was tired of constant criticism on NTV and asked for the remote so he could turn off his television set.

For Putin, turning off his own TV was not enough — he had to silence everyone else's, too. NTV was destroyed within a year as its studios were seized in an early dawn raid on Holy Saturday in April, 2001. Within three years of Putin's coming to power, by June 2003, all the other private television networks were silenced too, with the state regaining its Soviet-era monopoly on the most important source of public information. And though there was no single "moment" that could be said to mark Russia's transition from its imperfect democracy of the 1990s to the perfect authoritarianism overseen by Putin today, the year 2003 was an important turning-point. After pulling the plug on Russia's last private TV network in June, Putin went after a prominent rival in October — the oil tycoon and Russia's richest man, Mikhail Khodorkovsky, who had the tenacity to accuse the government of corruption and funded opposition parties and civil society groups. Khodorkovsky was arrested in a raid on his private jet by FSB operatives while on a trip to Siberia, brought back to Moscow, and displayed on television sitting in a courtroom cage.

The goal was not only to silence Khodorkovsky but to send a message to the rest of Russia's business community: stay out of politics or end up like him. The message was heeded. (Khodorkovsky would spend a decade in Putin's prisons before being expelled to the West, Andropov-style, on the eve of the Sochi Olympics.) Finally, in December 2003, Russia held a parliamentary election that, for the first time since the end of Soviet rule, was assessed by international observers as "not fair," with the effect of banishing genuine opposition voices from the Duma and turning it into a rubber stamp. "Parliament is not a place for discussion" — this imperishable observation by Boris Gryzlov, the speaker of the Duma and Putin's party colleague, would be a fitting epitaph for future history books on Russia under Putin.

Corruption has always been a feature of Russian life, but the removal of checks and balances and the institutionalization of authoritarian rule under Putin enabled kleptocracy on a scale never seen before. Putin's personal friends — from his childhood, from his KGB days, and from his stint at the St. Petersburg mayor's office in the 1990s — sprung from obscurity to join the ranks of Europe's richest men, helped by lucrative no-bid government contracts and requisitioned private assets. Names like Arkady Rotenberg, Gennady Timchenko, and Igor Sechin have come to symbolize the crony capitalism of the Putin era. The much-maligned "oligarchs" of the 1990s paled in comparison. From time to time, glimpses from that world would come into public view, as with the contract to build a thirty-mile road for the Sochi Olympics that exceeded the cost of NASA's Mars exploration program; a $2-billion offshore account belonging to a cellist friend of Putin's, found among the Panama Papers; a $1.3 billion Italian-style palace reportedly constructed for Putin's

59

personal use on the Black Sea coast. For evident reasons, such stories never become subjects of tame parliamentary debates or state-controlled television programs.

～≋

As the screws tightened and conventional channels of political activity and public communication were shut off, Russians — especially the younger urban middle classes — began taking to the streets to voice opposition to Putin's rule. The protests snowballed in the winter of 2011–2012 as tens of thousands filled the streets of downtown Moscow to denounce a blatantly fraudulent parliamentary election, in which Putin's party secured "victory" through large-scale ballot-stuffing. Among the leading voices at those rallies was Boris Nemtsov, who — unlike many of his former colleagues in the Yeltsin-era establishment — was not willing to be complicit in Russia's turn to authoritarianism. "Putin, leave! You don't know your own people," he said, addressing a 100,000-strong crowd on Bolotnaya Square, across the river from the Kremlin, in December 2011. "You don't even understand why we are here. We are here because we have a sense of dignity. We are here because we are not slaves." Once the face of Russia's hopes for democracy in the 1990s — a successful regional governor, deputy prime minister, and presumed heir to the presidency — Nemtsov emerged as the most prominent opponent of Putin's corrupt and despotic rule, leading street protests, organizing local election victories for the opposition, successfully advocating for targeted Western sanctions on Putin's cronies and oligarchs.

He was too principled to be bought, too bold to be frightened, and too dangerous to be tolerated. On the evening of February 27, 2015, Nemtsov was gunned down, five bullets in the back, as he walked home across a bridge in front of the Kremlin. It was the most high-profile political assassination in the modern history of Russia. To this day, its organizers continue to be protected by the highest levels of the Russian government. An oversight report by the Organization for Security and Cooperation in Europe (OSCE) in 2020 has concluded that the reason for this continuing impunity is "not the capabilities of the Russian law enforcement, but political will." After all, one cannot be expected to investigate oneself.

The last public demonstration Nemtsov had led was against Putin's war against Ukraine. In September 2014, tens of thousands marched down Moscow's boulevards in protest at the Kremlin's aggression against Russia's close neighbor and traditional ally. Earlier that year, following a popular "revolution of dignity" that ousted a corrupt and authoritarian Ukrainian leader, Putin moved full-scale against that country, starting an unannounced but deadly war in eastern Ukraine under the guise of a phantom "separatist" conflict and formally annexing the Crimean Peninsula for Russia. This was the first time one European nation seized territory from another since the end of the Second World War. It was not the first time Putin crossed another country's borders, though: in 2008 his forces had attacked the former Soviet republic of Georgia, occupying (but not formally annexing) some twenty percent of its territory.

To Western leaders, the war on Ukraine came as a shock: one official statement after another derided Putin for "breaching international law," "violating commitments," and "passing a point of no-return." The only cause for shock, though, should have been how long the leaders of Western democracies had not only tolerated but enabled Putin and his regime — by lending him much-needed international legiti-

61

macy and by allowing his cronies to use Western countries and financial institutions as havens for their looted wealth. The late Vladimir Bukovsky, a famed Soviet-era dissident, once remarked that for many Western politicians the ability to fry their morning bacon on Soviet gas trumped any concern for human rights.

In this respect, not much has changed since the 1970s. In 2001, weeks after Putin's government seized control of NTV, President George W. Bush famously stated that he had "looked the man in the eye... [and] was able to get a sense of his soul." (An impossible feat, given Putin's remarkably soulless eyes.) Later he praised Putin as "a new style of leader, a reformer... a man who is going to make a huge difference in making the world more peaceful by working closely with the United States."

Barack Obama continued this line of rapprochement, beginning his presidency with a "reset" in relations with Putin following the Georgia war; trying (unsuccessfully) to block Congressional passage of the Magnitsky Act that imposed targeted visa and financial sanctions on Kremlin officials involved in human rights abuses; and publicly praising Putin for his "extraordinary work... on behalf of the Russian people." On March 5, 2012 — the day after Putin "won" an election characterized by what OSCE observers described as a lack of "real competition" and "abuse of government resources" — the Obama administration announced that "the United States congratulates the Russian people on the completion of the presidential elections, and looks forward to working with the president-elect." I vividly recall that we in the Russian opposition received the news of this endorsement as we stood in Moscow's Pushkin Square with thousands of people who came out to protest the sham vote. It was difficult to say whether the people on that square — and the millions around the country who shared their outlook — felt more mocked or insulted.

Glaringly, the next American president, Donald Trump, professed his personal admiration and even reverence for Putin, invited him back into the Group of Eight (from which he had been expelled after the annexation of Crimea), and appeared to equate Russian intelligence officers accused of meddling in American elections with Americans who had helped craft the Magnitsky Act. In a pointed episode in 2017 — remember how much symbols matter for the Kremlin — the Trump administration, acting through a friendly senator, tried to block the effort to name a street in front of the Russian embassy in Washington D.C. after Boris Nemtsov. The administration's attempt failed as the D.C. Council stepped in to legislate the street naming — the first commemoration of Nemtsov anywhere in the world — but the intention was telling.

In fairness, the policy of accommodation toward Putin (in a different historical era it would have been called "appeasement") was not limited to the United States. With rare exceptions, European leaders did little better. I will never forget a lavish banquet honoring Putin during his state visit to the United Kingdom in June 2003 (which I was covering as a journalist), with champagne toasts and merry renditions of "For He's a Jolly Good Fellow" — literally days after his government pulled the plug on Russia's last independent television network. The banquet was held at the London Guildhall, not far from the spot where, three years later, Russian agents, likely acting on Putin's personal orders, would poison Alexander Litvinenko, a former FSB officer turned political émigré, with radioactive polonium: an attack against a NATO citizen on NATO soil.

As history has repeatedly shown — and very clearly so in the case of Vladimir Putin — appeasement is not only morally wrong but also practically ineffective. By turning a blind eye to Putin's domestic abuses in the hope of being able to "do business" with him in international affairs, Western leaders ignored a fundamental maxim of Russian history: foreign policy is a reflection of domestic policy. Repression at home and aggression abroad follow each other. This interrelationship has been manifested throughout Russia's history, but perhaps never as pointedly as in the past three decades. Democratic aspirations at home in the 1990s were duly translated into progressive international posturing, from President Yeltsin's support for the independence of the Baltic States and Poland's NATO membership to Russia's own accession to the Council of Europe and the Group of Eight and its cooperation treaty with NATO that affirmed a "shared commitment to build a stable, peaceful and undivided Europe, whole and free." With Putin's authoritarian turn, Russian foreign policy was redirected to supporting dictators and rogue regimes all over the world, often through confrontation with democratic nations — including a direct military collision with U.S. forces in Syria in February 2018. Putin's national security strategy has designated NATO actions as "a threat"; one of his state-of-the-nation addresses featured a computer animation of a ballistic missile attack on Florida; Russian military exercises have included simulated nuclear strikes on NATO countries and allies; and state propaganda chief Dmitri Kiselev has boasted on the air about Russia's ability to "turn the U.S. into radioactive ash." Alongside the actual wars against Ukraine and Georgia, Putin's aggression has come in "hybrid" forms designed to undermine the security and sovereignty of others, from as near as the neighboring Belarus to as far as the Central African Republic.

There is no reason to expect a regime that violates its own laws and tramples on its own citizens to respect international norms or the interests of other nations. History, as they say, knows no "if," but one can only wonder what the world would look like today if Western leaders had taken a more principled stand against Putin's attacks on democracy early on.

The main purpose of historical analysis is not the study of the past — however fascinating it may be — but the preparation for the future. History has not been kind to Russia, but it has given it a number of openings for democratic change — and, no doubt, there will be another. To avoid repeating past mistakes, it is important to learn from them. The main reason for the failure of Russia's transition to democracy in the 1990s lay in the inability — or the unwillingness — on the part of its new democratic leadership to fully break with the Soviet past. While Russia moved toward free elections, media pluralism, open borders, and a market economy, it never went through a process of public reckoning with the crimes of the former regime. There was nothing like the Stasi Records Agency in the former East Germany, the Truth and Reconciliation Commission in post-apartheid South Africa, or the Office for the Documentation and the Investigation of the Crimes of Communism in the Czech Republic. Some of the Soviet archives were briefly opened — and quickly shut again.

Russia's Constitutional Court did rule in 1992 that "the governing structures of the Communist Party of the Soviet Union had been the initiators of repression... directed at millions" — but no practical consequences followed. A lustration bill restricting former Communist and KGB officials from positions of power was introduced in the Russian parliament, but was never adopted. The old regime remained only half-condemned. "Be careful, it's like dealing with a wounded beast," Bukovsky warned members of Yeltsin's government in the early 1990s. "If you don't finish it off, it will attack you." His warning came sadly true with Putin's political rise just a few years later. The lesson for those who will shepherd Russia's next transition to democracy is clear: symbols are not everything. It is not enough to shed the outward trappings of a dictatorship, not enough to change national anthems, topple monuments, and remove memorial plaques. The underlying problems must be identified and addressed — and only such a process of atonement and reform can guard against an authoritarian resurgence. The successful experience of many emerging democracies, from Chile to South Korea, testifies to this.

But the West should learn its lessons, too. Although the main reasons for Russia's botched democratic transition of the 1990s were undoubtedly domestic, the reformers could have been greatly helped by a promise of European and Euro-Atlantic integration — a promise that played such an important role in incentivizing successful post-communist transitions in other countries of Eastern and Central Europe. In February 1990, in his historic address to a joint session of the U.S. Congress, Václav Havel, the dissident playwright and new president of Czechoslovakia, framed that entire transition in terms of his country "returning to Europe." For many former Warsaw Pact states, this return meant not only a symbolic affirmation of their status as "fully" European but also tangible practical benefits to their citizens in the form of open markets, free trade, and visa-free travel. In many cases, this prospect provided a crucial impetus for policymakers to stay the course in the face of acute economic and social challenges.

No such prospect was given to Russia in the 1990s. Indeed, overtures from Moscow were often met with silence. On December 21, 1991, as NATO diplomats gathered at the alliance's headquarters in Brussels to meet with their counterparts from former Warsaw Pact countries, Russian Ambassador Nikolai Afanasyevsky read out a letter from President Yeltsin to NATO Secretary-General Manfred Wörner vowing to work toward "strengthening stability and cooperation on the European continent" and "raising a question of Russia's membership in NATO ... as a long-term political aim." According to contemporary press accounts, "NATO officials, from Secretary-General Wörner on down, seemed too taken aback by the Russian letter to give any coherent response." By the time Russian Foreign Minister Andrei Kozyrev finally received assurances from the Clinton administration that the United States would be open to Russian membership in NATO in 1995, the democratic window in Russia itself was rapidly closing. As for potential accession to the European Union — which, under the terms of the Maastricht Treaty, was supposed to be open to "any European state," Russia being the largest one — that prospect was not offered to Yeltsin's government even as a distant possibility. Western reluctance to accept the nascent democratic Russia as one of its own would later be skillfully played by Putin's propaganda to portray the community of democracies as inherently anti-Russian.

Many of those mistakes came not from malice but from unpreparedness, both in Russia and in the West. For many Western policymakers in the late 1980s, the very prospect of democratic changes in Russia seemed to be in the realm of fantasy — whether because of confident predictions by Kremlin-watchers that the Soviet regime was secure and stable, or because of the misguided (and offensive) stereotype that

Russians are somehow inherently unsuited for democracy — a stereotype that Ronald Reagan had described in his Westminster speech as "cultural condescension, or worse." In fact, it is a matter of historical record that when Russians were able to choose their fate in a free election — be it the State Duma election in 1906, the Constituent Assembly vote in 1917, or the presidential election in 1991 — they chose democracy over dictatorship, and by a landslide. Democratic reformers in Yeltsin's government were equally unprepared for the momentous task before them, making mistake after mistake and ignoring advice from those who knew better, including Bukovsky and the prominent pro-democracy lawmaker Galina Starovoitova, the author of the unsuccessful lustration bill. Honest mistakes were compounded by cynical schemes by those more interested in personal enrichment than in the success of Russia's democratic experiment. That unpreparedness of the early 1990s came with a high cost — primarily for Russia but also, eventually, for the West.

It is imperative that we not repeat this error. If Russian history is any guide, big political shifts in our country come unexpectedly — including for their own participants. It is unlikely that the Czar's interior minister, Vyacheslav von Plehve, a fervent advocate for a "small victorious war" with Japan in 1904, expected that war to result in Russia's first revolution a year later. In a speech in Zürich in January 1917, the exiled Bolshevik leader Vladimir Lenin told a group of Swiss social democrats that "we of the older generation may not live to see the decisive battles of this coming revolution," but the revolution in Russia began six weeks later. In early August 1991, as I remember myself, no one predicted that the Soviet regime would not survive to the end of the month — and the Soviet Union itself to the end of the year.

Today we hear familiar tunes, both from Kremlin propagandists and from their apologists in the West: that Putin's regime is secure; that he is popular among Russians; that any alternative would be worse. As proof we are supposed to accept the results of bogus elections, with opponents disqualified from the ballot, and Putin's public approval numbers in an unfree society where people are hesitant to share political opinions with strangers; and the false image of unanimity carefully crafted by state media. "There is no Russia without Putin," as Vyacheslav Volodin, the speaker of the Duma, has said publicly — perhaps the biggest insult to my country I have ever heard.

In truth — and despite the coercion and the pervasive propaganda — there are millions of Russians who have a different vision: one of a modern country that would respect its laws and play a constructive international role; that would be accountable to its own citizens and be respected rather than feared in the world. This Russia can already be seen — not in the dour halls of the rubberstamp legislature or in the staged shouting matches on state-run television, but in the hopes and the aspirations of Russia's youth, the people who never witnessed any political reality except Putin's but who are growing tired of a two-decade rule by one man whose circle increasingly resembles Leonid Brezhnev's ageing Politburo. Even with the inevitable skewing of public opinion, surveys conducted by the independent Levada Center in the run-up to Putin's sham plebiscite waiving presidential term limits in 2020 showed that the prospect of his continued rule split Russians fully in half, with most of those below the age of thirty in opposition. Perhaps more tellingly, a clear majority of Russians of all ages, 62 percent of them, wanted to age-limit Putin out of the presidency, while 59 percent said it was time for "decisive, large-scale" change in the country.

The signs of this coming change are unmistakable. In local elections across the country — most spectacularly in Moscow in 2019 — pro-regime candidates have been losing to technical spoilers and political no-names even after real opponents had been disqualified from running. It should be difficult to lose elections when the opposition is not on the ballot, but such is the growing public fatigue with the system that Putin's party is managing it — and this is likely to be repeated nation-wide in the parliamentary election in September. In a realiza-tion of the Putin's regime's greatest fear — its phobia after a series of "color revolutions" toppled authoritarian leaders in other post-Soviet states — Russians are increasingly willing to go to the streets to challenge the system — as hundreds of thousands did across the country, defying official threats and police violence, to protest the arrest of opposition leader Alexei Navalny in January.

With his skillful social media outreach, his unique appeal to the young generation, and his organizational prowess, Navalny has emerged as Putin's most dangerous challenger, attacking the regime not only over its repression, but also over its weakest spot: corruption. His investigative video detailing Putin's lavish palace on the Black Sea has been viewed by a hundred million people, more than the combined audiences of Russia's state television networks. The Kremlin has tried to silence Navalny in traditional ways: first, by an attempted poisoning, a method borrowed from the Soviet KGB and increasingly popular under Putin (it was tried — twice — against the author of this essay), then by arrest and impris-onment. The effect, it seems, has been the opposite, only strengthening Navalny's public appeal and moral clout. As history shows, most dictatorships fall not under the power of their opponents but under the weight of their own mistakes. It seems Putin's will not be an exception.

Boris Nemtsov had long predicted that demands for change in Russian society would reach a critical point around the mid-2020s — and while no one can say exactly when or how this will happen, the more far-sighted are already preparing: organizing grassroots campaigns; building, despite the regime's best efforts, a vibrant civil society on the ground; running in municipal elections to gain invaluable experience; learning to stand up for themselves in the face of police brutality during street demonstrations. Needless to say, any change in Russia can and should — and eventually will — come from Russians themselves. It is important, however, that Western democracies stay true to their values by refusing to accept or legitimize Putin's attempts at further usurpations of power (including an extension of his rule, in violation of the term limit, in 2024); by stopping the import of corruption into their markets and financial institutions and finally targeting the Kremlin's dark money abroad; by resisting calls for yet another "reset" or "détente" with an abusive and aggressive regime; and, above all, by engaging in dialogue with Russian society in anticipation of the task of integrating a post-Putin Russia into the community of law-abiding democracies — this time, for everyone's sake, successfully. Just imagine the difference a democratic Russia would make for the world. Sooner or later, that day will come. With the right efforts and a shared commitment, it may come a little more quickly.

PAUL STARR

Reckoning with ℵational Failure: The Case of Covid

Epidemics are not part of America's collective memory. The colonial era's smallpox and yellow fever epidemics, the three cholera epidemics of 1832, 1849, and 1866, the great flu pandemic of 1918 — none of these left a deep imprint on the national consciousness. None fit into a larger national story, at least none that Americans cared to tell. If the polio epidemic of the early twentieth century is remembered, it is mainly because it led to the polio vaccine and fits into a story about the triumph of medical science and American know-how. The AIDS epidemic is still a vivid memory in part because of its effect on the mobilization of the LBGT movement and an expanded vision of human rights. We Americans like our trage-dies to have a happy ending.

A practical, inventive, yes-we-can people: that is the version of America many of us remember hearing about and believing in from childhood. Until recently, contagious disease has not troubled that understanding, and for good reason — experience has given us grounds for confidence. Advances in medicine have subdued the most lethal contagions. Disease hangs over all of us individually, but it has not threatened our collective life, much less our sense of ourselves.

The Covid19 pandemic, however, will likely figure in our history in a way no previous national encounter with disease in the United States ever has. It is too big and disturbing a horror to be forgotten — not merely a medical story but also a social and cultural one: a story about a country unable to contain the forces of unreason within it. The American response to Covid19 has encapsulated an era when a nation that has always thought of itself as a success has had to confront the possibility that its luck has run out. At moments of crisis, from the Revolu-tion to the Civil War and two world wars, the United States has not only benefited from its institutions and its wealth. It has also been exceptionally fortunate in political leadership. But it was America's distinct misfortune in 2020 to confront a new and deadly virus at a time when a plague was already consuming its political life. Politics always matters for health and disease. Political decisions shape social structures and the allocation of resources, which in turn influence who gets sick and dies. Ordinarily, however, the chains of causality from politics to disease are long and complex. Not so this time. The impact of politics on the Covid19 pandemic was immediate and direct.

If Covid19 had struck in the decades before Donald Trump became president, it probably would not have mattered whether the administration in office was Republican or Democratic. The president would have turned to the nation's leading experts in public health and medicine, relied on their counsel, and rallied the nation to cooperate in stopping the spread of the disease. Unlike AIDS in the 1980s, Covid19 did not inherently provoke culture-war divisions. A minimally rational president of either party would have seen the pandemic as an opportunity of the same kind that presidents have had in wartime to rise above partisanship and become the nation's defender.

That is not to say the American response would have been ideal. It would have had to overcome the longstanding inequities of its healthcare system and its underinvestment in public health. And because Covid19 was a new threat, any administration might have made mistakes, especially at the beginning of the pandemic when critical scientific questions about the disease were clouded in uncertainty. But Trump did not simply make mistakes stemming from inadequate scientific knowledge or other factors beyond his control. He deliberately misled the public. He promoted bogus cures. He modeled antisocial behavior. He held rallies that put his own supporters and their communities at risk of infection, and he turned the White House itself into a superspreader venue. To suit his political interests, his aides muzzled scientists in the government and overruled the public health guidelines they developed. Above all, Trump so thoroughly politicized measures such as the adoption of masks and social distancing that he made the denial of scientific evidence and the defiance of scientific judgment into emblems of Republican identity. Sucked into Trump's world of "alternative facts" or lacking the courage to speak up, other national leaders of his party either supported him or kept silent.

Much of the historical significance of the Covid19

pandemic would be lost, however, if we reduced it to Trump and the Republicans who buckled under him. The failure in the national response to the pandemic is a larger story and a longer one. The forces of unreason in American politics have been building up on the right for some time. Talk radio, cable news, and social media have provided new channels for disseminating conspiracy stories and other falsehoods. Polarization has become a road to power. The "infodemic" that accompanied the pandemic reflected a prior pattern, a wider pattern — a pre-existing condition, you might say: the growing use of the internet and social media for disinformation and the desperate countervailing efforts to bring the technology under control to serve rational interests in wellbeing.

The Covid19 virus came to our shores when we were already in the throes of a different sort of virality. Contemporary changes in information technology have affected the pandemic in many ways. Technology has divided Americans along class and racial lines. People who could do their jobs online have been generally safe, healthy, and even prosperous, while those who have to do their work in person have been exposed to higher odds of infection and unemployment. The disparities in who got sick and died partly followed from that objective difference in risk. Covid19 entered a politically polarized and economically divided America, and it intensified the divisions.

As 2020 ended, the United States counted nearly 350,000 deaths from Covid19, putting it fourth among the world's large, high-income countries in deaths from the disease per 100,000 population, surpassed only by Belgium, Great Britain, and Italy. (The toll in the United States may reach 600,000 deaths in 2021, according to projections in late January.) The East Asian societies that successfully controlled the pandemic offer a stark contrast. While the United States had 100.6

Covid19 deaths per 100,000 population in 2020, Japan had a rate of 3 per 100,000, South Korea 2 per 100,000, and Taiwan and Thailand under 1. If the United States had been able to keep its rate to South Korea's 2 per 100,000 in 2020, we would have had only about 7,000 deaths instead of almost 350,000. In 2019 a survey of international experts in health security had rated America the best prepared nation in the world to deal with a pandemic. But those experts had overlooked a critical factor. They overlooked *politics*. The United States has been dealing with a pandemic in a time of political derangement.

Everything about the Covid19 pandemic, including where it struck first, came to be seen through the prism of partisan politics. The virus arrived early in 2020 in the blue states and had its most severe impact on Democratic constituencies, a pattern that influenced how Trump and other Republicans framed the crisis. The disease then spread into the red states and by the November election was taking its highest toll in those areas. But by then Republicans had so successfully excused Trump from responsibility and minimized the suffering from the pandemic that its rise in the red states appeared to have little or no impact on Trump's support there.

The early outbreaks of the virus in coastal cities had nothing to do with their Democratic politics. A contagious disease originating abroad and spreading through contact was bound to arrive first in metropolitan centers with international connections and spread most rapidly through densely populated urban areas. The demographic profile of the victims was also predictable, since those areas had large numbers of low-income racial minorities who suffered from high rates of diabetes, heart disease, and other conditions that made them especially vulnerable to the coronavirus. In the early months of 2020, no one had drugs or other means of treating the virus itself. As the numbers of patients surged during March and April, medical facilities in New York and elsewhere also lacked critical resources such as testing capacity and personal protective equipment. Instead of a coordinated national response, however, the Trump administration left the problem largely to state governments, forcing them to compete with one another as they sought out resources in short supply.

What would have happened if Covid19 had struck the red states first? While it is impossible to know for sure, Trump might well have responded with more urgency and been less inclined to say — as he did to a rally last year — that the pandemic was the Democrats' "new hoax." The early geography of the pandemic allowed the president and other Republicans to suggest that the problems of the blue states were their own fault, the result of their own leadership, indeed, their whole governing ethos. The president made it clear that he did not regard the cases and the deaths in politically hostile regions as his responsibility: "If you take the blue states out, we're at a level that I don't think anybody in the world would be at. We're really at a very low level." This was false: by September, when he made those remarks, the rate of new cases in the red states was substantially higher than in the blue states — and it was about to go much higher still.

The federal government's failure to stem the pandemic began with the delayed development of a test for the virus and a disorganized response to travelers from China and Europe. On January 13, two days after Chinese scientists published the genome for the novel coronavirus, the World Health Organization issued a protocol for creating a diagnostic test. (The virus would later be named "severe acute respiratory syndrome coronavirus 2," or SARS-CoV-2, the cause of the disease Covid19.) While several countries immediately deployed a test using those instructions, the Centers for Disease Control and Prevention in Atlanta was unable to do so until February 28, a full forty-six days later. As the *Washington Post* subsequently reported, "The agency squandered weeks as it pursued a test design far more complicated than the WHO version and as its scientists wrestled with failures that regulators would later trace to a contaminated lab." The Food and Drug Administration, which could have approved alternative tests, also failed to act expeditiously. Even after a workable test was approved, the government failed to ramp up testing at commercial and university laboratories, and testing shortages persisted for months. Although evidence began emerging in January that people who had no overt signs of illness could transmit the virus, CDC officials were slow to acknowledge that possibility and, with testing kits in short supply, did not recommend testing individuals who had been exposed but reported no symptoms.

Although the testing failure originated within the CDC, the delay in correcting it and the persistent testing shortages reflected a failure of leadership at the highest levels of government. In 2018, Trump had shut down the Directorate for Global Health Security and Biodefense in the National Security Council, which is part of the White House. (President Biden has restored it.) When problems developed in global supply chains for N95 masks, chemical reagents for tests, and other resources, Trump turned instead to an ad hoc White House team of business consultants assembled by his son-in-law, which proved unequal to the task.

The delay in both testing and recognition of asymptomatic transmission contributed to the failure to identify foreign travelers carrying the virus into the country in early 2020. From mid-January to the end of February, while other countries began identifying and isolating carriers of the virus, the United States did not have the requisite diagnostic technology. On January 31, the day after the WHO declared a global health emergency, Trump announced restrictions on travel by non-citizens from China. But during the next two months, an estimated 40,000 returning citizens and others who fell under various exceptions to the travel ban arrived from China, and were often subject to nothing more than cursory questioning before being sent on their way and told to quarantine voluntarily for two weeks. Although local public health authorities were supposed to check with them later, the follow-up was haphazard. In any case, the virus had already entered the country during January, when at least 13,000 travelers a day had been arriving on flights from China. Trump announced restrictions on European travel on March 11, but as later genomic tracing would show, travelers had already brought a European strain of the virus to New York at least a month earlier. Although the travel restrictions may have bought some time, they were too little and too late, and enforcement was too lax and disorganized, to prevent the virus from gaining a foothold.

The United States could still have kept infection rates low if in the early spring it had adopted policies that reflected the evolving scientific understanding of the virus and its transmission. Those policies would have included the general promotion of masks and social distancing and the development of the three-part regime that other countries established for extensive testing, isolation of the infected, and systematic tracing of their contacts. Instead, the White House followed an erratic course from February to April before turning against a national public health effort and undermining a rational response to the pandemic.

Trump was so concerned about the appearance of a growing pandemic that he sought to stifle public warnings from health officials that were aimed at persuading Americans of the need for change. Talking privately with the journalist Bob Woodward, Trump clearly recognized the seriousness of the disease: "This is deadly stuff. You just breathe the air and that's how it's passed. ... It's also more deadly than even your strenuous flus." Publicly, however, he was saying there was nothing to worry about. On February 25, 2020 Trump said he thought the coronavirus was "a problem that's going to go away." So he was enraged when on that same day Dr. Nancy Messonnier, director of the National Center for Immunization and Respiratory Diseases at the CDC, issued a scientifically warranted warning that community spread of the virus was inevitable and Americans needed to consider drastic changes in their everyday lives, triggering a sharp fall in the stock market. CDC officials were thereafter directed to clear all public statements about Covid19 with the White House, and Messonnier was sidelined. The politicization of the pandemic was complete. Two days later Trump publicly speculated that, "like a miracle," the virus might just disappear.

National politics kept interfering with national competence. Trump also undermined the adoption of masks when the CDC changed its recommendations on their use. At first, partly for fear of exacerbating shortages of N95 and surgical masks for medical use, both the WHO and CDC did not recommend that the public at large obtain masks. Basing their judgment on research on earlier diseases, scientists also disagreed during the early months of 2020 about whether ordinary cloth masks would be effective in preventing transmission of the coronavirus. Some were emphatically opposed. "Stop buying masks!" the Surgeon General Jerome Adams tweeted on February 19. "They are not effective in preventing general public from catching #Coronavirus." This was an instance of a legitimate mistake made at a point when knowledge of the virus was just developing.

Yet a scientific consensus in favor of public use of cloth masks emerged as evidence began to demonstrate that masks did limit transmission, indeed that they were crucial for the general public because people who contracted the virus were most likely to infect others before they developed symptoms. But when the CDC on April 3 recommended that Americans wear "non-medical, cloth masks" in public places, the president said, "I don't see it for myself." Not only did he and other members of his administration ignore the guidance; the president mocked people who did wear masks.

Trump turned decisively against a concerted national effort during the spring. On March 16, he agreed to adopt federal guidelines for "15 Days to Slow the Spread," including recommendations for Americans to work from home whenever possible and to avoid discretionary travel and shopping trips, eating or drinking at bars and restaurants, and gathering in groups of ten or more people. Reluctantly, at the end of March he extended those guidelines for another fifteen days. By then a group of states, most of them led by Democratic governors, had issued more comprehensive stay-at-home orders. Research has shown that the measures adopted in March and April prevented millions of cases, "flattening the curve" and thereby, in the short term, preventing hospitals and other facilities from being overwhelmed, as they had earlier been in northern Italy and New York City.

That delay was supposed to provide time to establish a testing-isolating-tracing regime and to identify targeted measures for limiting spread so as to allow communities in stages to resume normal activities. Targeted measures, such as closing bars, restaurants, and large indoor gatherings, would have had far less cost to the economy than across-the-board lockdowns. But it was not long before Trump became impatient with restrictions at any level. Some of his advisers told him that the pandemic was ebbing, just the rationale he was looking for to abandon all regulation. For a few days in mid-April, it seemed as though Trump was going to insist that the response to the pandemic be entirely under his own control. "When somebody is the president of the United States," he said, "the authority is total and that's the way it's got to be." Three days later, however, as part of what aides called a "state authority handoff," the White House coronavirus task force issued reopening guidelines, and Trump told the governors, "You're going to call your own shots." But he didn't mean that, either. Ignoring his own administration's criteria for relaxing restrictions, he began tweeting denunciations of Democratic governors who failed to "liberate" their states.

During the spring, the president was increasingly at odds with the scientific community and his own government's public health officials. Shunting aside the experts, he took over the daily public briefings on the pandemic, using that platform to make boasts, give false reassurances, and pass along misinformation, most notoriously about an unproven and later discredited treatment (the infamous hydroxychloroquine) and the potential value of injecting disinfectant to kill the coronavirus. In May, after officials including Anthony Fauci, director of the National Institute of Allergy and Infectious Diseases, recommended greatly increased testing, Trump said that testing was "overrated": "When you test, you find something is wrong with people. If we didn't do any testing, we would have very few cases." Repeatedly, White House aides intervened with the CDC to stop it from issuing public health guidelines that conflicted with Trump's political message. The CDC's chief of staff later told the *New York Times*, "Every time that the science clashed with the messaging, messaging won."

Trump's messaging, designed to further his political interests among his base, fostered a narrative among his supporters that the coronavirus was overblown, and that the disease was not nearly as serious or extensive as the media were saying. But the numbers of cases and deaths kept rising through the summer and fall as the virus raged in rural areas and red states that were spared earlier. Some Republican governors finally did adopt regulations concerning masks and social distancing, but others, such as the governor of South Dakota, Kristi Noem, refused to impose any restrictions. In June, at a time when Covid19 cases were still low in South Dakota, Noem invited Americans who liked how well the state was handling the coronavirus to come there. From August 7 to August 16, tens of thousands of motorcyclists arrived, converging on the small town of Sturgis for an annual motorcycle rally and spending time at its bars, restaurants, and tattoo parlors, generally without masks. By November, South Dakota's rate of cases and deaths was among the highest in the country.

Earlier in the year, when Trump and other Republicans blamed the blue states for high rates of Covid19, the leaders of those states were dealing with a crisis that had been thrust upon them by forces beyond their control. But the later surge of the virus in the red states occurred when more was known about limiting transmission, and Trump and Republican leaders such as Governor Noem refused to act on the basis of that knowledge. Indeed, they passed off failure as freedom. Their refusal to require masks and social distancing showed how dedicated they were to freedom and how indifferent to danger. And it worked: the voters of those states did not hold them responsible for being the superspreaders that they were. In the wake of the November election, an analysis showed that 93 percent of the counties in the nation with the highest numbers of new cases per capita voted for Trump.

While Trump and the Republican leadership were the immediate source of America's catastrophic failure in the pandemic, they did not act alone or in isolation. They had the active support of right-wing media, and they benefited from the unguarded channels for the dissemination of falsehood created over the preceding quarter-century. In the right-wing world, the coronavirus was not the big problem that it was being made out to be; on the contrary, the mainstream media and the "deep state" were in league with Democrats, deceiving the public about what was generally a mild illness, all in an effort to limit freedom and bring down the president. Hatred of government has long been the basis on which the dissimilar elements of the right — evangelicals, business interests, the anti-vaxxers and anti-taxers — have been able to unite. Now the same hatred was mobilized against public health measures.

Conspiracy stories are falsehoods of a particular kind, involving claims of massive collaboration in deception. The idea that climate change is a hoax requires believing that scientists all over the world have conspired in making up evidence of rising temperatures, melting polar ice, and other signs of global warming. The idea that the 2020 election was stolen from Trump requires believing that election officials all over the United States conspired in tampering with the results and that the judges who rejected those claims, including many Republican appointees, were all in on the "steal." And the idea that the Covid19 pandemic was overhyped requires believing that scientists, front-line health workers, and public health officials joined together in another gigantic conspiracy.

The attraction of the political right to conspiracy thinking is hardly new. But until the past quarter century, the Republican Party and mainstream media were generally able to limit the reach of the conspiracy-obsessed far right. By Trump's presidency, however, Republican leaders had mainstreamed the fringe. Figures who used to be consigned to the political wilderness had gained a dominant role in both the party and its principal channels of communication.

The effect of that shift on public health was already evident under Barack Obama. In 2009, when scientists warned that the fall would bring a particularly dangerous flu — the H1N1 strain — right-wing media figures opposed Obama's efforts to persuade Americans to get vaccinated. Glenn Beck, who had a Fox News program at the time, said that "you don't know if this [vaccine] is going to cause neurological damage like it did in the 1970s" and that he would do "the exact opposite" of what the government advised. Rush Limbaugh told his listeners, "I am not going to take it [the H1N1 vaccine], precisely because you are now telling me I must. . . . I don't want to take your vaccine. I don't get flu shots." According to an October 2009 Pew survey, Democrats were 50 percent more likely than Republicans to say they planned to get vaccinated. Skepticism about the vaccine among Republicans, according to a study by the political scientist Matthew Baum, was concentrated among those who relied on cable news, the internet, and talk radio rather than network television news. Republicans were predisposed against any Obama policy, but the key factor, Baum argues, was the breakup of the earlier "informational commons" that existed when Americans from different viewpoints watched the same TV news programs. The change in communication may have had real-world consequences in 2009: red states had both lower flu vaccination rates and higher death rates from the flu that year than blue states did.

By 2020, there was even less of an information commons as a result of the decline of newspapers and network television and the growth of social media and partisan websites. Republicans and Democrats had separate sources of information and often wholly opposed understanding of basic facts. Unlike the much-denounced mainstream news organs, the right-wing media proudly refused to observe such conventions of journalism as checking facts and making corrections. The social media platforms contributed to the spread of misinformation. As studies of online communication have shown, people are more likely to share false information than accurate information. False information has the advantage of triggering more powerful emotions. In addition, the clustering of likeminded people in social networks tends to encourage more extreme views, a process known as "group polarization." Facebook, YouTube, Twitter, and other social media also set their ranking algorithms to maximize "user engagement," which often meant directing people to extremist and unreliable sources. For example, even when users watched a scientifically reliable video about vaccines, YouTube's "up next" recommendation algorithm pointed them to an anti-vaccination video.

Until 2019, the social media platforms rejected any responsibility for the misinformation they were circulating about any subject, including health. Defending themselves as champions of free speech, they did not want to bear the costs of separating fact from falsehood and assuming the role that the press has long accepted. But in the midst of a resurgence of measles in mid-2019, Facebook and Twitter broke from their traditional policy and changed their ranking algorithms on vaccine information to favor authoritative medical sources. When people asked about vaccines, the platforms began directing them to the WHO and CDC, not to anti-vaccination groups with more followers.

When the Covid19 pandemic began, the social media platforms confronted the same issue. Physicians reported cases of patients taking deadly remedies recommended online, such as bleach and highly concentrated alcohol, or refusing professional advice, citing posts they had seen on Facebook. In late February 2020, however, the platforms began extending to Covid19 the policies that they had already adopted on vaccination. Facebook reported that during March it displayed warnings on about forty million posts related to the pandemic and that by late April had "removed hundreds of thousands of pieces of misinformation that could lead to imminent physical harm," such as claims that drinking bleach cures the virus. It was also directing people to reliable sources of information. But despite Facebook's actions, the sober messages of public health authorities were poor competition for the masters of misinformation. During April 2020, the top ten health misinformation sites on Facebook had four times as many views as the CDC, WHO, and eight other prominent health-care institutions.

The change in policy at Facebook and other social media platforms represented a major shift, but the companies were unable to stop the spread of misinformation. Repeatedly, claims that appeared first on the political fringe took off when groups or websites allied with the Republican Party shared or repeated them. Political legitimation was crucial to the spread of lies. For example, a video called "Plandemic," posted by its maker on Facebook and other platforms on May 4, showcased a discredited researcher who claimed that masks could make wearers sick, vaccines for the coronavirus would be dangerous, and Anthony Fauci and Bill Gates were planning to gain money and power through the pandemic. After being promoted by a QAnon page and anti-vaccine activists, Plandemic took off when Trumpian "Reopen America" groups in different states began sharing it. Within a week it had been viewed more than eight million times. Eventually social media platforms began taking it down, but the damage had been done.

Trump himself played a central role in the spread of misinformation. On July 27 he shared another video peddling misinformation, this one called "America's Frontline Doctors," helping it gain tens of millions of viewers for claims that masks did not work and hydroxychloroquine was a cure for Covid19. The video showcased several doctors of dubious reputation, including one doctor-pastor known for arguing that "demon sperm" in nighttime dreams cause disease in women. On September 1, during an interview with Laura Ingraham on Fox News, Trump cited a statistic supposedly showing that only 6 percent of reported Covid19 deaths were in fact due to the virus. That claim had gone from a Facebook post with stops along the way in a QAnon page and the right-wing website Gateway Pundit, eventually reaching a Trump campaign advisor, the president himself, and Fox's audience. These were not exceptional cases. A study by researchers at Cornell University, which analyzed 38 million articles about the pandemic, pinpointed one key driver of the "infodemic": the president, who was himself the source of 38 percent of what the researchers called the "misinformation conversation."

The role of Trump and other Republican leaders in spreading misinformation about the pandemic created what seemed, at the time, to be an impossible problem for the social media platforms and the news media. Although the platforms and the media could indicate the claims were false, they could not suppress them. Claims by a president and leaders of one of the two major parties are inherently newsworthy; the public has a right and a need to know what they are saying, even when what they say is untrue. After the November election, Facebook and Twitter did block Trump from communicating lies that the election had been stolen from him. But he was already on his way out; the companies were unwilling to de-platform him when he was still firmly in power and his lies about the virus aggravated the pandemic. If they had done so at that time, they might have saved many lives. But the largest burden of responsibility for what Trump said and did properly belongs with him and the party that put him in office and continued to support him.

By any reasonable standard, the United States failed in its response to the pandemic in 2020. Its mortality rate exceeded that of most peer countries in the West, and it was astonishingly higher than East Asian societies such as South Korea and Japan. Changes in life expectancy offer a particularly telling measure of how great a loss Americans suffered, and who suffered the most. According to a preliminary medium estimate (which will probably turn out to be low), the pandemic brought about a decline of 1.13 years in life expectancy for Americans in 2020. Beneath that overall decline lay enormous disparities by race: a decline of .68 years for whites, 2.1 years for African Americans, and 3.05 years for Latinos. The bigger losses in life expectancy for African Americans and Latinos stemmed from greater susceptibility to Covid19 at younger ages in those groups as well as higher mortality rates from the disease. The deaths among whites were disproportionately among the aged, particularly residents of nursing homes. A toxic combination of ageism and racism lay behind the right-wing view that the pandemic was overblown, or that the disease should be allowed to spread until the country reached "herd immunity."

The damage from the pandemic goes beyond lives lost. Many survivors suffer from "long covid," which may impair their physical and mental health for years to come. Other long-term consequences will result from the disparate impact on families of the pandemic recession and the shutdown of in-person education. Whole sectors of the economy have been devastated, including many small businesses that have closed for good.

How to explain the catastrophic performance of the United States? A number of commentators have pointed to American individualism. The East Asian statistics that I have cited, for example, draw the response that those societies are too different culturally for a comparison to be valid. Not only did they impose stricter regulations, but their citizens, acting in a more communitarian spirit, also complied. According to the cultural argument, Americans would never have accepted such rules because of a deep-seated individualism that rejects governmental regulation of personal behavior. Individualism used to be an explanation of American achievements; in the pandemic it became an excuse for American failure.

Fortunately, we have some empirical evidence on whether regulations requiring masks made a difference in the United States. During the summer of 2020, Kansas conducted what amounted to a test of the efficacy of mask mandates. As a red state that might be presumed to be hostile to government regulation of personal behavior, Kansas is an instructive case. In July, the governor issued an executive order that mandated the use of masks in public places, while allowing counties to opt out. In an analysis of trends before and after the order went into effect, the CDC and Kansas Department of Health found that Covid19 incidence fell 6 percent in counties with the mask mandate and rose by 100 percent in the counties that rejected it. These results, the CDC report noted, were consistent with "declines in COVID-19 cases observed in 15 states and the District of Columbia, which mandated masks, compared with states that did not have mask mandates."

During the same period when Kansas enacted its partial mandate, Trump and his advisers debated whether the president should adopt a mask mandate for the country. According to the *Washington Post*, internal Trump campaign polling data in July showed that more than seventy percent of voters in states targeted by the campaign favored "mandatory masks at least indoors when in public, and even a majority of Republicans support this." One of the pollster's slides read, "Voters favor mask-wearing while keeping the economy open" and support Trump "issuing an executive order mandating the use of masks in public places." As part of this internal discussion, according to a *New York Times* report, Jared Kushner argued that embracing masks was a "no brainer" because Trump could say they were a key to enjoying the freedom to go safely to sports arenas and restaurants. But Trump concluded that "I'm not doing a mask mandate" after the White House chief of staff Mark Meadows warned that the base would "revolt" and that the president might not have the necessary legal authority, a point that had not worried Trump when he adopted other policies, such as excluding non-citizens from the Census count used for reapportionment.

Since a mask mandate by Trump might have had ample public support, including from Republican voters, it seems difficult to argue that America's individualist culture was the determining factor in the failure to adopt a mandate. Individualism might explain resistance to mask mandates if it had only one possible interpretation, which political leaders are unable to change. But even most libertarians accept a limit on individual liberty when actions threaten direct harm to others, as does the failure to wear a mask during a pandemic. Individualism was not the culprit. Political leaders also have the ability to shape opinion; as president, Trump radically shifted Republican sentiment on some issues, such as trade. As Kushner suggested, Trump could have spun "freedom" in favor of a mask mandate on the grounds that it would enlarge Americans' freedom to enter public places in safety. The party that bills itself as the "party of life" could easily have found a rationale for Americans to avoid killing their grandparents and their co-workers. Trump may have thought, like Meadows, that his base would not tolerate a shift on masks, and perhaps some of them would not have tolerated it. But he may just have misconstrued his own political self-interest.

Another cultural explanation for American behavior during the pandemic points to dominant notions of masculinity. According to this interpretation, the use of masks and other protections run up against the social pressures on men to display fearlessness and a willingness to take risks. Some evidence does support the idea that gender affected the use of masks. During August-September 2020, Gallup asked respondents, "Do you always wear a mask when you can't maintain social distancing in indoor settings?" Among Democrats, 90 percent of men and 93 percent of women said they did. Among Republicans, 40 percent of men and 56 percent of women said they did. While gender mattered in the responses, political identity mattered more.

To be sure, gender affects political identity — the gender gap in voting has reached unprecedented levels in recent years — and Trump made use of gender stereotypes in ridiculing masks, just as he drew on anti-government individualism to oppose regulations. But those cultural tendencies did not determine his choices. Even from the standpoint of his political self-interest, Trump could have chosen to pursue power a different way. By the summer of 2020 he may have dug himself in, but if he had acted differently in the early spring, public attitudes and social behavior regarding masks and other protections might have evolved differently despite the individualism and hyper-masculinity championed on the right.

The role of culture in explaining America's national failure is similar to that of race and social inequality. American culture did not determine the choices that Trump made, but it allowed him to believe those choices would work. The appeals to individualism and masculinity were resonant enough among Republican voters to be a plausible short-term political strategy, even if ultimately disastrous for the country. Similarly, the racial and other socioeconomic disparities in the pandemic allowed Republican leaders and the right-wing media to say the coronavirus was overblown. After all, they were not talking to the groups who were suffering the most. Republicans had a different frame of reference. Even as millions of Americans lost their livelihoods, Trump kept pointing to the stock market, which hit new highs in 2020. Just as Trump's response to the pandemic might have been different if the virus had first hit the red states instead of the blue states, his response might have been different if the pandemic had primarily hit a white, affluent population and had a bigger impact on the stock market and corporate America.

I do not mean to say Trump drew his support only from a white and privileged base. White working-class voters continued to support him, and while he lost African Americans and Latinos, he did better among them in 2020 than in 2016. People do not necessarily make their voting decisions on the basis of accurate calculations of risk. The virus did not kill or make seriously ill the majority of people who caught it. Individuals might discount the risk of contracting Covid19 if most or all the people they knew who had tested positive had recovered. Moreover, if their understanding of the corona-virus came from right-wing media they might discount the risk entirely, whereas they might worry that Democrats would shut down the economy and put them out of work. During 2020 many people may also have just changed their baseline expectations of risk. The virus may have just become one of many uncertainties in life to be endured as normal, not a reason to change behavior.

As great a disaster as the pandemic was, it became normal-ized in a remarkably short time. By the final months of 2020, the number of Americans dying of the virus every day was about what the country had lost on September 11, 2001. But the shock had worn off, and it had become almost unimaginable that the United States would make the necessary changes in society and behavior to control the pandemic. Complacency about the virus had set in. Early failures had narrowed the field of alternatives. The rate of community spread was so high that contact tracing and testing appeared to be futile. The only solution became a technological fix — a vaccine.

America's national failure in the pandemic has ominous implications for other challenges that America faces. Asking people to wear masks was not asking much of them. That many Americans refused to adopt so simple a change is a discouraging sign for how they will respond to demands that require sacrifice, such as reforms that are needed to deal with global warming. Climate change has evoked the same denial and defiance from the right as the pandemic, the same disregard for science, the same attraction to conspiracy stories. And just as Republicans dismissed the virus as overblown even when cases and deaths were growing in the red states, so they seem determined to ignore the realities of climate change even when they strike close to home. Disasters, such as the fires on the West Coast and the hurricanes in the Gulf, may become normalized. Alternatives may become unimaginable. Lying and manipulation for narrow political and economic gain may be become so routine that they no longer cause shock or indignation.

The United States has had great achievements, but it has also been lucky to have capable leaders when it needed them most. Until 2016, it succeeded in keeping demagogues like Trump away from the presidency. The same forces of unreason were always there, but they now control one of America's two parties. Although Trump is no longer in office, the political derangement that brought him to power is not yet over. Nor can we count on the supposed genius of our institutions to control it; there is only a hard struggle ahead to save those institutions and to get them to work at least as well as they once did. The pandemic is a warning about looming dangers. It is a cautionary tale that Americans must not forget if we are to escape from the derangement that has already cost so many lives and that threatens everything that we hold dear.

HENRI COLE

Lament for the Maker

At the museum of his life,
his leather duffle coat is behind glass.
It felt like a poem-protection center.
It was my responsibility to go home,
put food out in the same place every day,
talk to the people who came to eat,
then organize them, food and poetry being
a nourishment that shares a syntax.
There were many back roads to this far town,
but at the end of a path over pluff mud
I lay my shield down and stretched out on a bank.
Wool-gatherer, day-dreamer, bird-dogger,
I was sorry to have to leave,
but my hands felt less tied.

Like herons in a grove — or rain on mountains
or in a deep ravine — the realm of the immortals
releases and renews us. We want to live as if
we are going to die tomorrow. We want to learn as if
we are going to live forever. We want our bodies
to belong to us. Wider seems the path. On the train,
there was maple viewing and word games: alone, atone,
bemoan, daemon: "Thy word is all, if we could spell."
The sun seemed hush-hush, then later,
like a sword sinking thru stone. At the hotel,
there was black tea and murmuring.
After supper and a bath, I felt glad,
drinking water at the sink,
though usually I despair.

Guns

Stick in the mud, old fart, what are you doing
to get the guns off the street? I am not here to pick
on anyone. But now that they have shot Yosi,
who ground my meat in Hingham, and his shiny pink
meat-truck is for sale, I feel desolate. A gun is
a vengeful machine exacting a price. A gun rejects
stillness. It wants to get off. A man can be vain —
almost like a god — but inside him is a carp biting
the muck of a lake. A man who speaks too softly
gets hit with a big stick and lopes along behind.
A gun is minatory. Still, a week of kindness is greater.
Run, hide, evacuate; don't fire, duck, take cover.
At Yosi's ceremony, his family put a gold cloth on his face.
Self-reliant, autonomous, tough, he lay in a shroud of silk.

Glass of Absinthe and Cigarette

This is a poem about a man who is dead.
Sodomy laws treated him like a second-class citizen.
There were ripple effects. With the aid of stimulants,
he spoke like a truthteller and hungered for touch.
Even when repugnant, his disinhibition seemed godlike,
and what came out of him ravished me.
Alas, tolerance builds rapidly, and many lines must be
insufflated to produce that all-is-right-in-the-world euphoria:
"Feeling good. R U there. Come right now."
To keep myself sane,
I fled, dear reader,
but I'd give my kingdom
to see myself in those
dilated black eyes again.

Slowly in Haste

Those leaf blowers sure make a lot of noise.
Since love is the way, we nuzzle in the morning,
but wake up to high-decibel screaming,
dust, and exhaust smoke. More and more, being myself
seems to oppose the nature of the world. I don't want
updated privacy statements; I don't want to accept
cookies; I don't want active-shooter drills.
Lustful, moody, shy, I want to keep revising myself,
like a protean creature, but in a smart-phone free,
non-GMO space. Something like the Quiet Car.
Not hands-free though:
I want to be adjusting the sails;
a realist trims the sails
and doesn't whine about the wind.

Don't get me wrong — my life didn't turn out as expected.
Who knows what to expect out there? After
a wandering path has led over weird abysses,
I am here at the kitchen table eating cage-free eggs.
I am a HE still. It would be okay if a horn blared to herald
a finish, like in a symphony ("slowly in haste").
We suffer the ravages of Time & Weather, like trees holding on
to their leaves for color-change. From spring to spring,
we eat and avoid predators. The past intrudes,
the present languishes, the future is uncertain.
I hate leaving friends when the Here is simple and happy.
As I put on the radio and drink a ginger ale,
tanks and missiles surround the garden,
the wild horses neigh.

Horace

We were driving North. A sign read,
There will be no more wilderness;
I thought of my grandfather's softness
whilst hugging him when I was a little boy.
It was as if God hadn't created us naked
or defenseless and we had all we needed.
It was as if wilderness would never cease to be.
Now we must attend to it or die.
Unlike the rat in good Horace, I am mostly content
with my lot. *Get out of the way*, I mutter,
when pain approaches. We live in such tragic times,
buffeted like stone more than flesh.
Yet each day the fulgent sun rises,
blackbirds gather on the wire.

BECCA ROTHFELD

Sanctimony Literature

As many have noted and some have lamented, politics are multiplying: these days everything seems to have one. The search term "the politics of" yields over a million results in my university's library database. There is "the politics of dirt," "the politics of sleep," and even the politics of abstracta, such as "presence" and "absence." Obviously political entities, such as "authoritarian rule," have politics, as do things that might seem to the uninitiated to be staunchly apolitical, such as "dogs" and "snow." In a quaint display of reactionary nostalgia, my thesaurus suggests that "governmental" is a synonym for "political," but the political has evidently bubbled beyond the bounds of the state apparatus by now. It would make little sense to speak of the "the government of dirt" or "the government of absence," but both of these things apparently have "a politics."

Many of these freshly politicized phenomena do not just *have* politics so much as they *are* political, no matter what else they might appear to be. Like Plato's forms, a thing's politics have come to constitute its true if invisible essence, or so the popular story goes. The ethical, for instance, has become political: there are more than nine thousand hits for "the politics of ethics," whatever that means, in the library database. The aesthetic, too, is on the verge of annexation. As Lauren Oyler observed in *Bookforum*, "anxieties about being a good person, surrounded by good people, pervade contemporary novels and criticism." By "good person," contemporary novelists and critics do not mean someone rational, as Plato did; or someone merciful, as Augustine did; or someone who regards others as ends rather than means, as Kant did; or someone who celebrates the singularity of others, as Buber did. Instead, a person qualifies as "good" only if she conforms to a specific set of political standards, her personal virtues be damned. The standards in question, of course, are the ones endorsed by the crudest, most online leftists. "A good person," Oyler explains in her criticism of her moralistic peers, "possesses a deep understanding of power structures and her relative place in them." This is not understood by Oyler's adversaries as merely one of the many aspects of goodness: rather, it is all that they suppose virtue to consist in.

That is to say, a good person is concerned about global warming; she #believeswomen; she voted for Bernie and posted about it on Instagram. Admittedly, she bullies Warren supporters from an anonymous Twitter account with a snake avatar, but this amounts to "punching up" and is therefore morally commendable. A good person acknowledges her privilege frequently, and when she apologizes for it, as she often does, she pledges to "Do the Work" (but uncharacteristically declines to demand adequate compensation). A good person understands that "owning the libs" is of paramount importance, though she doesn't know any libs personally, probably because she understands that good people do not ever associate with bad people. (In any case, she is ultimately opposed to ownership.) In a word, a good person has no unpredictable opinions, no friends with whom she disagrees about anything of any importance, no views that could not be distilled into slogans and printed on canvas tote bags, and no unruly appetites. (Naturally she is a vegan.)

This person shows up in contemporary fiction as character, author, and regulative ideal alike. She is Bobby in Sally Rooney's *Conversations with Friends*, Adam Gordon in Ben Lerner's *Topeka School*, and Mia Warren in Celeste Ng's *Little Fires Everywhere*. She is also the conscience of all three novels, and under her watchful and unforgiving eye a body of writing has emerged that we might call "sanctimony literature." Its flourishing, commercially and critically, is one of the most salient features about this moment in the politicization of culture.

Sanctimony literature is, in effect, an extension of social media: it is full of self-promotion and the airing of performatively righteous opinions. It exists largely to make poster-cum-authors look good and scrollers-cum-readers feel good for appreciating the poster-cum-authors' goodness. In "Everybody's Protest Novel," James Baldwin wrote of sententious reformist fiction like *Uncle Tom's Cabin* that "we receive a very definite thrill of virtue from the fact that we are reading such a book at all." Sanctimony literature has similarly affirming and consoling effects: it serves to make us feel proud that we share its ethical assumptions.

Though it purports to treat themes of great gravity and complexity, such as sexism and economic inequality, sanctimony literature is suspiciously easy to read. Perusing a sanctimony novel feels like binge-watching a series on Netflix or scrolling through Instagram, pausing every now and then to read an inspirational caption. (Unsurprisingly, Rooney's *Normal People* and Ng's *Little Fires* have both been adapted into popular TV shows.) The vocabulary of both texts is often unambitious, and the syntax undemanding, for despite the sanctimony novel's pretensions to subversion and system-smashing, it is usually formally unadventurous. (Ben Lerner, an inspired stylist, is a notable exception to this rule.) The little exploration that the genre permits is so easily digestible that it hardly constitutes experimentation at all: in place of Proustian effusions we get fragments, strewn strategically amid complete sentences, to signal that the text at hand is capital-L-Literary. Emma Cline's *The Girls*, a gem of a sanctimony novel, is full of such shards: "Mothers glancing around for their children, moved by some feeling they couldn't name. Women reaching for their boyfriend's hands." These slippery non-sentences may seem daringly ungrammatical, but they are so easy to gulp down. A good person knows that ethical consumption and creation are impossible under capitalism, so she sets out to write a blockbuster, reminding herself that naked clauses are Tweet-adjacent and therefore apt to sell better. Like the protest novels that Baldwin so deliciously excoriated, sanctimony novels contain morals that are, as he puts it, "neatly framed, and incontestable like those improving motoes sometimes found on the walls of furnished rooms."

Above all, sanctimony literature is defined by its efforts to demonstrate its Unimpeachably Good Politics in the manner of a child waving an impressive report card at her parents in hopes of a pat on the head. *The Topeka School* is admittedly stylistically sophisticated, but Lerner nonetheless makes sure to lambaste Trump in no uncertain terms, lest we mistake his narrator's adolescent wrongthink for his own mature worldview. In the final scene of the novel, the author's alter-ego attends a protest against Immigration and Customs Enforcement, nefariously known as ICE. Flush with the sense of his own bravery, he reflects that "It embarrassed me, it always had, but I forced myself to participate, to be a part of a tiny public speaking, a public learning slowly how to speak again." In *Conversations with Friends* and *Normal People*, two fine exemplars of the sanctimony tradition, Sally Rooney reminds us over and over that her characters, like their author, are Marxists with the Right Opinions. "I'm gay, and Frances is a communist," one character in *Conversations* announces as she introduces herself and her friend to some new acquaintances. Later, Frances the communist avows that she "want[s] to destroy capitalism and consider[s] masculinity personally oppressive." In *Normal People*, one character remarks that an injustice has occurred for reasons she cannot comprehend: "it's something to do with capitalism," she concludes gravely. Her interlocuter replies dolefully, "Yeah, everything is, that's the problem, isn't it?"

These books — millennial agit-prop, millennial middle-brow — are inflated and animated by an unshakable faith in their own rectitude. Impossibly foreign to their guiding sensibility are such characters as Henrich von Kleist's Michael Kohlhaas, the mesmerizingly bloodthirsty protagonist of *Michael Kohlhaas*, or Philip Roth's Portnoy, the venomously sexist yet perversely charismatic anti-hero of *Portnoy's Complaint*. Now all the eponyms read Gramsci, respect women, and recycle. When and if they do make minor political gaffes, they acknowledge their faults and repent immediately, in a desperate bid to stave off the inevitable torrent of external criticism. In the era of sanctimony literature, Oyler writes mockingly, "a good person is not perfect (she has read enough not to fall for that trap), but she is self-aware."

Traps though they may be, these displays of preemptive self-flagellation have proved commercially irresistible, which is to say that they have elicited the coveted pats on the head in the form of prizes and plaudits. Their authors closely resemble masochistic Tweeters eager to cancel themselves before any of their enemies has a chance to close in for the kill. As Ligaya Mishan explained in her incisive genealogy of "cancellation" in the *New York Times T Magazine*,

> On Twitter, people speak scoffingly of canceling themselves...There's the hope that if we have the grace to cancel ourselves first, our ostracism will be temporary, a mere vacation from social media. Absolution is reduced to performance, a walk with a bowed head through jeers and splattered mud.

Mishan's prognosis may sound exaggerated — but recall the self-erasing contrition of Jessica Krug, the white professor at George Washington University who confessed to posing as Afro-Puerto-Rican in a deranged and remorseful blog post. "You should absolutely cancel me,", she imperishably declared, "and I absolutely cancel myself." The literary sanctimonists are likewise tripping over themselves to repent loudly and in print.

Often they do so by explicitly renouncing their past failures. *The Topeka School* is a sort of rejoinder to Lerner's first two novels, both of which sparkle because they take a mordantly ambivalent stance towards a narrator who is craven yet sympathetic. Sometimes they do so by introducing politically suspect characters solely for the sake of loudly disavowing them. It is telling that both Rooney and Lerner pit themselves against debaters who believe in earnest engagement with opposing positions: Rooney's villain of choice in *Normal People* is a college debater who defends freedom of speech, and Lerner's adversary in *The Topeka School* is a high school debate coach who urges his students to consider conservative arguments. Their respective protagonists flirt with these corrupt influences not because they suspect that thinking through Bad Politics might prove philosophically fertile, but rather so that they can demonstrate personal growth when they finally denounce disagreement for good. The enemy is anyone who would countenance the Wrong Position even for the sake of rebutting it. Beware the contamination that may result from exposure to the other side even in a good-faith exchange. Protect yourself! Lerner and Rooney demonstrate their piety by practicing what they preach: their novels are both exercises in retiring intellectual curiosity, and the result is a literature of consummate self-cancellation.

It is probably just as well, at least in the case of the sanctimonists, that aesthetics is dissolving into politics, because novels that cancel themselves and all their wayward characters do not make for strong art. For one thing, they are stupefyingly smug. As the critic Nathan Goldman has remarked about the passage in *The Topeka School* in which Lerner's protagonist recollects how much he loved performing cunnilingus on his high school love interest,

To be sure, the tone playfully mocks the young Adam's self-seriousness, self-congratulation, and self-regard. But it also reaffirms his understanding of himself — an understanding his parents share — as an outsider to the world of crude misogyny which, though it is his milieu, remains fundamentally external to the proto-feminist, Ivy-bound poet who goes down on his girlfriend.

It is not insignificant that so much of Lerner's novel ridicules his adolescent alter ego for being such a "man child," a term with which he intends to highlight the link between masculinity and childishness but which in fact illuminates the link between sanctimony literature and "young adult" fiction, colloquially known as YA. In truth, YA is something of a misnomer, as the books that qualify are not really for young adults so much as they are for tantrum-prone children. Now, there is nothing wrong with fiction written for ten-year-olds, much of which I loved when I was ten; but just as *Lolita* would fail as a children's book, a novel supposedly composed for moral and intellectual adults errs when it offers up moral nuggets that would sustain a fourth grader. Baldwin disparagingly compares *Uncle Tom's Cabin* to *Little Women*, and it is flooring how many recent literary hits are likewise set in the simplified ethical universe of adolescence: both of Rooney's novels are about college students, Lerner's is about a high schooler, Ng's *Little Fires Everywhere* is sort of about parents but largely about their teenaged children, the protagonist of Cline's *The Girls* is fourteen, the viral story "Cat Person" follows a jaded college student, and so on and on.

Sanctimony literature is aesthetically wanting not only because its language and moral outlook are juvenile, but also because its characters are not human agents so much as avatars of identity categories. In *Normal People* and *The Topeka School*, evil debaters are no more than roughly sketched ambassadors for unpalatable conservatism. In *The Girls,* a sexist cult that doubles as a symbol for The Patriarchy effaces the subjectivity of its female members. The book is indeed about girls, members of a group defined by their abuse at the hands of lecherous men. The cult's leader, Russell, is sexism personified. Though he is modelled on Charles Manson, he is stripped of the murderer's more memorable quirks: according to the logic of sanctimony literature, to represent someone evil as interesting or even idiosyncratic is necessarily to "glorify" him. (In this sense, the greatest anti-sanctimonist text of all time is *Paradise Lost*, with its irresistible portrait of Satan.)

All three of these novels and their characters lack what Lionel Trilling called "the personal vision affirming itself against the institutional with the peculiar passionateness of art." Their approach is familiar. In accordance with the tenets of progressivism, the collective and the systemic are their primary units of interest. In activist contexts, of course, a focus on structural reform is sensible: it seems manifest that, say, the anti-racism movement would be better served by prison abolition than by milquetoast corporate trainings in which white people are urged to fortify their fragile psyches. But a novel is not a social movement, nor is it a piece of political theory, and good fiction homes in on particular people — people who are shaped by their social environments, to be sure, but who are also so irreducibly singular as to amount to more than just epiphenomena of their conditions. As Trilling cautions in an essay on John Dos Passos, written in an earlier era of progressive piety, "too insistent a cry against the importance of the individual quality is a sick cry." And as Baldwin warned a generation later, there is not much to be gained from attempting to "lop" the human "down to the status of time-saving invention. He is, after all, not merely a member of a Society or a Group or a deplorable conundrum to be explained by Science. He is — and how old-fashioned the words sound! — something more than that, something resolutely indefinable, unpredictable." Irving Howe, who wrote an important book on the political novel, echoes both Trilling and Baldwin when he reflects that his literary contemporaries believe it beneath them to consider "anything so gauche as human experience or obsolete as human beings."

You do not need to deny that people's habits of mind are to a significant extent the product of their material contexts in order to accept the essential corrective of Trilling, Howe, and Baldwin's bold anti-reductionist approach. It might turn out, though I doubt that it will, that people are, at the most foundational level, nothing but accretions of social circumstance — but even if it does, we will have to persist in perpetuating the fruitful fiction of personality if we are to produce profound and persuasive novels. Fiction flourishes when it reflects actual individual existence, and no matter how enthusiastically theorists accept a "systemic" analysis of art in principle, few manage to experience themselves, their lovers, or their enemies as reducible to socio-economic tokens in practice. In our daily interactions, Trilling notes, "we do not easily tolerate people who are content to ascribe their personal — I do not mean their practical — failures to circumstances alone." This is not to say that we are not sometimes delusional: it is only to say that fiction succeeds when it captures our real, if perhaps mistaken, sense of self. Trilling goes still further, asserting that social and economic determinism's inability to account for our basic experience of individuality is a strike against its truth. And Baldwin, too, carries his critique of the politicization of art in a similar direction: "the failure of the protest novel lies in its rejection of life, the human being, the denial of his beauty, dread, power, in its insistence that it is his categorization which is real and which cannot be transcended." The upshot is not that we should abandon social and economic analysis altogether — Trilling, Howe, and Baldwin were all, to say the least, sophisticated social and political thinkers— but rather that we should not export a method well-suited to political criticism into the foreign province of fiction, where it frequently deserves no place. Heretical as it sounds, there are realms of life in which politics does not always belong. After all, as Baldwin rightly observes, "literature and sociology are not one and the same."

Of course, even in the realm of the novel, concern with morality is not misplaced. If sanctimony literature is soporific, it is not because it portrays people who strive to live ethically. Trying to be good is an important — if not the only important and not always the most important — part of being a person, and nothing that is human can be alien to literature. There are plenty of honest and unsentimental fictions about people trying their best to be good, or to figure out what goodness entails. Vasily Grossman's monumental *Life and Fate* is in large part about Viktor Shtrum's struggle to retain his integrity in the face of totalitarian pressures, and an entire planet away, Jane Austen's *Pride and Prejudice* follows Elizabeth's Bennet's vexed efforts to judge her acquaintances with charity and justice. These are careful and complex creations that neither lapse into homily nor shy away from ethical conundrums.

They succeed in part because they resist Manichean temptations: both are populated with characters who are neither angelic nor diabolical but morally mottled, compound creatures, as real people are. Elizabeth Bennet is usually a sharp judge of character, but she occasionally succumbs to the

113

prejudices of the title. Her certainty in the infallibility of her initial impressions prevents her from grasping that Mr. Darcy is well-meaning, despite his apparent standoffishness. For his part, Mr. Darcy can be pretentious, though he is ultimately honorable. And in his reduced and terrifying circumstances Viktor Shtrum also vacillates, alternately colluding with and defying his Stalinist oppressors. The sanctimonists maintain a tidily bifurcated interest in good people and bad people, when in fact what they should be studying is the good and the bad in all people — the full murk of human motivation, the tangle of tensions and contradictions, of desires and principles, that is the permanent condition of human choice.

Sanctimony literature errs, then, not because it ventures into moral territory, but because it displays no genuine curiosity about what it really means to be good, and is blind to the distinction between morality and moralism, and exhibits no doubt about its own probity. Isn't it funny that a good person, as envisioned by Lerner and Rooney, is exactly like Lerner and Rooney and all of their readers? And isn't it striking that all these Lerner-clones and Rooney-clones are depicted as irreproachably upstanding, while all of their enemies are represented as one-dimensionally irredeemable? The heroes and heroines of sanctimony literature are so steeped in self-satisfaction that they provide an inadvertent moral lesson. It turns out that someone can have all the *de rigueur* political opinions without thereby achieving any measure of meaningful ethical success. A novel's goodness *is* bound up with its beauty, but there is more to goodness than boilerplate leftist fervor.

If I think a little rhetorical ribbing about the "politics of every-thing" crowd is in order, it is because I wish to combat sanctimony literature's resistance to self-examination and its accompanying humorlessness, even stylistically. But I would hardly deny the obvious, namely that the way in which a society is organized has some bearing on the art that its denizens produce. Nor would I deny that there may be something fruitful about analyses that delve into an artwork's political context. Patently, it is profitable to read the black novelist Nella Larsen with reference to the history of American racism, or to read the Jewish poet Paul Celan with the Holocaust in mind. Indeed, it is hard for me to think of any book that would not be illuminated by a discussion of the conditions of its production. Even books that are about the chilly detachment of the aesthetic domain are the artifacts of a particular time, place, and worldview. Readers and writers are also people, which is to say that they are always members of political communities and are therefore always situated at what Trilling once called "the bloody crossroads where literature and politics meet." Authors who attempt to withdraw from political and social life, like Thoreau, are defined indirectly by the political affiliations they reject; writers who oppose the regimes in power, like Victor Serge, are members of political communities of resisters.

But everything that I have just described about the historical circumstances of the imagination is truistic. The question is not whether aesthetics is political in this anodyne sense but rather whether political value is the supreme value, the only sort of value — and, by extension, whether *every* analysis of *every* artwork must *always* advert to political factors, on pain of moral and evaluative failure. Is it permissible to write anything about Celan that emphasizes his choice of imagery rather than his heritage? Is he only a Holocaust survivor? Is there anything to be gained by praising his work's formal qualities without delving into his traumatic past? A related question is whether an artwork that is politically suspect could nonetheless show a degree of aesthetic promise. *Portnoy's Complaint* is manically sexist: must its locker-room lechery vitiate its sense of humor? And, really, are there no great conservative novels?

I am not sure whether anyone is enough of an avowed zealot of politicization to insist outright that there is no point in discussing the formal features of Celan's poetry, or that *Portnoy's Complaint* cannot be funny because it is sometimes misogynist. The novelist Viet Than Nguyen came closest to recommending the omnipotence of politics in an absurd *New York Times* column in which he urged his fellow writers to write exclusively political fiction in the wake of the Trump presidency. "What will writers do when the outrage is over? Will they go back to writing about flowers and moons?" he asks, as if flowers, wilting in warming temperatures, were not an appropriate object of political regard — and as if flowers and moons could only ever matter for political reasons.

In practice, many writers who do not go so far as to explicitly endorse such a cartoonishly extreme position nonetheless behave as if they regarded political virtue as the only or most important kind. Why else would they so often act as if criticizing a book's politics were tantamount to issuing a wholesale aesthetic indictment? Why else would they so often intimate that literature can only matter if it has salutary political effects? Why else, for instance, would the novelist Lauren Groff take to Twitter to assert that the political turmoil of the Trump era could have been averted if "a small percentage of Republicans read up to two books a year?" If Tweets such as Groff's are a perennial scourge — if literary people are often compelled to shout from the rooftops that books can spark revolution and save the world — it is because many of them are unable to conceive of something mattering for apolitical reasons. Expostulations such as Groff's are the logical endpoint of a culture in which we desperately want to regard literature as a worthy pursuit but cannot admit that aesthetic and ethical worth count as such. If books have to make a political difference in order to make any difference at all, then dedicated readers are left to stake out a losing position, for it is simply not plausible that literature will ever tank capitalism or keep the ice caps from melting.

This is not to say that works of literature have never had any tangible political effects. On the contrary, a handful of books — often the worst ones, aesthetically speaking — have had outsize influence: for all its flaws and immaturities, *Uncle Tom's Cabin* ignited a nation-wide debate about the horrors of slavery. But if political utility on the ground were the only measure of a book's value, we would be hard-pressed to defend the vast majority of masterpieces, among them *Moby Dick, The Wings of the Dove, A Remembrance of Things Past,* and so on. Did Proust change the world? I think he did, but not in the way the activists want to change it. Even more obviously political fictions, such as *Invisible Man* and *The Yellow Wallpaper,* did not yield many immediate or concrete reforms. Admittedly, books that do not directly launch social movements can raise political awareness, which may qualify as a virtue whether or not it ultimately precipitates action. But do we really want to say that this is the only way a work of literature can succeed? Do we really want to conclude that the merits of *Days of Abandonment* and *Beloved* are limited to their rather obvious political implications?

A person is allowed to have many priorities. In fact, she must have many priorities. She can — and she should — care about both beauty and justice. Problems arise not because writers are doing their best to balance a range of sometimes conflicting commitments, but because they seek to resolve the tensions by convincing themselves that there are no conflicts to speak of. If essays about madeleines and memories are to be shrunk to political gestures, then the Proustian does not have to deviate from the dogmas of the day or admit that she is failing by her own professed standards. But her delusion is as self-serving as it is dangerous. The fact is, you have not discharged your political duties by writing a Marxist analysis of Henry James, and even if you routinely criticize poetry with "bad politics," you have no excuse to skip the protest. If your primary goal is to become as politically righteous as possible, you would do better to become an organizer, a labor lawyer, an investigative journalist, or a politician — all dignified careers that double as admirable expressions of citizenship.

So should you fling these critical observations to the floor and rush out onto the streets, pounding your chest and shrieking? Not necessarily. Organizers, labor lawyers, investigative journalists, and (some) politicians are commendable, but there are many ways to strive for different iterations of the good. The Grand Canyon is majestic, but it didn't vote for Sanders (given its location, it more likely would have voted for Trump); *Babette's Feast* is a compositionally perfect film about the euphoric maximalism proper to both religious revelation and artistic creation, but it has absolutely nothing to do with #believingwomen. Maybe we could coax a political lesson out of Gerard Manley Hopkins' racked sonnets, but why on earth should we try? Nor do political merit and moral merit always overlap. Political virtue may be a species of ethical virtue, but there are ethical qualities that cannot be construed as merely political boons. The authorial voice that declaims loudly in

118

The Topeka School opposes racism, sexism, and xenophobia, but it is still objectionably self-congratulatory. At times it is even patronizing, and its condescension betrays a lack of respect for — or even a lack of belief in — its readers' moral agency. Rooney's characters are communists, but they are also insufferably hubristic (so much so that they often seem more like caricatures than like real human beings.) Plenty of people advocate for universal healthcare while inflicting interpersonal injury; there are any number of political paragons who fail as parents, lovers, teachers, and friends. (In a better literature than the sanctimonists', the frequent distance between our ideals and our practices would itself be the subject of interesting novels.)

Materialists often scoff at calls for compassion, as if the injunction to cultivate private kindness amounts to an alibi for public inaction. But if we abandon the fiction that all value is political, we can see that it is possible to recommend compassion without recommending it as a political strategy. Philanthropy is not a replacement for material redistribution, but that doesn't mean there is nothing to be said for being generous to the people around you. Even progressives are reprehensible when they are narcissistic, sadistic, rectitudinous, dogmatic, patronizing, hectoring, and dismissive. Sanctimony literature may champion admirable political aims, but it does so at too high an ethical cost: it flattens complicated moral landscapes into children's jungle gyms and addresses its readers as if they were prepubescent. And these ethical failings, it turns out, are not irrelevant to the genre's enormous aesthetic deficiencies.

As long as we are wedded to a narrow conception of the ethical as inseparable from the political, it will be hard for us to trace much of a link between the ethical and the aesthetic:

as sanctimony literature demonstrates, books with politically upstanding characters and politically saintly sensibilities are often pat and pappy. But once we renovate our notion of the ethical, we can see how it might come to stand in a more intimate relation to the aesthetic — and how a novel lacking a certain sort of moral complexity might therefore suffer artistically. Lionel Trilling knew this.

In his early examination (and commendation) of E.M. Forster, the critic wisely insisted that rich writing must display what he called "moral realism." This, he clarifies, "is not the awareness of morality itself but of the contradictions, paradoxes, and dangers of living the moral life." In a later essay he added that "to act against social injustice is right and noble" but "to choose to act so does not settle all moral problems but on the contrary generates new ones of an especially difficult sort." "Moral realism" becomes important precisely when people are most committed to "moral righteousness": at such times, among them the era in which the anti-Stalinist Trilling lived, we will drown in "books that point out the bad conditions, that praise us for taking progressive attitudes," but we will lack "books that raise questions in our minds not only about the conditions but about ourselves, that lead us to refine our motives and ask what might lie behind our good impulses." He continues, in a passage worth quoting, as it were, liberally, "Moral indignation, which has been said to be the favorite emotion of the middle class, may be in itself an exquisite pleasure. To understand this does not invalidate moral indignation but only sets up the conditions on which it ought to be entertained." In other words, we should be suspicious of artifacts that serve primarily to assure us of our own heroism.

Trilling's awareness of the pratfalls of moral self-congratulation drove him to criticize his own political allies more harshly and incisively than he criticized his opponents. Though he famously wrote, in 1950, that conservatives propound neither thoughts nor theories but "irritable mental gestures which seek to resemble ideas," he is far more frequently critical of liberals than he is of their — and his own — rivals. He admires Forster precisely because the novelist "is at war with the liberal imagination," and this despite the writer's "long commitment to the doctrines of liberalism." Trilling, too, was a champion of liberal causes, but he was also a lifelong adversary of the sententiousness to which liberalism often gives rise. He praises Forster for dashing the kind of liberal imagination according to which "good is good and bad is bad" and balks at dappled articles like "good-and-evil," for which reason its representatives "have always moved in an aura of self-congratulation. They sustain themselves by flattering themselves with intentions and they dismiss as reactionary whoever questions them." The liberals whom Trilling made a career of targeting "play the old intellectual game of antagonistic principles. It is an attractive game because it gives us the sensation of thinking, and its first rule is that if one of the two opposed principles is wrong, the other is necessarily right."

Now dissolve for a moment to the digitized present. The comfortable antinomies for which Trilling arraigned liberals have recently been given a new and frighteningly powerful technological foundation. As Christian Lorentzen pointed out in *Harper's* a few years ago, the intellectual and aesthetic horizons of contemporary liberals and liberal-analogs are exhausted by the limited options afforded by social media — like or dislike, upvote or downvote. It is all Rotten Tomatoes. The contemporary liberal — and just as often, the contemporary progressive -- is uncomfortable in that necessary wilder-

121

ness called "the middle," which Trilling once described as "the only honest place to be."

All this may come as a surprise to those anxious to cast Trilling as the liberal par excellence, or even as an early neoliberal, which is of course the ultimate smear. But when Trilling states at the beginning of *The Liberal Imagination* that liberalism "is not only the dominant but the sole intellectual tradition" in the United States, he does not regard this as grounds for celebration so much as an occasion for vigilance: "a criticism which has at heart the interests of liberalism might find its most useful work not in confirming liberalism in its sense of general rightness but in putting under some degree of pressure the liberal ideas and assumptions of the present time." That was one of the most renowned sentences of its era, and deservedly so. Far from endorsing neoliberalism, Trilling does not understand "liberalism" to pick out any particular economic arrangement: instead, he sees it as "a large tendency rather than a concrete body of doctrine." It must always be on guard against complacency, self-assurance, and the pre-reflective acceptance of a self-aggrandizing ideology that takes the place of a modest and discomfiting idea.

That certain contemporary critics think of Trilling as something approaching a reactionary is further evidence of their mental poverty. For them, anyone who rejects any aspect of the standard leftist package must therefore be a reactionary. Dislike! Downvote! Own the Libs! "To the simple mind," Trilling wrote premonitorily, "the mention of complication looks like a kind of malice, and to the mind under great stress the suggestion of something 'behind' the apparent fact looks like a call to quietism, like mere shilly-shallying." But in reality uncertainty is not spinelessness, it is the first step on the bumpy path towards responsible conviction. It is not enough to want morality, "not even enough to work for it — we must want it and work for it with intelligence." We are lost when a "'cherished goal' forbids that we stop to consider how we reach it, or if we may not destroy it in trying to reach it the wrong way." To wit: Might the relentless production of hyper-commercialized novels that practically adapt themselves to the screen undermine a laudable anti-corporate agenda? Might inciting moral panics about the tech overlords on social media line the same coffers that we purport to want to empty? Might a novel that aspires to fight sexism fail if it is crammed with women who look for all the world like nothing more than blobs of doughy victimhood?

Moral realism helps us see how our methods conflict with our motives. It is a vital antidote to the progressive who "thinks chiefly of his own good will and prefers not to know that the goodwill generated its own problems, that the love of humanity has its own vices and the love of truth own sensibilities. There is a morality of morality." Moral realism is the morality of morality and is therefore a specifically ethical virtue, though a contemporary sensibility may struggle to recognize it as such, for it does not convey many readily legible principles, much less does it urge us to reduce our meat consumption or stop writing about the moon. Trilling's *New York Times* obituary reported, in 1975, with a twinge of disappointment, that "as a critic he founded no school and left no group of disciples closely associated with his name." But that is the measure of his accomplishment: instead of instructing us in which propositions to believe, Trilling's criticism models the art of thinking without a mold and without a foregone conclusion. This is what makes him so invigorating to read: he was sympathetic to Marx, but he was not a Marxist; he was fascinated by Freud, but he was not

123

a Freudian; he delighted in form, but he was not a formalist; he was a liberal, but he was suspicious of liberalism; he was a close student of society, but he was not convinced that the human element could be wholly reduced to its circumstances.

"On the one hand," he wrote, "class is character, soul, and destiny, and...on the other hand class is not finally determining." In our unfortunate intellectual situation, such a pronouncement sounds almost incomprehensible. It is unlike "all the great absolutes," which are "dull when discussed in themselves." It does not fit neatly into the upvote/downvote dichotomy: we are genuinely unsure what will follow. And the very reason that Trilling is so interesting is also the reason that sanctimony literature is so boring: because absolutes are dead ends. We know at the outset of a sanctimony novel that good (the skinny leftists) will triumph over evil (the balding libertarians). We know what the canvas tote bags will look like and that the characters will all eat seitan. We know that a certain style of intellectual and emotional conformity will trouble neither the characters nor their creators.

And worst of all, we also know exactly what goodness, in the circumscribed world of the novels in question, boils down to. What we are denied is the intellectual excitement of trying to answer the exceedingly complicated question of what a morally serious person should be like. It is because sanctimony literature eschews moral realism that it foregoes the sort of style that might at last confer substance. We already have enough politics; now it is time for us to find an ethics; and if we are demanding of our skills and our sensibilities, an aesthetics may follow. If we cannot have enough good people, we may still aspire to more good books.

ENRIQUE KRAUZE

A Modest Utopia

I.

Every quixotic idea has its origins in books of chivalry.
Mine began in reading about English political history in the
eighteenth century. From Macaulay and Namier, I learned how
the Whig Party governed England for seventy years on the basis
of a parliamentary majority secured through a corrupt system
and fraudulent elections. This strange situation was most
memorably portrayed by Hogarth, with his scathing paintings
and engravings of rotten boroughs where even the dead were
allowed a vote. But then a set of sudden reforms, allied with
the emergence of a free press, ushered in genuine competition
between parties. The story ended well.

Reading this in Mexico, reflecting on this saga of political progress, an obvious thought immediately occurred to me: if this happened in England two centuries ago, why not in Mexico now? The result was an essay called "For a Democracy Without Adjectives," which I published in 1984 in *Vuelta*, an extraordinary journal founded in 1976 by Octavio Paz, where I worked as deputy editor. In left-wing circles, it was common to degrade democracy by adding adjectives such as "bourgeois" and "formal." What we needed, in my view, was democracy, period. Without adjectives, without condescension, without the fantasy that there is something better.

No sooner had my essay appeared than the government instructed its hired writers to attack my proposal as both senseless and dangerous. The journalistic, academic, and political Left, still wedded to the paradigm of the socialist revolution, came out against me as well, trotting out the old Marxist clichés about the falsity and inadequacy of democracy. The National Action Party (PAN), which since 1939 had gradually sought to construct a citizenry that recognized the worth of free elections, was at that time a center-right presence in Mexican politics, but it was weak. Nobody, or almost nobody, saw that the democratic liberal alternative proposed in 1910 by Francisco I. Madero to counteract the dictator Porfirio Díaz was the right and proper way out for Mexico. Madero led the first and very brief phase of the Mexican Revolution. In 1911, he was elected president in fair and free elections. He presided over a purely democratic regime for fifteen months and was overthrown and murdered in a coup backed by the American ambassador. This started the violent phase of the revolution that lasted until 1920 and left one million people dead, after which Mexico abandoned Madero's democratic ideal. The PRI was founded in 1929 and

126

held total power until the end of the century.

Liberal democracy, I argued, was also a solution for Latin America more generally, as it seemed to be indicated by the rejection of military governments in the 1980s in Argentina, Peru, Bolivia, Brazil, and Uruguay. These countries, each by degrees and all by the holding of elections, were moving in that direction. But liberal democracy was still not viewed positively by the region as a whole, with the notable exceptions of Venezuela and Costa Rica. In fact, in Colombia and Peru, as well as in Central America, the most viable means to power was still the one mapped out by the Cuban revolution, whose prestige remained intact in Latin American universities and among Latin American intellectuals.

The Sandinista revolution in Nicaragua, for example. In 1984, *Vuelta* published Gabriel Zaid's "Nicaragua: The Enigma of the Elections," in which Zaid declared that the Sandinistas had the perfect card to play in order to discredit American "aggression": they could simply call elections, from which one of their number would undoubtedly emerge triumphant. They used liberal means for illiberal — more precisely, dictatorial — ends. This anti-Sandinista heresy cost Zaid dear: in Mexico, and across Latin America, the left vilified him as an ally of Reagan. That same year, on being awarded the Frankfurt International Book Fair Prize, Octavio Paz called for exactly the same thing: democracy in Nicaragua. The response to his challenge was a symbolic lynching: outside his home on Paseo de la Reforma in Mexico City, protestors burned posters bearing the image of his face.

The next year, the front cover of *Vuelta*'s April issue was devoted to an essay by Octavio Paz called "PRI: Time's Up." Paz bravely argued that the PRI must open the way for profound political reform. The PRI was an ingenious kind of dictatorship, but a dictatorship nonetheless. Elections were organized by the Interior Ministry, and the PRI won every legislative and executive position all over the country. This closed political structure, which had been in operation for six decades, struck Paz as unsustainable and wrong. And indeed it was. The power wielded by the president was not only excessive, it bordered on the imperial: the Chamber of Deputies and the Senate, the Supreme Court of Justice, the governors and legislatures of all thirty-two states, answered directly to him. The so-called "Mexican Republic," which on paper, in the Constitution, was "representative, democratic, and federal," in practice verged on an absolute monarchy, a monarchy of a party, with the outgoing president choosing his successor at six-year intervals. The single lever of power in Mexico was the PRI, the Party of the Institutionalized Revolution, which properly speaking was not a party at all, but rather a machine geared for the winning of elections, as well as an efficient social mobility agency and patronage network in the way that it doled out public money and public positions. And there was yet another undemocratic feature to this alleged democracy: freedom of expression was limited to a few newspapers. (It was little more than a whimper on radio and it was non-existent on television.)

The history of dissent is often best documented in journals, and so *Vuelta* again: in that same issue in April 1985, Zaid had a piece called "Scenarios For The End of The PRI," among which he included a major earthquake — an actual earthquake, he was not speaking metaphorically — that would lead to the total discrediting of the political system. He was prophetic: the earthquake came to pass in September of that year, a terrible natural catastrophe. The incompetence of the government's response exposed its failings to all, and many Mexicans in central and northern Mexico began to believe that democracy might be a possibility. Various other factors added to this new awareness, among them the PRI's disastrous handling of Mexico's oil revenues, which in 1982 led the country to default on its sovereign debt.

As the evidence of the PRI's damage continued to mount, the left began to react to this demand for change by non-revolutionary means. Two years after I made my proposal for a democracy without adjectives, the distinguished Trotskyite historian Adolfo Gilly published an essay admitting that the idea might be worth taking seriously. The title of his piece was "A Modest Utopia." It was a sign of the times. With the involvement of parties on the left and the right, of unions, students, the teaching class, intellectuals, journalists, businesspeople, and broad, plural movements all throughout civil society, Mexico was beginning its move to democracy. Significantly, electoral fraud started to be seen as a national embarrassment. In 1988, one such fraud snatched victory from the hands of the presidential candidate Cuauhtémoc Cárdenas, who could at that point have put out a call for a revolution but instead opted for the historic decision of creating the Party of the Democratic Revolution (PRD), which for the first time in Mexico's history unified every leftist grouping. Elections took place again in 1994 and 2000, the latter organized and overseen by the Federal Electoral Institute, an independent body. Ernesto Zedillo, the twentieth century's last PRI president, behaved in an exemplary fashion and facilitated an orderly and peaceful transition.

Finally, at the turn of the century, the seemingly impossible happened: Mexico, the country of the Aztec *tlatoani*, of the Spanish viceroys, of the caudillos, of the imperial presidents, put an end to seven decades of PRI rule and elected Vicente Fox, a PAN candidate. A pluralistic Congress was also elected, with the three main parties represented. Perhaps for the first time since a distant experiment in the 1800s, there was full autonomy for the Supreme Court of Justice. Government at the state level enjoyed hitherto unknown independence. There was unfettered freedom of expression in the written press, and on radio and television too. "Democracy without adjectives" no longer seemed so quixotic.

II.

"Stick to my theory and you won't go wrong," my beloved teacher, the historian Richard M. Morse, once said to me. Over the course of a twenty-year friendship, he never took issue with my essays on behalf of liberal democracy in Mexico, nor with my critical history of paternalist and personalist rule in Mexico from 1810 to 1996. But Morse did not agree with my premises. His entire body of work on Ibero-America — as he preferred to call Latin America — emphasized the unlikelihood, the impossibility even, of liberal democracy ever fully taking root in these countries. And the strangest part about his theory was his insistence that the inappropriateness of liberal democracy to the region was not a reason for complaint. Who was this American historian who was disqualifying us from the moral and political order to which so many of us aspired, from the greatest political arrangements ever devised?

Though he was a distinguished and admired teacher at places such as Yale, Stanford and the Wilson Center in Washington (where he was director of the Latin American Center), Morse was not an ordinary academic, but rather a thinker in the mold of Miguel de Unamuno and José Ortega y Gasset, with a passion for Ibero-American culture. Born in New Jersey in 1922, he was the scion of one of New England's oldest families, for generations deeply involved in commerce with

Asia. One of his forebears was the inventor of the famous code. Morse began his academic career at Princeton, where he was a disciple of the critics Allen Tate and R. P. Blackmur. There he edited *The Nassau Literary Review*, in whose pages he published reports, stories, and a play inspired by a series of trips in the early 1940s to Cuba, Venezuela, Chile, Argentina, and Mexico. In Chile he met the Minister of Health, a young socialist who argued that the United States owed a historical debt to the South American countries. His name was Salvador Allende. In Mexico he interviewed Pablo Neruda (who was the Chilean ambassador) and the philosopher José Vasconcelos. Morse enlisted in the Army in 1943, seeing action in the Pacific, and on his return enrolled at Columbia University, where he studied under Américo Castro, the great historian of Spain's blended Arabic, Christian, and Jewish past. From him Morse learned the rich possibilities of the comparative cultural method.

Perhaps his most significant mentor was Frank Tannenbaum. An anarchist in his younger days, Tannenbaum developed a peculiar sensibility trained on exposing the darker aspects of life in the United States. He wrote books on inhumane prison conditions, on slavery's cultural legacy, on racism in the South, on social inequality. And this sensibility also put him in sympathy with the Mexican Revolution. Between 1929 and 1951, Tannenbaum wrote three important books on Mexico and several more on Latin America. From him Morse learned that Ibero-America is not a crooked branch on the Western trunk but a civilization in its own right, with values — such as the peaceful coexistence and free mixture of races and cultures — from which the United States had a great deal to learn.

On his travels through the continent, Morse had picked up on a feature of Latin American society that moved him deeply:

"Not that Latin America was a racial paradise, but at least the differences in color did not eclipse the human presence." This social blessing became personal when he met the woman who would turn out to be his interpreter of Latin American life. Her name was Emerante de Pradines. Born in 1918, a great-granddaughter of the founder of Haiti, the daughter of a celebrated musician, and in her own right a classical dancer and a student of Martha Graham, Emy met Richard in New York, where, in 1954, they were married. This inter-racial union cost them socially, professionally, and within their own families. In a time of acute racial discrimination in the United States, the couple set up in Puerto Rico, where Dick (as he was known to us) took a teaching post at the university. They lived there between 1958 and 1961, and had two children. Emy was beautiful — she would often wear a headpiece with flowers in it, which can be seen on the cover of the LP *Voodoo,* her recording of Haitian songs. Enveloped in this magical sensibility, Morse returned from Ibero-America bewitched. His intellectual interest in "the other America" had become an existential choice. Hence his determination to get to the bottom of the "historical nature" of the two Americas, and to display to the world (and to himself) the riches of the path that he had chosen.

I understood none of this when I met him in 1981. One day, as I was going through proofs of *Vuelta,* I got a call from Morse asking me to join him for breakfast. I gladly agreed. Some years earlier I had read his essay "The Inheritance of New Spain" in *Plural,* which was the predecessor of *Vuelta.* In it Morse for the first time compared the Weberian idea of political patrimonialism with the Thomist Spanish state that for three centuries had ruled Spain's overseas territories without its legitimacy ever being disputed. This was a novel and significant idea, which Octavio Paz went on to assimilate in his numerous essays on Mexican history. Paz was persuaded by Morse's view of the persistence of that order ("Thomist" in Morse's terms, "patrimonialist" according to Weber) in the Mexican regime in the run-up to the revolution. The quasi-monarchical PRI also functioned in effect as the heir of that old conception, in a body politic that was presided over by the presidential head — a Hispanic, corporatist, durable, and inclusive edifice in which there was room for all the supposedly antagonistic classes. Not a democracy, but not a tyranny either. What a surprise: the key to the political history of Mexico was to be found in Thomas Aquinas! How could I not want to meet the man who came up with such a notion?

We went for coffee in Mexico City and talked for hours. I asked him where the idea of Thomism as a founding philosophy in Ibero-America had originated. "It's a long story," he said, "and I'm pulling it together in the book I'm about to finish." This book was *Prospero's Mirror*, a comparative study of the cultures of North and South America, for which he considered it necessary to go back to their shared historical basis, all the way to the medieval past. Only in this way, Morse believed, could the fundamental differences be grasped: the imperatives of the political unification of an island in the case of England, the imperatives of the incorporation of the new American world in the case of Spain. And then, without further ado, he embarked on a detailed narration of the "preparatory role" played by Peter Abelard, the twelfth-century scholastic, in the modern philosophical tradition. From that point onward, Morse claimed, by way of the embryonically experimental, tolerant, pluralist work of William of Ockham, a trajectory emerged that was to lead to the great scientific, philosophical, and religious revolutions of the Middle Ages and the Renaissance, culminating in two distinct "historical paths."

133

A Modest Utopia

In the anglophone world, which was enthusiastic in its embrace of those revolutions, the path led to Hobbes and Locke, the founding fathers of English political culture in the seventeenth century. But a century earlier, Iberian thought had inaugurated another path when it adopted Thomas Aquinas as an authority. With the "architectural feat" (as Morse called it) of the *Summa Theologica* as their starting point, three generations of Spanish philosophers, jurists, and theologians had constructed the "cultural premises" of the Hispanic sphere: the Dominican Francisco de Vitoria (1483-1546), his followers Domingo de Soto (1494-1560) and Melchor Cano (1509-1560), both also Dominicans, and the Jesuits Juan de Mariana (1536-1624) and Francisco Suárez (1548-1617). "They had the ascendancy," Morse told me, and then came another surprise: "but they had a formidable adversary, who was not an Englishman but an Italian." He was referring to Machiavelli. Needless to say, I came away dazzled by all this.

These ideas were first published in Morse's famous essay "A Theory of Spanish Government," which appeared in 1954. It brought to the table the "Machiavellian" elements of late fifteenth- and early-sixteenth century Spanish rule. Ferdinand II of Aragon himself seemed to embody the prince imagined by Machiavelli (who in fact saw him as such, in *The Prince* as well the *Discourses on Livy*). Isabella I of Castile, by contrast, represented the "Thomist" vision of absolute monarchy. This dichotomy between Renaissance and medieval ideals had long ago been "a gut feeling," Morse wrote, but over the years he discovered that his intuition had ample foundation in Spanish intellectual history of that era. Although in Spain the tension had been resolved in favor of Thomism, Morse maintained that the Machiavellian element — present, to a different degree, in the conquistadors Cortés and Pizarro — was to persist in a latent or "recessive" state for almost three centuries.

It emerged again, it exploded, in the form of the Ibero-American caudillos who arose out of the wars of independence in the nineteenth century. At the close of the eighteenth century, Spanish America, "hierarchical, multiform, pre-capitalist, was poorly prepared for enlightened absolutism, and far less for any sort of Lockean constitutionalism." But a direction was open that would have been unthinkable three hundred years earlier: nothing less than the fusion of the two prototypes, the Thomist state and the Machiavellian *caudillismo,* leading to new varieties of legitimate rule. This was the final and most unexpected theme in Morse's electrifying essay. Ten years later, in the essay "The Heritage of Latin America," Morse charted this correlation between Thomist and Machiavellian ideas against the Weberian categories of patrimonial and charismatic rule.

Prospero's Mirror has never been published in English, but a year after our fateful meeting it was published in Spanish. Owing to that book, which I have read countless times, our friendship began. I had discovered Morse's code.

He began the section that he called "The Iberian Path" — the course taken in the fifteenth and sixteenth centuries — with a quotation from *The Tragic Sense of Life* by Miguel de Unamuno:

> I feel that I have within me a medieval soul, and I believe that the soul of my country is medieval, that it has perforce passed through the Renaissance, the Reformation, and the Revolution — learning from them, yes, but without allowing them to touch the soul.

A Modest Utopia

Spain had indeed "passed through" those mutations, as well as the scientific revolutions of the Middle Ages, virtually untouched. And this resistance was not a question of religion alone. In this sense, the north-south religious axis — the great distinction between the Protestant north and the Catholic south — was neither unique nor essential. After all, Italy and France, both Catholic, had adopted the scientific and philosophical precursors to modernity.

The persistence of Spain's "medieval soul" was owed to a variety of causes: the relative weakness of the feudal lords (versus the autonomy of their counterparts in England, France, and Italy); the power of the ancient Spanish cities at their peak; the growing power of the Castilian crown in the face of liberal Aragon; the centuries-long centralizing efforts of the Reconquista, the culmination of which coincided with the discovery of America. Combined with the early-sixteenth-century challenge of Lutheranism, which unified the Iberian Peninsula against it, the revelation of the New World turned out to be decisive. The imperative of integrating a Christian legal system into the indigenous societies was the determining cause in the Spanish taking up Thomism again. It was a philosophy particularly apt to the task. "The Spanish turn to Thomism," Morse observed, "is explained... by the need to reconcile the rationale of a modern state with the assertions of an ecumenical world order [...] and to adapt the requirements of Christian life to the task of making non-Christian peoples a part of European civilization."

This titanic task — inaugurated a full century before England's first colonial ventures — would go a long way to explaining the concentration of Spanish intellectual efforts on theological, philosophical, juridical, and moral speculation from the sixteenth century onwards. Almost across the board, mathematics and natural sciences were overlooked. Nor were the Spanish universities centers of independent thought: they were institutions isolated from the outside world and designed to produce servants of the state.

Morse did not claim that the Thomist revival in Spain was the whole story; *Prospero's Mirror* alludes also to Spanish humanism of the sixteenth century. But this atmosphere of relative pluralism and openness, which was characteristic of the reign of Carlos V, finally came down on the side of a "Thomist" consensus on "the nature of government: its sources of legitimacy, the proper reach of its power, its responsibility in guaranteeing justice and fairness, and its 'civilizing' mission with regards non-Christian people in its domain and overseas." In short, it was the discovery, settlement, and conversion of Latin America that led to the Thomist turn in Spanish imperial policy. The ideas did not impose themselves on reality; the reality imposed itself on the ideas.

The accession of Philip II (1556-1598) definitively set the course against all "the heretics of our time": humanists, Erasmians, followers of Luther, readers of Machiavelli. It was during Phillip's reign, in Morse's view, that the structure of imperial Spain assumed the form that would (in essence) prevail until 1810. This Thomist mold would have a bearing on all spheres of life: political, religious, juridical, economic, social, academic, intellectual. And nothing could have been further from the Thomist interpretation of power and its ecumenical Christian vocation than the ideas expounded in *The Prince*: the state as the art (artifice, occupation, practice; not moral theory) of governing. These were irreconcilable visions, and the conflict between them reached beyond the borders of Spain. Though Aquinas' philosophy represented a new solution for the unprecedented circumstance of having discovered America, for various thinkers he was emblematic of the old way: thoroughly Christian, oriented towards the common good, inspired by faith as much as by reason, following the dictates of natural law inscribed by God in man's conscience. Machiavelli, by contrast, represented the modern way: removed from religious inspiration, pessimistic (or realistic) when it came to the goodness of man, oriented to the exercise of power and the establishment of stable states inspired by the patriotic, republican ideals of the classical world, and all of this in line with the dictates of reason.

In Morse's account, it was not Machiavelli's "absolutism" that made his Spanish critics uncomfortable (this was anyway shared by the Spanish state), but the threat of tyranny in a political order in which divine providence had been expelled from the workings of history. In 1559, three years into Phillip's reign, and after an intense debate, Machiavelli's masterpiece was added to the list of banned books. Morse contended that the neo-scholastics succeeded in preventing the influx of Machiavellianism into Spain between the sixteenth century and the dawn of the nineteenth century. The theologian who elaborated the legal, religious, and moral foundations of the relations with the non-Christian peoples and territories of Latin America was Francisco de Vitoria. But the thinker who was responsible for what Morse called "the Spanish political choice," that is, the philosophical foundation of the Spanish state as a legitimate structure of rule, was Francisco Suarez.

Suárez, who was born in Spain in 1548 and died in Portugal in 1617, was the author of thirty works on metaphysics, theology, law, and politics. In his system, mankind comes to the political by way of morality, metaphysics, and religion. For him, "the state is an ordered entity in which the wills of the collective and of the prince harmonize according to natural law and the interest of the *felicitas civitatis*, or common good." The Suárezist state had certain fundamental features which, with slight differences between the Hapsburg and Bourbon dynasties, were in effect throughout the seventeenth and eighteenth centuries. Paternalism, for a start: in Suárez's design, the state is an "organic architecture," an "edifice built to last," a "mystical body," at the head of which stands a father who fully exercises the "dominant legal authority" over his subjects. This constitutes an "absolutism tempered by ethics, by Natural Law... and maintaining the common good as a goal." This paternalistic and tutelary concept of power presupposes the predominance of immutable natural law over fallible human laws: "Society and the body politic are conceived as though they were ordered by the objectives and external precepts of natural law, not by the dictates of individual consciences." Moreover, sovereignty passes ineluctably from the people to the monarch. For Suárez, the people are the original depositories of sovereignty (which originates in God), but there is an underlying political pact (*pactum translationis*) whereby the people not only delegates this sovereignty to the prince or monarch, but actually disposes of it. The monarchs are not mere "mandatories," as in the English tradition or even that of the French Revolution, custodians of a freely revocable power. In the Thomist tradition, power is total, undivided, and difficult to revoke: "The people have the same obligations as the king to the pact made with him, and cannot claim back the ceded authority so long as the prince abides by the conditions of the pact and the norms of justice."

Suarez was careful to provide for a popular right to insurrection and even to tyrannicide; but in order to reach such an extreme measure (which was never put into practice in the history of the Spanish monarchy, unlike in England and France) the tyrant and the injustice had to be "public and manifest," and in no case could revenge be the motive for revolt. The execution of a monarch was the correction of the monarchy, not the abolition of it. And finally Suarez's state was characterized by a corporatist centralization. Medieval customs had deep roots in this political edifice: society was organized in strata and associations that related to each other not directly but through the monarch, from whom emanated all public initiatives, prebends, concessions, and mercies of the kingdom, and whose figure was the underlying source of the social energy. This state was a profoundly medieval entity.

Those are the premises that propped up the political edifice of Spanish monarchy and Spanish statehood until 1810, when the wars of independence broke out in Latin America. The legacy of this political culture, according to Morse, would remain active for the following two decades, with one very surprising component: the resurrection of Machiavelli, whose work was not so much read as embodied by caudillos from Mexico to Patagonia.

III.

In the glorious year 1810, the disappearance of the paternalist monarch, who was sanctioned by tradition and faith, discredited the existing Spanish bureaucracy. At this hinge point in Latin-American history, the most urgent challenge was to identify a substitute authority that would enjoy the approval of the populace. Thus it was that the intellectual and political elites of Latin America, trapped between the impossibility of a return to the imperial Spanish order and the immediate reality of the strongmen produced by the movement for independence, sought to adopt liberal constitutionalism.

This dream — as Morse called it — did not last long. By the third decade of the nineteenth century, the region had left behind that first moment of republican idealism. Other such moments would come, but they would prove just as fragile and fleeting. No less than Simón Bolívar himself experienced this disenchantment with what he called "the republics of the air," which he considered legalist and removed from the complex social and racial actualities of the nascent South America. Morse suggests that Bolívar, in his search for an alternative, discerned a solution that had a clear imperial and "Thomist" thrust:

> Bolívar, South America's most famous leader, was caught between the vision of an amphictyony or "league of neighbors" of the Hispano-American peoples and the clear awareness of the local, feudal oligarchies and the peasants tied to the land that could only give rise to purely phantasmal nations. It is reasonable to suppose that the term amphictyony, used by Bolívar and proper to the neoclassicism of the idea, deep down represented his instinct for Hispanic unity rooted in a heritage that had medieval overtones.

141

Bolívar called his vision Great Colombia. Morse speculated that "if Bolívar had not feared being like Napoleon, and had abandoned the George Washington model, perhaps the destiny of the Great Colombia would have been saved."

In other words, had Bolívar embraced (with modern overtones, in a somewhat republican or, even better, monarchical form) the Thomist concept of the "built-to-last" corporatist order, Bolívar would have found the legitimating formula that was required to unify the new nations. This did not happen. The Congress of Panama organized by Bolívar in

A Modest Utopia

1826 offered the first hint of an Ibero-American project, but that was as far as it went. Any attempt to regulate the region's internal issues at a continental level was abandoned. Bolívar, as they say of futile endeavors, was ploughing the sea.

Beyond the world of ideas and plans, in the void of legitimacy left behind by the collapse of the Spanish edifice, the people followed the surviving captains of the wars of independence. They were akin to the Italian *condottieri* of the Renaissance era. Machiavelli's mark was reborn in these men of daggers and pitchforks, these new conquistadors: the caudillos. "On almost every page of his *Discourses* and even in *The Prince*," Morse explains, "Machiavelli's advice could almost be based on the exploits of the caudillos." It was hugely important, for example, in establishing the rule of charisma. "There is nothing more certain nor more necessary in the halting of an enraged crowd," Machiavelli instructed in his *Discourses*, "than the presence of a man worthy of veneration and who projects this image." Another requirement for personalist rule was an intimate knowledge of "the nature of the rivers and the lakes, [to be able to] measure the expanses of the lakes and the mountains, the land, the depths of the valleys," which was prescribed in *The Prince*. These prescriptions were met to an astonishing degree in what we know from the memoirs of José Antonio Páez, both a companion to and an adversary of Bolívar, the "great lancer" of the Venezuelan plains. And, Morse continued, the same went for the likes of Facundo Quiroga in Argentina, José Gervasio Artigas in Uruguay, and Andrés de Santa Cruz in Bolivia.

The problem is that legitimacy based purely on charisma cannot hold. Machiavelli himself recognized the need for the prince to govern according to "laws that provide security for the people as a whole." The prince's command "cannot last if the administration of the kingdom lies with the men of one sole individual; it is advisable therefore that the government should in the end be the work of many and be upheld by many." This transition from the leadership of a homegrown caudillo to a "republic" (nominal but at least stable) required that the government be established on the basis of certain "original principles." Translated to Ibero-America, these ideas meant laying the foundations for a "paternalism oriented towards the public good." Should this fail to be achieved, the social groupings — some of them predominantly indigenous — would go back to being as scattered as they always had been. With the Thomist foundation lost, and the threat of a pure but unsustainable leadership system under charismatic caudillos, Ibero- America's early days were marked by attempts to avoid being engulfed by violence and anarchy, and to build relatively stable and legitimate governments.

The solution devised by the countries of Latin America was a compromise between Thomism and Machiavellianism, with an added veneer of Lockean constitutionalism. These sources of legitimacy corresponded to Weber's famous classification: charismatic, traditional, legal-rational. (Morse, like Weber, was careful to emphasize the "ideal" nature of these types, which never exist in their "pure" state.) Morse concluded that over the course of a century, from the end of the era of independence to the early decades of the twentieth century, three "modes of stability" emerged.

The first "mode of stability" had at its core a charismatic leader who was associated with a project symbolically greater than himself but actually centered on his person: Bolívar's

143

Andean federation, Francisco Morazán's Central American union, the constitutionalism of Benito Juárez in Mexico, and even Gabriel García Moreno's theocratic state in Ecuador. Another variety of this type is represented by the military caudillos who imposed themselves on society by seduction and by force: Juan Manuel de Rosas in Argentina, Antonio López de Santa Anna in Mexico, and Doctor Francia (known as *el Supremo*) in Paraguay. Towards the end of the nineteenth century, the presence of European capital in Ibero-America favored a third kind of individual leadership: the caudillo-presidents who made a formal show of respect for constitutionalism, most notably Porfirio Díaz.

The second attempt at stability adhered to patrimonialism, the traditional kind of legitimacy put forward by Weber, which in Ibero-America had Thomism as its origin. This was no longer a matter of reinstating the absolute monarchy of the Hapsburgs, or of literally applying Francisco Suárez's doctrine. Instead it involved the creation of a new order inspired by the paradigm that had demonstrated its effectiveness over the course of three hundred years. Chile was an example. In Morse's account: "A businessman from Valparaíso, Diego Portales... [came up with] a document with a considerable aura of legitimacy. The constitution of 1833 created a strong executive without stripping Congress or the Courts of their counterbalancing powers. The first president, General Prieto, had the aristocratic bearing that Portales lacked: a steadfast Catholic, Prieto was unswerving in spite of the various political factions. The first presidents discharged their duties in double periods: the winning candidate was chosen by his predecessor. Thus, the paternal structure of the Spanish state was preserved, with the concessions to Anglo-French constitutionalism necessary to maintain the image of a republic that had impugned the monarchic regime."

Yet the most complete application of the traditional or "Thomist" model in the twentieth century was undoubtedly the case of post-revolutionary Mexico. Most notable here was the survival of the old Spanish mold in society, politics, culture, and economy — Suárezism in a Mexican setting. After an insurrection against a tyrant, the Revolution went back to the origin: once again, all the riches that lay beneath the earth became the property of the state, as they had under the Spanish crown. The cooperative system of *ejidos*, through which land was distributed among the peasants, was named in commemoration of the communal lots in old municipal Spain. The indigenous once more enjoyed a special protection; rural and industrial workers alike sheltered under the paternalism of the state. The capitalists, administrators, and businesspeople, along with the labor unions among professionals and teachers, were drawn towards the politico-administrative nucleus of the government and then, only secondarily, towards competitive interaction.

And then there was the third route, the "rational" route, to stability: a competent bureaucracy and public respect for the law. The example cited by Morse for this model was Argentina, which between 1860 and 1946 attempted "a modified version of liberal democracy." On the basis of new affluence linked to the export of grain and livestock, and in spite of the marked concentration of wealth and power in the rural oligarchy, Argentina succeeded in integrating the great influx of immigrants and generating a middle class. With this foundation, and assisted by ethnic homogeneity and technological advances, "a series of statesman-presidents were able to promote and guide the development of Argentina, conforming to a reasonable degree with the Lockean constitution of 1853." The power struggles of that time did not pave the way to tyrannical rule, but to the advent in 1890 of a liberal party of the middle classes, the Radical Party, which rode a number of important electoral reforms (free suffrage, the right for votes to be secret) to take the presidency in 1916. And yet, in Morse's judgement, the Radical Party put a brake on the social and economic progress, on the advancement of workers and the urban middle classes, and it was weak in the face of the landowning oligarchy. The price was high: "Only in this context would the frustrated middle classes succumb to the lowest sort of demagoguery, and to Juan Domingo Perón."

For Morse, the experience of the twentieth century showed the durability of Thomism allied with the charismatic legitimacy of the Machiavellian kind, whose liberal-democratic constitutionalism was mainly for show. Not only that: Morse would declare that only on this basis could Latin American nations, and stable and legitimate governments, be constructed. (Morse had no interest in analyzing the military dictatorships of the southern cone, such as those of Argentina and Chile, because they were merely tyrannies without any legitimacy.)

In 1989, a collection of Morse's essays, called *New World Soundings*, was published by the Johns Hopkins University Press. Six years later, in homage to his work, we put out a translation of the book at the small press that we had founded at *Vuelta*. At the end of his long and winding journey — forty years of scholarship and reflection on Latin America — Morse enumerated his "premises" for the construction of Latin American governments. They may be summarized in a "ten commandments" of political rule in Ibero-America:

- The lived world is natural, it is not a human project. "In these countries, the feeling that man constructs his world and is responsible for it is less deep and less widespread than in other places."

- Disdain for written law. "This innate feeling for natural law is accompanied by a less formal attitude towards the laws formulated by man."

- Indifference to electoral processes. "It is difficult for free elections to summon the mystique conferred on them in Protestant countries."

- Disdain for parties and for democratic practice, including legislative procedure and voluntary, rationalized political participation.

- Tolerance for illegality. The primacy of natural law over written law means a tolerance for even criminal practices and customs which in other societies go punished, but in these societies are seen as "natural."

- An absolute handover of power to the ruler. The sovereign people surrenders power to the ruler; it does not merely delegate it. That is, in Latin America the old, original pact between the people and the monarch remains intact.

- The right to insurrection. The people conserve "a keen sense of fair treatment and of natural justice" and "are not indifferent to abuses of the power they have given away." This is why uprisings and revolutions — so commonplace in Latin America — tend to be born out of grievances against an authority that has become illegitimate. The insurrection needs no elaborate program: it is enough for it to seek to reclaim a sovereignty that has been tyrannically abused.

- Non-ideological charisma. A legitimate government needs neither a defined ideology, nor a plan to bring about an immediate and effective redistribution of wealth, nor a majority of the vote. A legitimate government requires only "a profound sense of the moral urgency" often embodied in "charismatic leaders with a special psycho-cultural appeal." Tyrants cannot enjoy legitimacy.

- Formal appeal to the constitutional order. Once in power, to overcome personalism — or in Weber's terms, to routinize the charisma — the leader must stress the importance of the literal application of the law as a means for the institutionalization of the government.

- The personal ruler is the head and the center of the nation. Like the Spanish monarch, "the national government [...] functions as the source of energy, coordination and leadership for the unions, corporate entities, institutions, various social strata and geographic regions."

Morse, then, was not exactly an enemy of liberal constitutionalism in Ibero-America, but neither was he its friend. He settled on an understanding of the region's political prospects that was deeply cultural and deeply pessimistic about the possibilities of liberal democracy.

IV.

Richard Morse died in Haiti in 2001, when the turn-of-the-century democratic euphoria was at its peak. At that bright moment in history there was nothing to suggest that I needed to reconsider his illiberal theory of the "cultural premises" of Ibero-American politics. I had moved away from it in a more optimistic direction, to the cause of democratic liberalism, and I felt certain that I was right to have done so. History seemed to be justifying my hope.

And then Hugo Chávez appeared. I was sufficiently interested in his case that I decided to travel to Venezuela to write a book about him. *Power and Delirium*, I called it. Every single one of Morse's ten commandments was evident in Chavez, with an additional element: as well as the charismatic legitimacy of the president and the traditional legitimacy of the paternalist corporate state, there was the legitimacy of the ballot box. Chávez realized that the armed forces were not necessary for the establishment of a dictatorship: he could instead monopolize public truth, and rewrite history, and close down freedom of expression, and keep his electoral base in a condition of permanent mobilization, and invent enemies within and without, and distribute money, and call elections that he would almost always win. Encouraged by Fidel Castro, Chavez's inspiration and spiritual father, his model was also taken up in Bolivia and Ecuador. There was no need for Argentina to adopt it because Chavismo was, in essence, the mode of domination exercised by Perón and Evita, which, with astonishing continuity, has remained in force for over seventy years.

In parallel with Chávez's rise, a charismatic leader the same age and with very similar attributes emerged in my own country, in the shape of Andrés Manuel López Obrador, the

149

president of Mexico, widely known as AMLO. He fought and lost the presidential elections of 2006 and 2012 but, undeterred, he ran again in 2018. All of Morse's ten commandments were evident in him too, but he added a new spirit: the spirit of messianism. Lopez Obrador genuinely feels himself to be Mexico's redeemer. AMLO is not just another populist; he is a populist who wears the nimbus of holy anger. He has compared himself to Jesus, feeling equally crucified by his opponents. And now he is both Jesus and Caesar.

AMLO sees himself — and many Mexicans share his view — as a political redeemer. He is the way, the truth, and the light of the people. And in such a salvific framework, everything about his rule falls into place. Redeemers, after all, do not lose; or if they do, the world also loses. In AMLO's view, his doom would be Mexico's doom. Redeemers, moreover, will spend their entire lifetime in the struggle for power. Once it is attained, always in the name of the people, always in communion with the people, these redeemers want it all, without divisions, deviations, or dissents. And they seek to retain power in perpetuity, until their last breath.

In my attempt to understand the phenomenon of Lopez Obrador, I wrote a book in the run-up to the 2018 elections, already convinced that he was going to win. It was called *El pueblo soy yo*, or *I Am The People*, and it is an anatomy of Latin American populism. In writing it I went back to Morse's theory of Latin American history. My book became, in fact, a dialogue with Morse. He was no longer nearby, in his Georgetown home where we shared so much, so our debate took place entirely in my head. I certainly needed to revisit his arguments in order to try to refute them. Was he correct to warn me that liberal democracy in these countries, in my country, is a chimera?

I chose to write him a long letter in which I sought to rehabilitate the liberal tradition of Ibero-America in the twentieth century. In part, it read:

> In your work you pay little attention to the Ibero-American countries which, well into the twentieth century, succeeded in building precisely that liberal legitimacy, those Lockean arrangements, that seemed inauthentic to you. At the same time, you overlook various political figures and intellectuals from the nineteenth century who sought to consolidate a reasonably democratic liberal order. Above all I think of Andrés Bello, the early mentor of Simón Bolívar and the father of the Chilean Constitution. An unforgivable omission. What would have become of Diego Portales without Bello? It was fortunate that the authoritarian Portales placed his trust in the eminent humanist, philologist, poet, philosopher and legislator Bello, educated in England and with a deep knowledge of its political philosophies, the creator of the Chilean Civil Code. Bello's permanent exile from Venezuela since the eve of the Revolution of Independence in 1810 — he represented his newborn republic in England and stayed there for two decades — was an irreparable loss for his native country and an abiding blessing for Chile, where he established himself in 1829. It wasn't the Thomist model that saved Chile; it was Bello, the most learned man of his time. You don't so much as mention him.
>
> And what would have become of Mexico without the separation of the church and state, and that modicum of institutional structure that we owe to the liberals of

the generation of *la Reforma*, the founding fathers of
Mexican liberal thought, laws, and institutions in the
mid-nineteenth century. You do mention Juárez — but
he was not, as you suggest, a Machiavellian caudillo who
used the Constitution of 1857 as a trick to consolidate
power. He was a reader of Benjamin Constant, a liberal of
the kind you have little time for. And the Constitution
was not a trick. His was a government that respected the
division of power, the law, and the institutions, and also
individual liberty and individual security.

You were quite right to leave aside the tyrants that
populate our history: Juan Vicente Gómez, Trujillo,
Somoza, Stroessner, Pinochet, Argentina's military
juntas, and so many more. They had force without legitimacy, and your work was looking for sources and forms
of legitimacy. But these nineteenth- and twentieth-century tyrants and the "legitimate" dictators you adduce
(such as Perón and Castro) had something significant in
common: a disdain for democracy, for liberalism, and
for freedom of expression. These liberal qualities, along
with almost all the elements constitutive of "Lockean"
liberalism, did not merit your attention.

Yet a modest page in the press, with its ferocious caricatures and satirical verses, its incendiary articles and its
great prose writers, was always raised against all of the
dictators. Journalists and writers such as Juan Montalvo,
Juan Bautista Alberdi, Domingo Faustino Sarmiento,
José María Luis Mora, Francisco Zarco, Manuel González
Prada, and José Martí. And many more. All would have
joined the republican Martí in saying: "About the tyrant?

About the tyrant say everything, say more!" Many went to jail, many were cast out, some were killed. But however precariously, and against terrible risks, they persisted in their vocation of liberty. With the arrival of the twentieth century, freedom of expression was consolidated in the countries with the deepest democratic vocation, such as Chile, Costa Rica, Uruguay, and Colombia. There are newspapers still in print today that have been in circulation without a break for a century and a half. These historical newspapers are living monuments to liberty. They have been bastions in times of confusion, manipulation, and lies. And you ignored them.

What would Morse have made of Latin American populism in the twenty-first century, of this populist golden age? Combining elements of his theory, I can imagine his collective portrait of various Ibero-American leaders on the left and the right. A charismatic leader with "a special psycho-cultural appeal" comes to power by means of the ballot box and, with all the excitement of the demagogues of old, promises to establish again the traditional order, the arcadia of the past. A utopia is just around the corner. But since the reality of things does not comply with such reactionary plans, and since the leader harbors ambitions of retaining power in perpetuity, and since democracy and liberty are for him — a Machiavellian, when all is said and done — only the means for securing absolute power, he will go on to undermine, slowly or at breakneck speed, the freedoms, the laws, and the institutions of democracy, until they have all been stifled or destroyed.

We may recognize this dark portrait in every day's headlines. It describes the political decline of our own times. And what would Morse have made of the ominous replication

153

of this Ibero-American archetype in the United States, in the person of Donald Trump? I am sure that, being a believer in democracy, he would have condemned it, but to my mind his advice would have remained the same: "Stick to my theory and you won't go wrong." I did stick to it, inasmuch as it explains a great deal about Ibero-American political history — or rather, I stuck only to a part of it, because its erudite portraiture is incomplete. It egregiously omits the liberal tradition, which has fitfully accomplished a great deal in various Latin American countries, and which is still alive. And so in the end I abandoned my friend's teachings on historical grounds, because of what it omits, and on moral grounds, because I do not wish to give up hope.

I am quite certain that there is no charismatic, populist, patrimonialist, culturally reactionary, corporatist, paternalist, Thomist-Machiavellian solution to the weaknesses and inequalities of Latin America. Only the decency and the rationality and the patience of a liberal order offer us a chance. We must remember and honor those ideas, because ideas are the seeds of political possibilities: without the idea of freedom there will be no freedom. It is true that such liberalism is not exactly the bulk of our cultural inheritance, but neither is it without precedent at this late date in the history of Latin American societies. There are times in the lives of individuals and nations, moreover, when we must modify and even reject some of what we inherited. For injustice is also a significant part of what was bequeathed to us.

Perhaps my quixotic idea is not so quixotic after all. Perhaps Macaulay and Namier are indeed relevant to the future of Latin America. Perhaps it is still possible to rescue "democracy without adjectives" for Mexico, and even for Venezuela and Cuba. After all, our inheritance is manifold and multivocal: it contains two political traditions, two theories of legitimacy, two visions of how and why we should live peaceably and fairly together. Thomas Aquinas, Niccolò Machiavelli, and Francisco Suárez are still alive. But so, too, are Andrés Bello, and all those brave journalists and liberal politicians of the nineteenth century, and all our democrats of the twentieth century, such as Francisco I. Madero, Rómulo Betancourt, Daniel Cosío Villegas, Octavio Paz, and Mario Vargas Llosa. My master Morse and I will go on debating forever. I pray that he is wrong.

WILLIAM DERESIEWICZ

The Individual Nuisance

A single sentence sufficed to seal my veneration for Harold Rosenberg. It comes in the midst of the bravura conclusion of "The Intellectual and His Future," an essay from 1965. "One does not *possess* mental freedom and detachment," it reads, "one participates in them." Here was a dictum worthy of adoption as a creed. "Intellectual" is not a title, an honorific, or a job description. It is a daily aspiration.

Rosenberg is remembered, if he is remembered at all, as one of the leading American art critics of the twentieth century, the coiner of the term "action painting" to describe the work of Jackson Pollock, Willem de Kooning, and other

Abstract Expressionists, and it was for that reason, several years ago, that I turned to his work. What I discovered was not an art critic but a full-spectrum intellectual who thought about art. He also thought about poetry, politics, theater, fiction, society, sociology, Marx, Marxism, Judaism, the media, and the nature of the intellectual himself.

And he did it all better than just about anyone I had ever encountered. He was Trilling without the solemnity, Kazin with a wider, more ironic mind (to name two earlier infatuations among the New York intellectuals). His point of view was comic in the deepest sense. An outsider by temperament as well as conviction, he looked at everything from the outside, accepting nothing — no movement, no figure, no social fiction, no educated formula — at its own estimation. His most potent rhetorical weapon was satire — the whiff of caricature, the gust of common sense. "Far from being goaded to their parts by police agents hidden in the wings"—this in reference to the vogue of self-confession among postwar ex-radicals — "the guilty here had to force their way onto the stage. [Whitaker] Chambers himself, that witness of witnesses...describes how close he came to breaking under the ordeal of getting the notice of people whose vital interests he was determined to defend." But Rosenberg wasn't merely a debunker. He believed in things: in art, in the struggle to come to terms with reality, in the individual. He was skeptical of "thought," but he believed in thinking.

Other intellectuals saw through collective illusions. Rosenberg saw through the illusions of other intellectuals. The criticism of kitsch art or popular culture, a highbrow hobby in the new age of mass entertainment, was nothing, he wrote, but another form of kitsch — kitsch ideas. "There is only one way to quarantine kitsch: by being too busy with art." Notions of the "other-directed" "organization man," promulgated in the

The Individual Nuisance

1950s as descriptions of the new American type (and clichés of thought to this day), were in reality projections, he explains, on the part of the new caste of intellectual placemen who were swarming the postwar bureaucracies. "Today Orgmen reproduce themselves like fruit flies in whatever is organized, whether it be a political party or a museum of advanced art." As for "alienation," that great midcentury bugaboo and talking point, not only does Rosenberg not deplore it, he sees it as a virtue, a failure "to participate emotionally and intellectually in the fictions and conventions of mass culture."

He was fearless in the face of reputation. T.S. Eliot (then at his zenith), having made an idol of "tradition," had led American poetry into a cul-de-sac of academicism. *1984*, all but sacred at the time, was marked by "frigid rationality and paranoiacally lifeless prose." Auden and Spender, darlings of the cultural left for their politically "responsible" poetry, avoided responsibility for individual experience and social reflection alike. "When I first encountered the gravity of Lionel Trilling," Rosenberg writes, "I did not get the joke; it took some time to realize that there wasn't any."

Upon his death in 1978, Hilton Kramer, the chief art critic of the *New York Times* and himself a prominent figure in intellectual New York, eulogized him as "the quintessential New York intellectual." For the essayist Seymour Krim, reflecting on the same occasion, Rosenberg had been the most intelligent critic writing in English. As for his physical presence, Krim reported, "Harold looked and shone like the Lion of Judah. He was about 6'4," a really heroic-looking prince among the bookish intellectuals…a sort of matinee idol of the intellectual underground" who had passed "a lot of lean years bucking all the Establishments." His passing, Krim observed, "sweeps a period with it."

Harold Rosenberg was born in Brooklyn in 1906. He spent a year at City College, then three at Brooklyn Law School, but he would later say that he'd received his education on the steps of the New York Public Library. After graduation, he plunged into Village bohemia, befriending artists (de Kooning was an early and crucial encounter) and inheriting the twin legacies of the New York intellectuals: Marxism and modernism. He joined the League of American Writers, a radical organization, wrote for *New Masses* and *Art Front*, and dreamed of becoming a poet. (A small volume, *Trance Above the Streets*, appeared in 1942.) During the Depression, he kept himself afloat by writing for the WPA, moving to Washington in 1938 to become the art editor of its American Guide Series, then staying after Pearl Harbor to work for the Office of War Information.

After the war, and back in New York, Rosenberg became a stalwart of the little magazines: *Commentary*, *Encounter*, *Dissent*, and, of course, *Partisan Review*. He found an apartment on Tenth Street, a rotting Village block that sheltered tramps, a poolroom, and a collection of obscure American painters who were in the process of transforming art. "The Herd of Independent Minds," an essay whose title became a catchphrase, appeared in 1948; "The American Action Painters," which birthed another, in 1952. His first collection, *The Tradition of the New* (its title soon a third), appeared in 1959. Within a few years, he was lecturing at Princeton and writing for *Esquire*, *Vogue*, and the *New Yorker*. "The beggarly Jewish radicals of the 30s," Kazin wrote in 1963, "are now the ruling cultural pundits of American society."

Eight more collections would follow in the space of fourteen years (the most important is *Discovering the Present*, which, with *The Tradition of the New*, contains his finest work). In 1966 (he was already sixty), Rosenberg became a member of the University of Chicago's exalted Committee on Social Thought, and, the following year, art critic for the *New Yorker*, positions that he held until his death. (Most of the later collections consist of pieces from the magazine.) The bucker of Establishments had stormed them, but he never relinquished his outsider stance. American society, he wrote in "The Intellectual and His Future," is replete with obstacles to independent thought, including institutional ones. "The intellectual, however, is adept at finding the cracks in society through which to crawl around the obstacles, whether he eludes them in the university, on a park bench, or in an insurance office."

Marxism and modernism. From Marx, Rosenberg acquired a sensitivity to history — above all, to historical action, or more precisely, historical acting. A touchstone was *The Eighteenth Brumaire of Louis Bonaparte*, the work in which Marx famously declares that everything in history happens twice, the first time as tragedy, the second time as farce. Louis Bonaparte assumes the costume of Napoleon and dubs himself Napoleon III. "Luther donned the mask," Marx writes, "of the Apostle Paul." Rosenberg develops the idea: those who wish to seize control of history — political figures, revolutionaries — invariably cast themselves as reenactors of a prior revolution. History becomes a play, with roles, scripts, sets, and above all, a plot — a predetermined outcome, guided by a self-appointed hero.

For Marx, the final hero would be a collective one, the proletariat, who would free humanity from history, its nightmare repetitions, by dispensing with historical make-believe and acting in the sober consciousness of actual conditions. But "one hundred years after...the publication of *The Communist Manifesto*," Rosenberg writes in 1948, "the simplification of history has not been brought about." Instead, the players of the nineteenth century have been replaced by a new and more malevolent form of farceur:

> The heroes of our time [Hitler, Stalin, de Gaulle] belong
> to contrived rather than spontaneous myths — on
> that account often evoking even more fanaticism than
> formerly as a psychological protection against disbelief...

> The comic nature of the twentieth-century hero is
> instinctively recognized the moment he makes his
> entrance upon the stage: in the popular phrase, "At first
> nobody took him seriously." The clown-hero retali-
> ates to the ridicule of the world by exposing the lack
> of seriousness of the rest of the cast, of all the exist-
> ing historical actors. The leader without a program
> challenges all opposing classes, parties, governments,
> individuals, to live up to *their* programs. And since all are
> playing a comedy of pretense, "the adventurer who took
> the comedy as plain comedy was bound to win."

The notion of politics as theater remained salient for Rosenberg throughout his career — more and more so, indeed, as the media tightened its grip and political events became performances contrived to hold its interest. For the most part, however, he turned the metaphors of drama — role, action, mask — in a different direction. For it was not only the statesman or revolutionary who aspired to play a part, in his conception; it was, of necessity, every modern person. To be modern is to be cut off from the past, from the traditions that told you who you are and where you belong. "Since he is not bound to anything given," Rosenberg writes, modern man "is capable of playing countless roles" — the many roles that society offers him — "but only as an actor," aware of his disguise. Not content to be an actor, though, "he takes up the slack between himself and social reality," between ego and role — who he feels himself to be and who he appears as to others — "by creating illusory selves," fantasy projections of (as we would say today) a "real me." But, like Louis Bonaparte, he copies those selves from available models: "Socrates, for example, or Christ, or some revolutionist clothed in the glamour of the times" (one thinks of Che Guevara, Johnny Rotten, Kurt Cobain, each with their legions of imitators). "Members of every class surrender themselves to artificially constructed mass egos."

But modernism demonstrated an alternative. Social roles, prefabricated selves, conformity, illusion: all these could be resisted. The problem of the modern self — the problem of identity — remained. The solution was to treat it as a problem. Rosenberg's artistic heroes made the search for self — the effort to create a self — the content of their practice and the subject of their art. Before they were painters, however, those heroes were poets (poetry, remember, was his youthful aspiration): Rimbaud, Mallarmé, and Valéry, the leading French Symbolists, together with their predecessors, Poe and Baudelaire. "I is another," said Rimbaud, and, as Rosenberg explains the process in an early essay, those figures sought, through programs of spiritual experimentation enacted in verse, to conjure up that other.

162

"Whoever undertakes to create soon finds himself engaged in creating himself," Rosenberg would later write, and he found his greatest self-creators in the artists whom he dubbed the action painters: Pollock, de Kooning, Adolph Gottlieb, Philip Guston, with Hans Hoffman and Arshile Gorky as important precursors. Rosenberg did not evince much interest in what he referred to as "formal modernism, or modernist formalism," the run of work from the Impressionists through the early twentieth century (Manet, Cézanne, Picasso, Matisse). Formal exploration never engaged him as such. Rosenberg tunes in when art confronts the modern crisis, when art itself becomes a crisis. That is to say, with World War I, with Dada and Surrealism. By 1914, he writes, the formal tradition was moribund. The art that followed, which he called "*modern* modern art," "arises from the conviction that the forms of Western culture...have permanently collapsed." Dada declared "that anything can be art"; Surrealism, that "poetry is the substance of painting." Both were forms of anti-art, and both turned art in the direction of philosophy, psychology, politics, and metaphysics.

Those developments were slow to register on this side of the Atlantic. The 1930s were, in any case, a time when art was flattened underneath the dictates of leftist political orthodoxy. But in the 1940s painting started over, as it were, in the United States. In "Parable of American Painting," the piece with which he chose to start his first collection, Rosenberg, thinking of the War of Independence — when files of British infantry were picked off from behind the trees by scruffy colonials — distinguishes between "Redcoats" and "Coonskins." The Redcoats fall because they think they're still in England, fighting on the rolling greenswards, instead of looking at the landscape that is actually in front of them. They are victims of style: they see

163

what they've been taught to see. The Coonskin starts with where he is and tries to act accordingly. "Coonskinism is the search for the principle that applies, even if it applies only once." Whitman was a Coonskin. "What have I?" he said. "I have all to *make*."

Until the 1940s, Rosenberg explains, the great majority of American painters were Redcoats, projecting European styles onto American landscapes and streets. But the action painters had absorbed the "*modern* modern" point: there were no styles anymore — none with any force or claim. They needed to begin from the beginning. At the same time, though, they "shared...the intuition that there is nothing worth painting. No object, but also no idea." All that was left was the self, which they couldn't so much paint as paint into existence. Action, says Rosenberg, of any kind, "embodies decisions in which one comes to recognize oneself." The action painter starts with no design or expectation, no subject or thought. He makes a mark — a stroke, a drip — and the action begins. Each mark begets the next within a kind of dance. The artist thinks in paint, with his eyes and his hand. The canvas talks back, "to provoke him into a dramatic dialogue. Each stroke ha[s] to be a decision and [i]s answered by a new question."

Rosenberg was fond of pointing out that many of the action painters were immigrants, people for whom the question of identity was especially urgent. (Pollock was an immigrant from Wyoming.) Nor was it an accident, he thought, that the movement arose in America, that land of immigrants, transients, and strangers, and in "a century of displaced persons, of people moving from one class into another, from one national context into another." Still, while the action painter lands upon the shore of each new canvas free of preconceptions or intentions, like the immigrant

164

he does not land there free of the past. That past consists of everything he has seen, especially art. The *modern* modern artist "picks his way among the bits and pieces of the cultural heritage and puts together whatever seems capable of carrying a meaning." The action painter, in particular, "starts an action and observes what kind of image it will magnetize out of the formal accretions piled up in his mind." Tradition, like paint, becomes something to think with.

A painting so produced, says Rosenberg, is not an object but an event. It is a "fragment," a "sketch," not a whole so much as "a succession of wholes" (de Kooning's famous *Woman I*, he tells us, was "repainted daily for almost two years"), one whose end, the point at which the artist steps away for good, is as arbitrary as its beginning. "And after an interval," in "a civilization in which the cultures of all times and places are being blended and destroyed," these wholes perforce disintegrate. In modernity, says Rosenberg, there are no masterpieces, objects that endure — not for any dearth of creative energy, but because the conditions, the stable traditions, no longer exist. Indeed, as they circulate through reproductions in books and magazines, in the discourse of critics, journalists, and art historians, as they are taken up and set aside by curators, spectators, and artists themselves, as they lose or pick up speed and spin in their "passage through the social orbit," the masterpieces of the past are also now events. "The *Mona Lisa* arrives from Paris and is greeted at the dock like a movie star." "All that is solid melts into air," wrote Marx. "All that is holy is profaned."

"To be a new man," says Rosenberg, "is not a condition but an effort." ("One does not *possess* mental freedom and detachment, one participates in them.") Coonskins can turn into Redcoats, if they let themselves become a style — in fact, it happens more often than not. Just the initial breakthrough into newness can require an endeavor of years. "The American...who searched for genuine art has been fated to spend half his life in blind alleys," Rosenberg writes. "Often it required a second 'birth' to get him out of them. One thinks of the radical break in the careers of Rothko, Guston, Gottlieb, Kline" — or of that archetypal Coonskin, Whitman. The artists whom Rosenberg most esteemed were two for whom no question was ever settled, no label was ever sufficient, one-man avant-gardes who sustained their radicalism across a span of decades: his old friend de Kooning, "the foremost painter of the postwar world," and Saul Steinberg, a figure about whom the art world could never decide if he even counted as an artist.

They and other artists are the model individuals, in Rosenberg's conception; they show us what it means and what it takes to be one. And the individual, even more than art, was for Rosenberg the highest value. Not individualism, in the sense of libertarian conservatism, or of thinking that people are not conditioned by their social context — he took leave of Marxism, but he didn't take leave of his senses — but the individual: the person who thinks for himself, who acts on his own responsibility, who stubbornly insists upon his separateness and independence.

That figure, he believed, was everywhere under assault. First, in his early years, by Marxism, or by what it had turned into, Leninism. In Leninism, the Party supplants the proletariat as the hero of history. And the Party, with the omniscience granted it by the infallible methods of dialectical materialism and the sacred texts of Marx and Lenin, is in absolute possession of the truth. The Communist, says Rosenberg, is thus "an intellectual who need not think." The rest of society, as in other orthodoxies, is divided into two groups: the sheep and the wolves, the simple folk who know not and the evil ones who know incorrectly. To the sheep, the uninitiated, the Communist adopts a benignly pedagogical stance, one composed in equal parts of tolerance and smugness. In Lenin's words, he patiently explains. But to the wolf, the independent intellectual, the individual who dares to challenge the Party's monopoly on understanding, the Communist is ruthless. Such a person must be canceled, and since at stake is nothing less than the salvation of humanity, any means to do so is acceptable.

After the war, the assault on the individual came from other directions. In one lay not Communists but ex-Communists, ex-radicals and former fellow travelers. Here began that vogue for self-confession — "Couch Liberalism," Rosenberg called it, meaning the analyst's couch — of which Whittaker Chambers ("St. John of the Couch") was the great exemplar. In *The End of Innocence*, the critic Leslie Fiedler went so far, to Rosenberg's disgust, as to indict the *anti*-Communist intellectual, to indict all intellectuals, for the sin of merely being intellectuals, for thinking and sounding like intellectuals and thereby separating themselves from "the Community," that idol of the 1950s. Rosenberg viewed with dismay (and sardonic amusement) the new generational style — "The Solid Look," the Brooks Brothers suit, the ideology of "babies, God, and job" — especially as it was taking hold among the younger intellectuals. For society had discovered that intellectuals were useful — in government, in universities, in public relations and advertising firms — provided they agreed to stop being intellectuals. Which most of them happily did. Having donned the mask of the Organization Man, "the gentlemen of the Left" became "hysterically antipathetic to whatever possessed its own physiognomy. The outstanding figures in modern art and literature were abused as 'mere individualists' unable to 'solve the problem of our time,'" and in the Cold War context, "'the end of innocence' meant, basically, an abusive goodbye to Karl Marx by shivering jobholders."

What bothered Rosenberg as much as anything about this *trahison des clercs* was its insistence on using the first-person plural. Fiedler was pointing his finger not at himself but at "us." Already by the late 1940s, writers such as Trilling and Edmund Wilson were stepping forward to interpret the "Communist experience" of the 1930s — to speak, that is, for Rosenberg's entire generation. Rosenberg, who never spoke for anybody but himself, refused to be enlisted. There are common situations, he said, but there is no common experience. Every person's is their own. His, for example, besides "'the thirties,'" contained "all sorts of anachronisms and cultural fragments: the Old Testament and the Gospels, Plato, eighteenth-century music, the notion of freedom as taught in the New York City school system, the fantastic emotional residues of the Jewish family." For individual experience, he said, "it is necessary to begin with the individual...one will not arrive at it by reflecting oneself in a 'we.'"

The argument occurs in "The Herd of Independent Minds," his great essay from 1948. The point of the title is not that the liberal elite is afflicted by groupthink (which is not to say that it isn't) but that it thinks of itself as a group. Mass culture, Rosenberg says, is predicated on the idea that everyone is alike, and it makes us over in its image, so that we come to see ourselves as alike. But there is also such a thing, he says, as "anti-mass-culture mass culture," the mass culture of the elite: "'significant' novels," "'highbrow' radio programs," "magazines designed for college professors" — the culture of "seriousness" and "social relevance." Characteristic of all mass culture is "the conviction that the artist ought to communicate the common experience of his audience." But since there is no common experience, the result is "contrived and unseeing art," rendered through a set of formulas, "by which the member of the audience learns from the author what he already knows" — "that together with others he is an ex-radical, or a Jew, or feels frustrated, or lives in a postwar world, or prefers freedom to tyranny."

By the same token, mass culture, including the anti-mass-culture of the educated herd, "must deny the validity of a single human being's effort to arrive at a consciousness of himself and of his situation" — must be hostile, that is, to genuine art. For "the genuine work of art...takes away from its audience its sense of knowing where it stands in relation to what has happened to it" — takes away, that is, the accepted versions of history, the official accounts of identity. It "suggests to the audience that its situation might be quite different than it had suspected." It brings us into a truer relationship to reality, but it brings us there, perforce, as individuals. "Along this rocky road to the actual it is only possible to go Indian file, one at a time, so that 'art' means 'breaking up the crowd' — not 'reflecting' its experience."

But above all, Rosenberg discerned the impulse to negate the individual in the art world itself. The heyday of Abstract Expressionism — the action painters, plus figures such as

Rothko, Ad Reinhardt, and Barnett Newman, the movement's mystical wing, who sought to purify their art into an ultimate transcendent sign — did not outlast the 1950s. AbEx was deposed by Pop art —Warhol, Lichtenstein, Oldenburg — succeeded, or joined, as the 1960s wore on, by Op ("optical") art, kinetic art, and minimalism and other varieties of formalism. All involved for Rosenberg a retreat from the things that he most valued in art. With Pop, he believed, art surrendered to the media; with Op art and kinetic art, to science. Formalism — which settled in as art-world orthodoxy, thanks in part to the dictatorial dogmatism of Clement Greenberg, Rosenberg's great rival among the midcentury critics — represented a rejection of content as such: of art's involvement with social, psychological, or spiritual questions, with anything outside itself. Gone in all these trends were the hand and the medium as instruments of discovery, the engagement of the self in the process of creation, the oppositionality and will to social transformation of the avant-garde.

Rosenberg viewed these developments — and this was characteristic of his thought across all its dimensions, part of what made him an intellectual who wrote about art rather than merely an art critic — in their historical and social context. After the war, the media itself had elevated both the profile and prestige of modern art. The result was the creation of what Rosenberg referred to as the "Vanguard Audience" — a mass audience for new art (an anti-mass mass, of course) that, priding itself on its sophistication, "could accept the new in its entirety, with all its conflicting assumptions or without any assumptions." The Vanguard Audience could not be shocked; it enjoyed affront and understood incomprehension. It did not embrace Cubism, or Surrealism, or Abstract Expressionism: it embraced them all indiscriminately. The new itself, in other words, became the highest value, became the only value. The new became a tradition: the tradition of the new, in Rosenberg's famous phrase, one that was "capable of evoking the automatic responses typical of a handed-down body of beliefs."

The artists who arrived in the 1950s and 1960s were happy to play to that audience. "Putting on a show developed a stronger appeal than the act of painting carried to a hesitant pause in the privacy of the studio." As for the audience itself, "after the strain of trying to respond to the riddles of Abstract Expressionism," "it preferred images taken in at a glance and 'glamorous' colors translatable into dress patterns." Warhol grasped that art, for them, was something not to scrutinize but be "aware of." Like Robert Rauschenberg and Jasper Johns (artists for whom Rosenberg had little use), he understood that people liked to see things they already knew: Brillo boxes, American flags, the collages of everyday objects that Rauschenberg rebranded as "combines."

Tending to the Vanguard Audience, as both a cause and a beneficiary of art's new visibility, was a vastly expanded institutional apparatus: galleries by the hundreds, collectors large and small, arts councils, traveling exhibitions, university departments and museums, "editors, curators, art historians, archivists, biographers, publishers, columnists, TV and radio programmers, photographers, catalogue writers." The market, newly flush, turned art into a commodity, but the academics and museums turned it into something more insidious: a form of knowledge. A crowd of words surrounded the work: wall texts, exhibition catalogs, monographs, interviews. Never mind trying to feel your way, in silence and stillness, into a spontaneous aesthetic response. Artist, date, "period," style, authorized interpretation: now you *knew*. Art was recruited

The Individual Nuisance

for programs of public education, as the curator displaced the artist at the center of the enterprise. Shows turned into theses that you walk through, with paintings "function[ing] as illustrations to bring out the critical or cultural concept" (for example, "The Nude Through the Ages"). Exhibitions "more and more take on the character of art books, presenting wall-scale duplicates of the publications that will result from them." Art turned into "culture" — a form of living death.

As art became institutionalized, the artist became a creature of institutions: that is, a professional — respectable, well groomed, a solid citizen. The Abstract Expressionists, the painters of Tenth Street — cranky, alienated, socially marginal, down at the heels — were the last in the line of artistic bohemians that stretched back to the Impressionists. Training in a studio gave way to training at a university, the half-a-lifetime's search in blind alleys to the smoothly ascendant career. The artist "abandon[ed] his shamanistic role, and the rites required to realize it" — Cézanne's anxiety, Surrealist self-estrangement, de Kooning's "failure" — all of which posed "an impediment to the good life of professionals," and to the characteristic goal of professionals, success. As art was drawn into the orbit of the university, its values drifted toward the academic, toward art conceived of as a set of problems and solutions, things you could rationalize, train, and explain — line, plane, form, color. Hence the reign of formalism, and the emergence of the artist "who conceives picture making in terms of technical recipes, but who is entirely ignorant of the role of art in the struggles of the modern spirit." The avant-garde lived on, but only as a simulacrum of itself, a "socially reconciled avant-garde," sponsored by the NEA and sustained by "the myth of rebellion." Revolution, like the new, had become a tradition, and overturned nothing.

172

To the effacement of the individual in all its forms, Rosenberg offered no solutions, certainly no systemic ones. His only solution was to be an individual—or rather ("one does not *possess*...") to try. This, he believed, is always in our power. "For the individual," he said, "the last voice in the issue of being or not being himself is still his own." And to help us, there is art. One of the reasons he deplored the conversion of art into knowledge, of paintings into pictures in books, images on television, and slides in the classroom, is that "the direct experience of art" — up close, in person, just you and the work — "contributes a lively sensation of ignorance." Before a genuine work of art, one is left with questions, not answers. Which is to say, one starts to think.

There is art, and, for us, there is the work of Harold Rosenberg. It should be obvious by now that my attraction to this man derives not only from his iridescent mind, his swooping prose, but from the relevance of his ideas to the present moment. I won't insult the reader's intelligence by drawing out the application of his picture of the "clown-hero" who "retaliates to the ridicule of the world," the "leader without a program" whose self-contrived myth "evoke[s] even more fanaticism than formerly as a psychological protection against disbelief." I will only note that we live in an age when the self-contrived myth has become a universal — as it were, a democratic — possession. Rosenberg wrote of the construction of illusory selves, devices to bridge the abyss between ego and role. Now, thanks to the wonders of social media and the miracles of the Instagram filter (not to mention of the plastic surgeon's office), that construction is literal. Yet it remains, overwhelmingly, an act not of creation but of imitation: of

The Individual Nuisance

celebrities, "influencers," fictional heroes and superheroes, themselves copied one from another. We are everywhere invited to bullshit ourselves, and we everywhere comply. The clown-hero, in full theatrical makeup, calls his army of fanatics to the capital, and they arrive arrayed for cosplay. In seeking to understand our current malaise, our great contemporary deficit of being, we could do worse than start there.

Remember also that the artificially constructed egos that Rosenberg spoke of were mass ones, the self submerged within the herd. And the crisis of the individual, as he described it, has only deepened in the decades since his diagnosis. We need only think about the transformation, since the post-war years, of the meaning of the word "identity." Having once referred to a unique and hard-won self-conception wrested from experience — that which made you you and no one else — it now denotes the reverse. Your identity today is that which assigns you, at birth, to your group. Rosenberg said that there are common situations but only individual experiences. The identity-mongers also invoke experience (or "lived experience," as if there were another kind), but only to align it with collective scripts. Today we say "me too." To say "not me" is to invite anathematization.

The Party may be dead, but its functions live anew. Again today we have the orthodoxy of the Left as Rosenberg described it: sacred texts and prophets (Foucault, Butler, Kendi), omniscience conferred by a set of infallible formulas ("cultural appropriation," "white fragility"), pedantic smugness, messianic intolerance, consensus enforced by the standing threat of professional or social death. We certainly have no shortage of intellectuals who need not think, pundits and critics whose minds appear incapable of containing a thought that wasn't put there by the zeitgeist. If our public discourse has become so numbingly predictable, especially on the left, that is largely because it is dominated by individuals who can tell you their opinion of a thing before they've even heard of it.

In art we are back to the 1930s. Art must toe the ideological line. As for the mass audience, the herd, its demands are now explicit and belligerent. The artist must speak for the group (the one to which she's willy-nilly been assigned), never for herself as an individual, "a single human being." Which is to say, she must allow the group—or rather, its self-appointed ideological commissars—to speak through her. The word today is not "reflect" but "represent": affirm rather than disrupt, as Rosenberg put it, the audience's "sense of knowing where it stands in relation to what has happened to it." Woe be unto those who dare to shock instead of pander, or who refuse the injunction to "stay in your lane." Anti-mass mass culture is also still with us, the culture of the educated elite, with its fake rebellions and its moral self-flattery: NPR, the *New York Times*, the *New Yorker*, et al., together with the cultural products — always scrupulously woke — to which they give assent. One thing, though, has changed since Rosenberg's day. Elite mass culture hardly even pretends anymore to be interested in art — in art, that is, as opposed to entertainment, high art as opposed to kitsch. Art is too hard, too subtle, too complex, too time-consuming, altogether too recalcitrant. The professional would rather watch Netflix; the "cultural critic" would rather pontificate about the TikTok trend. Rosenberg didn't think that kitsch was even worth bothering to attack. Now it rules the world.

As for me, it is Rosenberg's example, even more than his ideas, that is bracing. He was a thinker who maintained the stance, with respect not only to society but also to his fellow intellectuals, of the artist — of the rare artist, such as de Kooning or Steinberg, who never ceases to be a true one. Even

175

bohemias, he wrote, become conformities. "The artist thus finds it necessary to exist on the edge of the edge," and that is exactly what he did. He kept faith with his estrangement. He was the greatest of the New York intellectuals, and also the least characteristic. He ran with no packs and subscribed to no schools — nor did he attempt to found any. And he stayed in the stream. He knew that culture — art, thought — must always, if it is to live, be enacted: daily, continually, like de Kooning repainting a canvas. He faced the modern crisis, the disorientation of perpetual change, without swerving right or left, toward nostalgia for what was or utopian expectations of what will be. His only direction was forward: through problems, through questions, through doubt.

Late in life, Rosenberg composed the introduction to a volume of de Kooning's work. Its peroration, with a few adjustments, applies to its author himself:

> De Kooning has never attempted to attribute political meaning to his work...Yet under the conditions of the ideological pressure characteristic of the past forty years, unbending adherence to individual spontaneity and independence is itself a quasi-political position... Improvised unities such as de Kooning's are the only alternative to modern philosophies of social salvation which, while they appeal for recruits in the name of a richer life for the individual, consistently shove him aside in practice. De Kooning's art testifies to a refusal to be either recruited or pushed aside... He is the nuisance of the individual "I am" in an age of collective credos and styles.

BENJAMIN MOSER

Hals at Nightfall

The "war against water," the Dutch struggle to wrest their country from the sea, is strangely invisible now. Concerns about global warming are just that, global. The little local struggles — the rush to get the livestock to higher ground, the nervous pacing along the village dam — belong to dangers from olden days, like getting shipped off to suppress a tribal uprising in Sumatra, or contracting cholera from shit in the canal. Only the very old recall the last time things went wrong. The North Sea Flood of 1953 occasionally resurfaces in black-and-white photographs and television documentaries. Every Dutch person has seen these images, but they look as remote as the folk costumes that the people in them are wearing. Almost nobody has experienced the old ancestral terror: that water, looming, lapping, leaping, waiting to whisk you away.

This is because the flood of 1953 was the last of its kind. In its wake, the government embarked on one of the most elaborate engineering projects in history, the Delta Works; but the challenges for which they were designed are not the challenges, barely envisioned, of global warming. To ask whether those enormous barriers can withstand the new age of weather is to wonder how long the Netherlands can survive. With every freak hurricane and unexpected drought, we find ourselves, like every generation past, dwelling on eschatology. And when we imagine the collapse of dune and dike, among the many dark things that we imagine are the cultural losses such a cataclysm would bring. If the western Netherlands — all those cities, with all those museums and libraries — were swept into the sea, which treasures would we miss the most? It is a question that people in other increasingly vulnerable cities should increasingly be asking themselves.

The extraordinary artistic riches of the Netherlands notwithstanding, the answer to that chilling question, to this awful cultural triage, is surprisingly easy for me. It is to be found along a quiet street in Haarlem. There are many reasons for the art pilgrim to come to this city, halfway between Amsterdam and the ocean. Today virtually a suburb of Amsterdam, a few minutes from its central station, few cities have as distinguished a cultural tradition as Haarlem, a tradition honored in the museum that bears the name of its greatest painter. To see Frans Hals in his own place is to realize that not every artist travels well. Some can be seen anywhere: you can appreciate Titian better in Madrid, Paris, or Washington than in his hometown of Venice, where his works blend too seamlessly into the ambient splendor. Yet you will never understand the point of Carpaccio outside his own ghostly city, where his bizarre mythological tableaux glow with Egyptian mystery.

The Dutch, for the most part, are transportable. Most of them painted for living-room walls, and those can be found anywhere: one reason that, since medieval times, their works have been exported by the tens of thousands. If Holland disappeared, the achievement of its painters would still be visible all over the world, and we would know their Golden Age as we know those of Greece and Rome — from noble fragments. Enough Rembrandts and Vermeers would survive, even if *The Jewish Bride* and *The View of Delft* were not among them. But though many of Hals' greatest works are in foreign collections, you still have to come to Haarlem to see him. There, in eight gigantic paintings — placed end-to-end, they are twenty-three meters long — the Dutch Golden Age unfurls in portraits of members of Haarlem's charitable and military institutions. They show eighty-four people in all, painted over half a century.

179

In June 1902, to escape construction noise next door to his house in London, the American painter James Abbott McNeill Whistler fled across the North Sea. In The Hague, he met the German painter Georg Sauter, who was dismayed to see the state of Whistler's health. A drive to the beach at Scheveningen sufficed to exhaust him; and when Whistler spoke of going to nearby Haarlem, Sauter thought he was too frail.

The next day, he was amazed to find Whistler in Haarlem. They strolled past the pictures, from the earliest, painted in

Hals at Nightfall

1616, when Frans Hals was young, to the *Regentesses*, painted in 1664, when Hals was nearly as close to death as Whistler was now. Sauter's notes from the trip report, "Certainly no collection would give stronger support to Whistler's theory that a master grows in his art, from picture to picture, to the end, than that at Haarlem." The elderly painter warmed to the subject, and slid under the railing in order to view the pictures from closer by. The guard forced him to take a step back, and Whistler determined to wait until the other visitors were gone.

At last, wrote Sauter, "We were indeed alone with Franz Hals. Now nothing could keep him away from the canvases; particularly the groups of old men and women got their full share of appreciation." Whistler clambered onto a chair, "absolutely into raptures over the old women, admiring everything; his exclamation of joy came out now at the top of his voice, now in the most tender, almost caressing whisper: 'Look at it — just look; look at the beautiful colour — the flesh — look at the white — that black — look how those ribbons are put in. Oh, what a swell he was — can you see it all? — and the character — how he realized it.'"

And then: "Moving with his hand so near the picture as if he wanted to caress it in every detail, he screamed with joy: 'Oh, I must touch it — just for the fun of it,' and he moved tenderly with his fingers over the face of one of the old women." The guards indulged the sick painter — who miraculously managed to make it back to London. He hardly left his house again. The construction banged on. Soon he was dead.

The care lavished on the building that now houses the Frans Hals Museum seems at odds with its original purpose, a nursing home. Such buildings amazed foreign visitors, who were more used to seeing such outlays reserved for princes or bishops. The Old Men's House was an expression of dedication to the infirm, and before it became a museum it served as an orphanage, a further advertisement, in mortar and brick, for Dutch moral excellence.

Hals was young when construction began, in 1607. With its spacious rooms and tranquil garden, the Old Men's House speaks of wealth sagely deployed, of a well-ordered civilization. So does the collection's centerpiece, Hals' group portraits. Swooshing with silk, dripping with lace, they nonetheless convey a dignity that, even at its most celebratory, is never ostentatious: these are people who deserved their golden age.

Yet the life of the artist who created the pictures — the person for whom the building is named — speaks of a poverty so extreme that the modern mind struggles to fathom it. Rembrandt died poor, but enjoyed long periods of affluence, even magnificence; Hals, from before his birth till after his death, was trailed by such destitution that most of what we know of his life comes from the annals of the small-claims court. When he was born, his father was involved in a lawsuit arising from his brother's estate. The question, which dragged on for nearly a year, involved a rapier, a doublet (a men's jacket), six shirts, and a pair of stockings. The records of this dispute survived. The record of Frans' birth has not. Though we do not know the exact date, we know he came into the world in Antwerp toward the end of 1582 — which is to say, in the middle of an atrocity.

The Dutch Revolt began as a reaction of the Netherlands — attached by inheritance to the crown of Spain — to punitive taxation, tyrannical government, and brutal

Hals at Nightfall

religious repression. The revolt was centered in Antwerp, the mercantile and banking capital of Europe, which was being reduced to a colonial tributary, its preachers tortured, its treasury milked to finance wars in faraway lands. By the time of Hals' birth, the city had been reduced by wave after wave of destruction. In 1566, the Protestants purged the churches of what they saw as idols, an act of defiance against king and church that was answered, ten years later, by a sack of the city: eighteen thousand people were killed in three days. In historical terms, the "Spanish Fury" meant the end of Antwerp as the entrepôt of the North.

In personal terms, for the survivors, it meant nothing good, especially if they, like Hals' parents, were poor to begin with. His father was a shearer — a man who cut wool from sheep — one of the many artisans in a cloth-making industry that never recovered from the attacks. In an economic and military context that made six shirts and a pair of stockings a treasure worth fighting over, more violence was to come. Around the time of Frans Hals' birth, another fury broke out. The Prince of Orange invited the brother of the King of France to lead the liberated provinces; but the Duke, unwilling to be a constitutional monarch, attacked his own city of Antwerp. The coup resulted in a humiliating defeat, hundreds of troops hacked to death by the outraged citizenry. But the "French Fury" weakened Antwerp still further. And the next summer, the Spanish returned. After a year of starvation and horror, the city fell. From then on, the northern and the southern Netherlands were severed. The Dutch blockaded Antwerp for two centuries. Over half its population fled, among them the Hals family. They settled in Haarlem—also besieged and plundered by the Spanish. But the Spanish left Haarlem in 1577, and never returned.

By the time these thousands of Flemish immigrants arrived, Haarlem was being rebuilt. The skills that these sophisticated people brought revitalized the city's trade, including the cloth trade that employed Hals' father, Franchois. The city prospered. The Hals family did not. In 1599, to make good a debt incurred by purchasing half a cow, Franchois was forced to cede the entirety of his household goods.

A pair of stockings, half a cow: the tone was set. Frans Hals would be sued, in 1624, for payment for a jacket (three guilders and six stuivers). In 1627, he would be sued for seven guilders for a delivery of butter and cheese. In 1629, a baker sued him for five guilders and seventeen stuivers. In 1631, he was sued over his failure to pay for some meat for which he had agreed to pay 42 guilders; thirteen were still outstanding. In 1634, he was sued for twenty-three guilders for bread. (He had exchanged a painting for the bread, not enough to cover the debt.) In 1636, another baker sued him. In 1640, he was sued for thirty-three guilders for rent. In 1642, he was sued for five guilders for a bed. In 1644, he was sued for five guilders and two stuivers for the purchase of canvas. In 1647, he owed his shoemaker fifty-nine guilders and eight stuivers. In 1649, two of his grandchildren were admitted to the orphanage, their parents deceased and he and his wife unable to care for them. The next year, a local bartender sued him. The year after that, his wife was sued for four guilders for not paying for a box. When his ailing son Claes made a will in 1656, he allowed his parents to choose among his gray coat, his "worst outfit," or one Flemish pound (six guilders).

So it went. If one knew Frans Hals only through the scarce documents that chronicle his life, one would be utterly unprepared for the sumptuous paintings that deck the halls of the museum that bears his name. If his life was petty, his

Hals at Nightfall

work was lavish. Perhaps more than any other Dutch painter of his time, his impulse was celebratory, and as notable for everything it omits as for everything it includes.

There are no still lifes. There are no landscapes or seascapes or cityscapes or — surprisingly, for a man with something like fourteen children — nudes. Notwithstanding the odd skull, his pictures are bereft of allusive symbols; we vainly comb them for *mementi mori*. And though a pair of evangelists turned up in the basement of a Ukrainian museum in the 1950s, they bear not the slightest whiff of religion. Frans Hals' subject was people, specifically the people of Haarlem.

His first known portrait — still in his museum — shows Jacobus Zaffius, a Catholic who, in 1578, witnessed the destruction of Haarlem's holy images, and was imprisoned for protesting. In 1611, when this picture was painted, Zaffius was a figure who looked to the wars of religion and independence — to Haarlem's past. The man who painted him pointed to the future. Hals was not quite young — almost thirty — when he painted Zaffius. It was a late start. At that age, Paulus Potter was dead; Carl Fabritius had two years to live. Despite the many hurdles that he faced in his life, Hals would live far longer than any prominent Dutch painter. He died in 1666, age eighty-four, fully twenty years older than Rembrandt was when he died — and Rembrandt was considered old, and had outlived most of his colleagues.

The vitality that propelled Hals through a long life is visible, already, in this early picture. The paint is laid on in liberal scrapes. Though the colors are few — black and brown for Zaffius' clothing, yellows and reds and whites for his face and beard — Hals wrings every nuance out of them. "He doesn't have a single black, but twenty-seven different blacks," wrote another painter, who thought he was Rembrandt's equal. That painter — Vincent van Gogh — was one of many moderns who found a model in Hals. Whistler called his painting of his mother "Arrangement in Grey and Black No. 1," a title that could have served for any number of Hals' paintings. Only Rembrandt and Hals placed such unembarrassed emphasis on the artifice of their art, a break with tradition that would not be taken up again until the nineteenth century.

Yet all these whorls and scratches inevitably resolve into Haarlemers who, though centuries dead, illustrate the paradox that makes Hals' work so fascinating. Blatantly artificial — yet so alive that his subjects always seem to have been snapped *in flagrante*, as if by a canny street photographer. Roman Vishniac's Warsaw, Vivian Maier's Chicago, Henri Cartier-Bresson's Paris: they all descend from Frans Hals' Haarlem.

In Hals' technique, the moderns found a lineage — and in his subjects, too. After a visit to Haarlem, Manet made up his mind to become a painter of his own time. Hals had discovered the range of humanity even in a small city, and alongside the grandees and the flush merchants he showed the common folk: a bartender tallying her customers' drinks on the wall; a series of fishermen's children; a sly hooker.

The city was small, but its citizens reflected the Dutch Republic's worldliness and ambition. Isaac Massa — a fluent Russian-speaker who was ennobled in Sweden, became the first Westerner to publish maps of Siberia, and wrote an account of the False Dimitri — puts in an appearance; and so does a man attired in one of the rare kimonos that the Dutch were allowed to export from Japan. The first person to paint the landscape of Brazil, Frans Post, sat for Hals. So did a man

185

Hals at Nightfall

who, though born in France, became as much a symbol of Dutch cultural achievement as Hals himself: René Descartes, who spent his adult life in Amsterdam, where, in a climate of intellectual freedom that had no equal anywhere in Europe, he composed his philosophical works, and was painted by Hals shortly before his death.

Alongside these eminences are people one would cross the street to avoid: a man who played an instrument that squawked so obnoxiously that neighbors would bribe him, with a coin, to get him to move along; and Malle Babbe, "Crazy Babs," known in local legend as the sorceress of Haarlem. Malle Babbe clutches a pewter mug of beer while an owl — a symbol of drunkenness, of the night-side — perches on her shoulder. Is she laughing? Grimacing? She is one of Hals' most ambiguous characters. Some find her *gezellig* — an overused word that means fun, sociable — the type of kind-hearted drunk you might spend a memorable evening with at the bar. Popular songs have been written that portray her as a prostitute, which seems unlikely. Others see a terrifying madwoman in the grip of alcoholism and mental illness.

186

She was a real person, named Barbara Claes, who has been traced in the records of the same asylum to which Hals' own son Pieter was committed. (Another of the tragedies that filled his life, recorded in the dry prose of bureaucracy.) In an age without euphemism, this institution was known as Het Dolhuys, "the madhouse." In an age without specific diagnosis of mental disabilities, it is hard to know what ailed her. Whatever her story, she surely never dreamed that she would remain a symbol of Haarlem centuries after her death, or that the city would honor her with a statue, complete with the owl on her shoulder. Her name and face are still known thanks to Hals' portrait, which — in our image-soaked world, in our dutiful trudges through "encyclopedic" museums — is that rare picture that, once it has been seen, can never be forgotten. *El sueño de la razón produce monstruos*, Goya famously wrote on an etching: the sleep of reason produces monsters. Owls descend on a dozing man, landing on his shoulder as they did, a hundred and fifty years before, on Hals' ominous woman, on Malle Babbe. Amid all the attainments of civilization — Goya showed the man respectably dressed — it is enough to close one's eyes to see the madhouse, the bailiff, the orphan, the drunk. (Enough, too, to open them.)

You enter the Frans Hals Museum through a monumental gate, take a right, buy your ticket in the bookstore, and then walk, counterclockwise, around the courtyard. The great Haarlem artists before Hals file past on the right side of the quadrilateral — and then, in the wing opposite the entrance, the first of the works that have attracted generations of artists to this city, the eight heroic group portraits, appear. No matter how many other pictures by Hals you have seen in real life — no matter how many times you have seen these particular pictures reproduced in books or on screen — you will not be prepared for their size and their impact.

The woozy idea of inspiration, of the artist's pleasure in his work, springs to life here. To see Hals paint — and his pictures give you the feeling that you are watching him paint — is to see a graceful young animal bouncing and jumping, delighting in everything he sees. A fork! A hat! A moustache! The artist never gets bored, or reverts to routine. Everything is a burst, a climax. The flash of the feasting militiamen, seated at their richly laden tables, clad in their fabulous garments, is rendered by a man who wields brushes as they wield swords, and whose technique matches his subjects so perfectly that it is impossible

Hals at Nightfall

to separate one from the other. The militiamen flaunt their pride, and so does the painter.

The earliest, *The Banquet of the Officers of the St. George Civic Guard*, dates to 1616, the beginning of Hals' career. Its colors are bright and cheerful, showing young men — many younger even than Hals — the flower of a triumphant nation at the height of its opulence. For them, the iconoclasms and the religious wars, the sieges and the massacres, would have been thrilling stories they had heard, as children, from the greatest generation.

Twenty-five years — another generation — later, Hals, now middle-aged, painted the regents of the St. Elizabeth Hospital, housed directly across from the museum. The colors have sobered, and the subject is different: the directors of a charitable foundation, the first such group painted in Haarlem. Gone is the sparkling silverware; the only metal visible is a clutch of coins dedicated to the care of the infirm. Here are people scratched together in paint — those twenty-seven blacks — who seem far more real than the smoother creations of other artists: life-like and life-sized. The man closest to the viewer is seen in profile, cocking an ear toward some invisible interloper who has walked in on their gathering. Through that gesture, the group acknowledges the viewer, and through their gestures they acknowledge each another.

Like a pianist whose fingers never allude to the deprivation that preceded his performance, or like a pirouetting ballerina whose dainty smile gives no hint of the blood in her shoes, his travails — his quibbles with the tailor, his dead children — have been pushed offstage. Hals is entirely at the service of an art that does not show daily life but that, by rising above it, elevates it. All the spectator sees is the *sprezzatura* of the prodigy. His light touch disguises something only his fellow painters can fully appreciate: nobody else can do this. His works are all of a piece, so much so that they seem to have been dashed onto canvas in a single inspired explosion. Technical research shows that these works took years. But the appearance of effortlessness — of a balance so refined that it seems inevitable — is the miraculous illusion of the virtuoso.

Yet the great virtuosi are not always the great artists. These are often those who, alongside their mastery, have that creepi-ness, that slightly-off-ness, that getting-under-your-skin-ness, which Freud called *das Unheimlische*. One feels the tension between spontaneity and obsession even in Hals' earliest works, but only as one is nearing the exit of the museum does "the uncanny" burst into full funereal flower. Here we find the regents and the regentesses of this very building, the Old Men's House, staring at us from across the ages: five women and six men, gathered in two very gloomy paintings. These are the works to which the dying Whistler paid homage, and they are so strikingly weird that it is no surprise he dragged himself here to touch them, or that a legend grew up around them. These pictures demand explanation.

The man with the floppy hat and the hangdog face is drunk, for example; and the crones, whose portrayal, it is said, was Hals' revenge for their forcing him to spend his last years in this institution. But the stories, however charming, are myths. An inebriated regent was unthinkable in a formal portrait — and Hals never lived in this building. But they thrive because we know there is more to these pictures than a meeting of the board. We know, for example, that these pictures were created by an octogenarian. We know that, if eighty is elderly now, it was nothing short of ancient then: given the life expectancy at the time, most residents of the Old Men's House were presumably much younger. We know

Hals at Nightfall

that these were the last pictures that Hals made. And we know that another twenty-five years — another generation — have passed since the St. Elizabeth's portrait.

Something has changed. If the earlier portraits are cohesive internally (the figures in their relation to each other) and externally (the figures in relation to the viewer), the regents and regentesses interact with nobody. As if sliced from other paintings and pasted into an amateuristic photomontage, they stand uncomfortably, pinned to a background, looking right and left, and above, and below — never at each other, and never at us.

In a traditional novel, one sentence leads to the next, one thought to another; in a sonata, an initial theme is coaxed into a more elaborate development, then brought back to a recapitulating conclusion. To see Hals' final, fragmented pictures is to understand that the earlier portraits were akin to well-constructed fictions, in which the chaos of experience has been pressed into a readable narrative, an artificial form. No matter how wild Hals' pictures seemed, they respected the classical order. Eye met eye; hand led to sleeve that led to elbow; one color led harmoniously to the next. Yet here, in these late masterpieces, the colors seem to have been frightened off. All that remains are the twenty-seven blacks, and an equal number of whites. Hands and heads emerge from darkness; and the people, especially taken together, look disembodied, ghostly.

"A lonely prince of a realm of spirits, from whom now only a chilling breath issued to terrify his most willing contemporaries, standing as they did aghast at these communications of which only at moments, only by exception, they could understand anything at all": thus Thomas Mann imagined Beethoven at the end of his life. Abandoning his audience, the artist created a style that was half breakdown, half liberation. Adorno was obsessed with this notion of a late style, and for decades plotted a book about it. (Of this book, appropriately, only fragments remain.) Late Beethoven did not show fullness or resolution; he showed, instead, the preposterousness of the very idea of unity, totality, narrative. The works that he created at the end showed him in the face of the dissolution of death, their broken nature suiting an artist who had outlived his time.

Such late works do not display a failure of unity or narrative. They display a willingness to transcend it. "Objective is the fractured landscape, subjective the light in which — alone — it glows into life," Adorno wrote. "He does not bring about their harmonious synthesis. As the power of dissociation, he tears them apart in time, in order perhaps, to preserve them for the eternal. In the history of art, late works are the catastrophes." The shattered illusion of totality is the catastrophe that we see in the Black Paintings of Goya or the last plays of Ibsen. Our perplexity and discomfort in the face of such works shows that aesthetic needs (for narrative, for visual unity) are grounded in emotion, and show that, as with incorrect punctuation, untuned instruments, or clashing colors, disjointedness and dissonance upsets us — physically, emotionally — more than we realize.

When we do realize it, still another displeasure arrives. It feels pathetic to be so troubled by a lack of harmony or synthesis, so dependent on the illusion of unity. We know that our own lives don't add up, and that such totalities are artificial. We know that the fractured landscape is the objective one; but that may be precisely the reason we expect art to provide that neatness and consolation. Looked at head-on, the fracture is unbearable. "The maturity of the late works does not resemble the kind one finds in fruit," Adorno wrote of Beethoven. "They are ... not round, but furrowed, even ravaged. Devoid of sweetness, bitter and spiny, they do not surrender themselves to mere delectation."

These were the fruits Hals painted; and when we try to taste them, we discover how prepared we are for delectation, how uncomfortable in the absence of sweetness. And this discovery opens the door to a more accurate appraisal of the world and our place within it. Such knowledge dispenses with devices that link one thought, one person, one figure, to the next, and that understand one phase of life as a positive evolution toward another. As in the Kabbalah, this view understands us as fragments of shattered vessels; but this most secular of painters withholds the prospect of redemption. All this, in these citizens of seventeenth-century Haarlem.

The regents and the regentesses are thrice late. They are painted by a man who has outlived his generation and buried his children. They show older people: not as old as the painter, but none quite young, and one of whom — the man rumored to be a drunk — seems to be disintegrating. And these people, painted by an old person, are in charge of a home for old people — the building where these pictures still hang. They are avatars of aging, of time, of decline, of mortality; ambassadors of what awaits us.

In the wilting flower, the fleeting days, the sunset, thousands of works of art ponder decline. They are melancholy, but they can be produced by young artists; and even when produced by older artists, they do not necessarily need to be composed in the fractured or anti-harmonious manner suggested by Adorno with the term "late style." Not every elderly artist develops — like Beethoven, Ibsen, or Goya—a distinctive late style. "His late works," Adorno wrote of Beethoven, "constitute a form of exile." In that word, exile, lies a possible key to Hals' monumental late paintings: not the exile that we usually imagine, an expulsion from city or country. One might always—at least theoretically—return to a place. These paintings show something more irrevocable. There is no going back for one who has outlived his own time.

Hals, the man who painted these pictures, was an exile from time itself. A home for the aged is a home for people alienated forever from whomever and wherever they once were. In temporality, no repatriation is possible. Its residents could once feed and wash by themselves, walk without effort, sleep without soiling the bed. Now they find themselves in a building that, no matter how lavishly appointed or caringly staffed, is the antechamber of death; and Frans Hals, no matter whether he lived in this building or a few streets away, inhabited the same room.

This is the institution over which the regents presided. In their spookiness, they resemble other representations of guardians of the crossroads. These are lords of the threshold, at the junction of this world and the next: liminal deities like Janus, who looks in two directions; Saint Peter, who keeps the keys to the Christian heaven; Papa Legba, who watches over the gates to the Vodou underworld, Guinee.

Malle Babbe shows the proximity of sanity to madness. The regents and the regentesses show a more unbridgeable distance. No landscape is more fractured than the region between life and death. "Touched by death," Adorno wrote, "the hand of the master sets free the masses of material that he used to form; its tears and fissures, witnesses to the finite powerlessness of the I confronted with Being, are its final work."

Hals at Nightfall

Beethoven's late works resolved into trills; Hals', into the tears and fissures of brushstrokes alone. The portraits of these eleven people add up to a portrait of a single man standing between this world and the next. These paintings loom at the junction between religion and art, and in their profanity they evoke a response that more explicit religious art seeks, but often fails to elicit. Their very indirectness lends them a mystic electricity. Perhaps the reason that I would save these works first when the flood comes, and the reason that they appealed to so many modern artists, is that they show how, in a churchless age, we might yet evoke the oceanic feeling, the sensation of infinity, that courses through our world. We are not really looking for answers. It may be that truth can only be glimpsed in pieces, in fragments, in the details whose whole escapes our purview. In certain moods, we feel defrauded by fiction, by harmony, and want to taste those bitter, spiny, darkening fruits.

194

CHAIM NACHMAN BIALIK

At the Bookcase

Accept my greetings, ancient scrolls,
and favor my kiss in your dusty slumber.
From sailing to foreign isles my soul has returned,
and like a wandering dove, trembling and with weary wings,
once more it knocks at the entrance to its childhood nest.
Do you recognize me? I am he!
Your bosom-child from way back, the abstinent one.
Of all the divine delights in the wide world
my early years knew only yours,
you were my garden on a hot summer's day
and on winter nights my pillow.
I learned to bundle my soul into your scrolls for safekeeping,
and to fold into your columns my holy dreams.
Do you still remember? — I have not forgotten —
In an alcove in a desolate house of study
I was the last of the last,
on my lips the fathers' prayers fluttered and died,
and in a hidden corner there, by your shelves,
the eternal flame flickered before my eyes and was gone.
In those days I was still young,
no bud had yet blossomed on my cheeks,
and wintry nights, tumultuous nights,
found me over an old book, its pages torn,
alone with the fears and the fantasies of my soul.
A darkening wick still heaved
as the oil in the lamp on the table was consumed;

in the bowels of the bookcase a mouse was scratching;
a coal in the fireplace released a final whisper —
and the fear of God made my flesh crawl
and my teeth chatter in terror.
It was a ghastly night, the most cursed of nights.
Outside, behind the clouded window,
a raging storm howled wildly,
the shutters broke, iron bolts and all,
the demons of destruction tore down the walls.
I saw my fortress exploded,
and I watched God's presence leave its place
as it stole out from under the curtain of the ark,
and the image of my grandfather's countenance,
my shelter and my support,
the mute witness and judge of my heart's nature —
it too disappeared from my sight and slipped away.
Only the flame in my lamp was still gasping for air,
twisting this way and that, leaping to its death,
when suddenly the window shattered
and everything was extinguished,
leaving me, a tender fledgling banished from its nest,
in the custody of the night and its dark spaces.....

196

And now, after times have passed,
the wheel of my life has returned me here
with my wrinkled brow and my wrinkled soul
and stationed me again before you, occulted ones,
scions of Lvov, Slavita, Amsterdam, and Frankfurt.
Once more my hand turns your pages
and my tired eyes grope between your lines,
quietly scouring the ornamented letters
to wrest from them the traces of my soul
and find the trails of its first stirrings
in the place of its birth and the house of its life.
You brought contentment to my youth — but behold,
my heart says nothing, and no teardrop quivers on my eyelid.
I look at you, I see you, elders, but I do not recognize you.
No penetrating eyes —
the doleful eyes of the venerable ancients —
any longer peer from your letters into the depths of my soul,
and no more do I hear their voices whispering
from a forgotten and unvisited grave.
Your columns of print are to me
like a broken strand of black pearls;
your pages have been widowed
and your every letter has been orphaned —
have my eyes dimmed and my ears grown heavy,
or is it you who have decayed, the eternal dead,
so that nothing remains of you in the land of the living?

197

And I, in vain, like a thief with a spade
tunneling underground without a lantern or a torch,
scraping through earthen caverns and tenebrous places,
digging day and night into your graves, deeper and deeper,
to seek hidden signs of life beyond the roots and below them —
while at that very moment they are above me,
in cities of men, they sound from hills and mountains,
their fruits clamor beneath the sun, the moon, and the stars,
they dance and seven times repeat their dance,
their roar crosses to the far ends of the sea —
and not even an echo reaches my ears.

Who knows,
if when I emerge back into the domain of the night
after hacking through tombs and ruins of the spirit
with nothing to show for it, nothing recovered,
except this spade that clings to my hand
and the dust of the ancestors on my fingers,
poorer and emptier than I was —
I will prostrate myself before the splendor of the night
and seek out a path to the mysteries that it holds
and a soft shelter in the folds of its black mantle,
and tired unto death I will summon it, and call out:
            come, night,
gather me up, magnificent night, cover me,
do not deny me, the fugitive from the graves —
my soul asks for rest, and infinite serenity.

Liberties

And you, divine stars,
allies of my spirit and interpreters of my heart,
why are you silent, wherefore are you silent?
Does your shimmer and gleam have nothing to tell me,
not even a clue to reveal to my heart?
Or perhaps you do, you do — but I have forgotten
        your language
and no longer hear your speech, the secret tongue?
Answer me, divine stars, for I am saddened.

Translated by Leon Wieseltier

DAVID NIRENBERG

Gods and Pathogens

What does piety have to do with public health? In several recent rulings concerning restrictions on in-person religious services during the pandemic, the Supreme Court has repeatedly confronted the question, but it is hardly a new one. Humans have probably been asking similar questions for as long as they have clustered together in sufficient densities to sustain the spread of pandemic pathogens: which is to say, for as long as they have been recording their history.

Pandemics and piety are sometimes opposed protagonists in well-known artifacts of that history. Homer's *Iliad* opens with the god Apollo, angered by the Greek king Agamemnon's mistreatment of his priest, driving "the foul pestilence along the host, and the people perished." Until the prophets were consulted and the god appeased, "the corpse fires burned everywhere." And in the Hebrew Bible it is not only the Egyptians who are punished by plagues. When the Israelites "lost patience" in *Numbers* 21 and "spoke against God and against Moses," "God sent fiery serpents among the people; their bite brought death to many in Israel." Only when the sinners confessed their errors did God teach Moses the cure.

We cannot call either of these two examples from roughly three millennia ago "historical," since we cannot be sure that either of these events actually occurred. But they certainly teach us something about the long history of human reaction to pandemic. In both we see theodicy at work: that is, an attempt to understand and to justify an epidemiological catastrophe in terms of the intentional action of gods or God — in these instances punitively, a plague as punishment for some error or sin in the people or the polity. As King Edward III of England put it in 1348, when the pandemic known as the bubonic plague or Black Death was devastating Asia, Europe, and North Africa: "Terrible is God towards the sons of men, and... those whom he loves he censures and chastises; that is, he punishes their shameful deeds in various ways during this mortal life so that they might not be condemned eternally." It was in order to do penance for those sins and appease the punishing deity that the king called for collective prayer in churches across his realms.

Older than the hills, but fresher than the grass. In March 2020, the month that the World Health Organization declared the COVID-19 a pandemic, the share of internet searches for prayer surged across the globe, among adherents of every faith, to the highest level ever recorded in the (short) history of Google Trends. And in early May last year, with much of the United States in "lockdown," Kraig Beyerlein, Kathryn Lofton, Geneviève Zubrzycki, and I administered a survey on COVID and religion in collaboration with the Associated Press-NORC Center for Public Affairs that found plenty of evidence for contemporary covid-19 theodicy. When asked about the coronavirus, sixty-three percent of Americans agreed that through it "God is telling humanity to change the way we are living." And fifty-five percent thought that God would protect them from infection. Both these views are characteristic of classical theodicy, though there are also important differences between them. For example, white evangelical Christians proved much more likely (sixty-seven percent) to think that God will protect them from infection, whereas black (seventy-eight percent) and Hispanic (sixty-five percent) Americans are much more likely to think God is demanding change. Perhaps we should speak of at least two pandemic theodicies in contemporary America, one more satisfied with the moral and social status quo, the other more critical.

In short, arguments about the relationship between piety, politics, and pandemics have a long and potentially instructive history. We find ourselves in need of that instruction, now that covid-19 has put similar arguments at the center of strident debate. In the United States, the pandemic has brought to the surface of public discourse a sharp divide between those who advocated public health measures to slow the spread of the disease, such as prohibitions on gatherings of large numbers of people in places of worship, and others who argue that such measures unconstitutionally restrict the exercise of religion. The divide may be more political than popular. In early May last year, a US District Court Judge granted Tabernacle Baptist Church of Nicholasville, Kentucky temporary restraint against Democratic Governor Andy Beshear's executive order prohibiting mass gatherings, and Republican Texas Governor Greg Abbott issued an executive order prohibiting local governments in the state from closing houses of worship. At that time, according to our poll, only 9 percent of Americans agreed that in-person religious services should be allowed without restrictions.

But regardless of their popularity, arguments about the relationship between religious liberties and public health are clearly shaping the response to the current pandemic in the United States, just as similar arguments did in the distant past. The draft guidance for re-opening the country put forward by the Centers for Disease Control and Prevention last spring included instructions on topics as varied as the use of dishes and utensils at restaurants and seating arrangements on buses and trains. It also included recommendations for houses of worship, such as warnings against sharing prayer books if in-person services were conducted. Objecting to the latter, the Trump administration rejected the CDC's draft. According to Roger Severino, the director of the Department of Health and Human Services' Office for Civil Rights, "governments have a duty to instruct the public on how to stay safe during this crisis and can absolutely do so without dictating to people how they should worship God."

Severino, previously chief operations officer of the Becket Fund for Religious Liberty, is a Harvard-trained lawyer, but he may be unaware that the word "crisis," with which he chose to describe our current predicament, is itself the result of a previous pandemic that produced very similar debates. Though the Greek word is very ancient (the philosopher Parmenides used *krisis* in the fifth century BC to denote the decision between being and not-being, truth and mere opinion), it took some two thousand years to enter English. It did so in the fifteenth-century translation of a fourteenth-century Latin treatise by Guy de Chauliac, who contracted the bubonic plague during its so-called second pandemic in 1348, while he was physician to the Pope in Avignon. He survived, and he left an account of the symptoms and the etiology of that dread disease. Chauliac's translator appropriated the word into English in a narrow medical sense: crisis is the moment of "determination," the point in the progress of a disease at which it becomes clear if you will get better or not. In the case of the bubonic plague, with an infection fatality rate above fifty percent, the answer was most often not.

Today the word "crisis" means a time of high uncertainty or emergency, and we can use it to speak, as Severino does, not only of health but also of economic, political, psychological, and spiritual crises caused by the pandemic. Perhaps we should speak too, as Parmenides might have, of a pandemic-induced intellectual crisis, a moment in which we feel the foundations of our knowledge tremble, and our habits for acting in and making sense of the cosmos suddenly seem insecure. How a society reacts in such moments is a matter of vital importance, not only because it affects who lives or dies but also because it shapes that society's future capacities for interpreting the world.

We were living in such a moment during the first months of the pandemic, bombarded by constantly changing observations about a virus whose symptoms, infectiousness, modes of spread, possible prevention and treatment, were not well understood. Even its lethality was widely disputed. Was its Infection Fatality Rate less than 1 percent, as the World Health Organization maintained? Or was it above a terrifying 10 percent, as early data from Italy, Spain, and some other countries suggested? Did asthma increase risk, or perhaps (as my doctor told me) decrease it? What about blood type? Did masks work, and if so, who should wear them? What amount of "social distancing" is sufficient? If my partner has a cough, should I move into a different bedroom? Can I hug my children? Can I visit my parents? All of us remember wanting answers to such questions as the disease spread.

Many called the situation "unprecedented," by which they could only mean either something as trivial as the observation that every historical moment is unique, or more substantively that this experience is without precedent in our privileged experience as inhabitants of a world with well-trained epidemiologists, widespread vaccination, and effective anti-biotics (none of which we should be taking for granted). Yet we are certainly not the first humans to experience a pandemic-induced intellectual crisis, and our reactions are in some ways similar to those who have come before us, not least in the potential of those reactions to produce conflicts between different systems of knowledge and value, such as religion and medicine, piety and public health. Since those conflicts clearly affect our possibilities for life (and death) in the present, we should want to ask: what can we learn from differences and similarities between present and past?

The most massive pandemic in human history was also the most recent. When the smallpox virus booked trans-oceanic passage with European explorers, it wiped out approximately ninety percent of the many millions of antibody-less inhabitants in each of the worlds Columbus and his successors "discovered." How did the Aztecs and the Incas, the Polynesians and the indigenous Australians, make sense of such a scale of disaster?

Gods and Pathogens

Did they observe the progress of the disease, the torments of the afflicted, and design measures in an attempt to counter its spread? Did they turn to their gods with renewed fervor, or abandon them as vain? Some of these deadly "first-contacts" between pox and indigenous peoples took place as recently as two centuries ago, but we cannot turn to them for actionable intelligence. It is a symptom of the appalling blindness of history that we know almost nothing about the crises that the pandemics of an earlier globalization produced in the societies that they destroyed.

Still, we do know a great deal about the cultural effects of a microbe whose earlier migrations produced the first, second, and third pandemics of the disease known generally as "the plague." The arrival of *yersinia pestis antiqua* in the sixth century brought the Byzantine empire of Justinian to its knees, and paved the way for the Islamic conquests of the Mediterranean and the Middle East a generation later. (Readers wanting more can turn to William Rosen's *Justinian's Flea*.) It was around 1345 that *yersinia pestis medievalis* began its journey, probably from central Asia, and in a little over five years had eliminated virtually half of the population of the Asian, European, and African land-masses that it reached. (To put the numbers in perspective, imagine that covid-19 had just killed ninety-nine million Americans.) The plague's third pandemic, *yersinia pestis orientalis*, reached San Francisco in 1902. Though much less deadly, it too had consequences, among them inducing Congress to make permanent the Chinese Exclusion Act as a law of these United States. Permanent, that is, until it was replaced by other immigration legislation nearly half a century later.

In the 1990s I spent a year as a graduate student in a beautiful late-medieval building in Barcelona's Gothic Quarter, called the Palace of the King's Lieutenant. Back then it housed the medieval archives of the Crown of Aragon, where I was researching the effects of the Black Death on violence against minorities. This past year, as I binged on coronavirus headlines and advice, I suddenly felt as if I understood for the first time what the king of Aragon in those terrible years, Peter the Ceremonious, must have felt as he waited for the plague to reach his lands, while reading the reports sent by his spies, agents, and ambassadors from more eastern locales where the plague had already struck. One of his informants observed that many people sit or lie down before becoming deathly ill. Perhaps, he deduced, the plague was spread by a poison "sprinkled on benches on which men sit and put up their feet." He strongly urged the king to avoid sitting down.

I read many letters like these that year, and I hope I did not smile with condescension at the desperate attempts of King Peter's people to turn observation into life-saving advice. Today I feel that they were engaged, as we are, in what the historian of science Lorraine Daston calls "ground-zero empiricism." "At moments of extreme scientific uncertainty," she writes, empirical "observation, usually treated as the poor relation of experiment and statistics in science, comes into its own. Suggestive single cases, striking anomalies, partial patterns, correlations as yet too faint to withstand statistical scrutiny, what works and what doesn't...." And she continues, speaking of covid, that "we are back in the age of ground-zero empiricism, and observing as if our lives depended on it."

The arrival of the Black Death to the Islamic and Christian world of the Middle Ages was also an age of ground-zero empiricism, as we can already see in the very earliest European reports of the plague, such as this one from Michele da Piazza, writing from Sicily in 1347: "It so happened that in the month

Gods and Pathogens

of October in the year of our Lord 1347, around the first of that month, twelve Genoese galleys, fleeing our Lord's wrath which came down upon them for their misdeeds, put in at the port of the city of Messina. They brought with them a plague that they carried down to the very marrow of their bones, so that if anyone so much as spoke to them, he was infected with a mortal sickness which brought on an immediate death that he could in no way avoid." In this record of "first contact" between Western Christians and the plague, we can already see two explanatory frameworks simultaneously deployed: theodicy — the Lord's wrath — and empiricism. The chronicler's observations may even have succeeded in distinguishing between the pneumonic and the bubonic variants of the plague. (The former is transmitted person to person by droplets coughed by the infected and is almost always fatal, while the latter, transmitted by the bites of infected fleas, had a mortality rate closer to fifty percent.) Other early observers, most famously Boccaccio in his *Decameron*, quickly and empirically observed that the clothing of the sick transmitted the disease to those who might wear it or touch it, presumably because of the fleas within it.

Governments seven hundred years ago were quick to respond to the Black Death in ways that today seem quite familiar. On May 2, 1348, for example, the town council of Pistoia ordered all borders closed, prohibited trade in goods believed to carry infection, and forbade gatherings of ten people or more, including funerals. These were just a few of the many public health measures listed in the ordinance, which ended with a coda: "Saving that anything in them which is contrary to the liberty of the church shall be null and void, and of no effect." Reading those ordinances today, it is easy enough to feel an empathetic shudder. We can feel the Pistoians weighing important values against one another: the demands of public health against the needs of trade, of politics, of ritual, of family. And we can follow them struggling with where to draw the line. The prohibition on gathering for funerals, for example, "shall not apply to the sons and daughters of the deceased, his blood brothers and sisters and their children, or to his grandchildren." (I could not help thinking of this particular exception as my wife's aunt lay dying of covid-19 in a locked-down Madrid, with no possibility of visits or of mourning.) "These ordinances are to be observed until 1 September, or until 1 November at the discretion of the elders and the gonfalonier." Even the shifting deadlines articulated for "re-opening" seem eerily familiar, as we debate endlessly what and when to shut down, when and what to reopen.

And what of that exceedingly unempirical coda? "Saving that anything in them which is contrary to the liberty of the church shall be null and void, and of no effect." Surely we differ here. We are the heirs of Enlightenment, and so we assume that we are utterly unlike denizens of the Middle Ages who lived long before the sciences and secularizing tendencies of modernity. We might imagine that the "Dark Ages" were incapable of perceiving potential conflicts between different explanatory frameworks such as theodicy and empirical medicine. Or that if they did perceive them, they would nevertheless wager entirely for God.

But even without public-opinion surveys, we may be confident that the vast majority of medieval people living through the advent of the plague would have agreed with the Americans today who have concluded from our tribulations that "God is telling humanity to change the way we are living." The Black Death provoked many a theodicy, in thought and in art, and many new devotional practices, some of which

Gods and Pathogens

(such as the flagellants) are still notorious. But if many contemporary Americans in this time of plague seem "medieval" in their interpretation of it, the opposite irony also is the case: medieval people were also and simultaneously capable of noticing the dangers of gathering for worship and ritual, thinking through conflicts between their religious inheritance and their "ground-zero empiricism," and insisting on prioritizing public health.

Consider just one treatise, entitled *Convincing the Inquirer about the Terrible Disease*, composed around 1349 by a Muslim physician living in the Islamic kingdom of Granada named Lisān al-Dīn ibn al-Khatīb. The author's position on the relationship between piety and empiricism is unambiguous: "One principle that cannot be ignored is that if the senses and observation oppose traditional evidence, the latter needs to be interpreted." In a pandemic, in other words, observation should be preferred over dogma.

Many Muslim scholars frowned on theories of contagion because they seemed to diminish the power of God by assigning agency to pathogens. But based on all observations, the author argued, "the correct course in this case [of the bubonic plague] is to interpret it according to what a group of those who affirm contagion say." Once you accept the theory of contagion and the observed patterns of infection, the need for quarantine is evident. "There are many texts that support this, such as [the Prophet's] saying, may God pray for Him and grant him peace: 'The sick should not be watered with the healthy.'" In fact, to ignore the empirical evidence of contagion and continue to allow gatherings or compel

210

attendance at mosques "is blasphemy against God, and holding the lives of Muslims to be cheap." Tantamount to suicide, it violates the Qur'an admonition "not to contribute to your destruction with your own hands."

Ibn al-Khatīb was not some obscure physician without influence or power. He was chancellor and chief minister of Granada, one of the most influential statesmen and historians of Islamic Spain and North Africa. He was credited with saving his sovereign from the plague by completely isolating him in the palace of the Alhambra for a year. (The Granadans noted with satisfaction that the Christian king of neighboring Castile, their greatest enemy, died of the disease.) However that may be, his explanations for the plague's spread do not seem significantly different from those one might expect from a public health expert advising governments today: "repeated contact with the infected at funerals, exposure to their clothing and items, living in close quarters, and overcrowding" as well as "mismanagement, carelessness and lack of awareness due to widespread ignorance and the absence of knowledge about these matters among the masses."

One wishes for ibn al-Khatīb's bluntness from all public health officials in the United States. If that wish is not fulfilled, it is at least in part because of ongoing struggles in this country over the relationship between public health and piety. Again, those struggles may not be as widespread as their prominence in political and legal discourse suggests. In our survey, we asked respondents, whether, during the coronavirus outbreak, each of the following should be allowed without any restrictions, allowed but with restrictions on crowd size or physical distancing, or not allowed at all in the United States. The results showed widespread support for restrictions on constitutionally protected activities in the context of this pandemic.

Gods and Pathogens

A meager nine percent of Americans thought at that time that in-person religious services should be allowed without restriction. Roughly the same number favored restrictions on freedom of political assembly. Moreover, the willingness to support restrictions on liberties seems to correspond to an evaluation of danger. There was much more support for drive-through religious services, and for allowing visits to parks (with restrictions), presumably because the public believed these to pose a lower risk of infection.

All this is hardly because Americans think that religious freedom is not important. In a survey on religious freedom that we conducted in February 2020, before the pandemic had reached the United States, the vast majority of respondents identified religious freedom as somewhat, very, or extremely important to them. In the May poll, respondents — especially white evangelical Christians — did express concern that the prohibition on in-person religious services might violate freedom of religion. Yet at the onset of the pandemic, before restrictions on worship had been hammered into a wedge issue for the presidential campaign, they overwhelmingly favored those restrictions. Here too, the responses seem to demonstrate some weighing of risks and freedoms against each other.

From these results we could conclude that Americans — like medieval Christians and Muslims — value religion and religious freedom, but that absent massive political effort, they do not necessarily think of these as a value independent of or absolute over others, such as public health. In our survey on religious freedom, we explicitly tested this assumption. We asked for respondents' views on children's vaccination exemptions based on religion. This religious exemption is allowed in many states in America, and is probably the vaccination exemption claimed with greatest frequency. We offered the following scenario: "A parent does not vaccinate their children because of religious beliefs against this practice, and the children are denied enrollment in public school because of its policy that all students must be vaccinated." Nearly three quarters replied that un-vaccinated children should indeed be denied enrollment, and that this denial does not constitute a violation of the child or parent's religious freedom.

These results may seem surprising, given the high visibility of religious freedom arguments in recent anti-vaccination movements and in politics and the courts during the current pandemic. That high visibility suggests that the public's ability to weigh competing claims of piety and public health will continue to be put to the test. The same is true of the abilities of our politicians and our courts. The United States Court of Appeals for the Ninth Circuit in San Francisco put the stakes clearly in its 2-1 ruling in *South Bay United Pentecostal Church, et al. v. Gavin Newsom, Governor Of California, et al.,* upholding the Governor's restrictions on religious services. "We're dealing here with a highly contagious and often fatal disease for which there presently is no known cure," the majority wrote, before quoting the famous dissent in a free-speech case by Justice Robert Jackson in 1949: "There is a danger that, if the Court does not temper its doctrinaire logic with a little practical wisdom, it will convert the constitutional Bill of Rights into a suicide pact." Last spring a more divided Supreme Court (5-4) upheld the Ninth Circuit's ruling, citing a different precedent *Marshall v. United States,* from 1974: when officials "'undertake...to act in areas fraught with medical and scientific uncertainties,' their latitude 'must be especially broad.'" By late November Amy Coney Barret had replaced Ruth Bader Ginsburg, and any such deference to officials acting in a crisis was a memory. Responding to an application from the Roman Catholic Diocese of Brooklyn and another from two synagogues, the Court ruled 5-4 that the restrictions violated the First Amendment's protection for the free exercise of religion.

In times of pestilential danger, facts and meanings will both be desperately sought. But the searches sometimes interfere with one another. Suicide pacts and latitude for ground-zero empiricism: I cannot help noting how similar (for now) the majority reasoning of our highest courts is to that of Ibn al-Khatib, the medieval chief minister of Muslim Granada, as he advocated anti-contagion measures such as the closure of mosques in the face of horrors hitherto unknown. When it comes to "medical and scientific uncertainties," the present day is much advanced from the Middle Ages. But when it comes to the capacity for suicide pacts between ideals, values, and liberties, perhaps not so much.

AGNES CALLARD

Romance Without Love, Love Without Romance

THE ETHICS OF BREAKUP

I have only ever had one friend as crazy as I am. Once we painted a giant fireplace onto the wall of her apartment as decoration for a dinner party we were hosting — and then, at the end of the party, she led our guests up the stairs onto the roof of the building, bringing with her a boombox playing Strauss. I climbed up the fire escape in a ballgown. I held out my hand. We waltzed with speed and gusto. Our friends and professors looked on, terrified: there was no railing. Another time she planned a scavenger hunt through San Francisco, and I found myself in a store selling sex toys, forced to examine each device meticulously to find the next clue. The finale of the scavenger hunt was at a disco, and she danced with me there, too, even though I had to cover my ears — I am very sensitive to sound — and there is nothing in the world dorkier than someone dancing with her hands over her ears.

I haven't done as much dancing in the seventeen years since I ended that relationship. The breakup happened like this: we had planned an elaborate outing in Sonoma County for her birthday. The picnic supplies alone took days to gather. We left early, and got home late, and, as she told me when she hugged me goodnight, everything in between had been perfect. It had been a perfect day. The next morning, I wrote her a letter telling her that I did not want to be friends with her anymore.

I had my reasons, of course. As I say, she is crazy. I am, too, but in a very different way. The immense effort it took for me to spend a whole day with her and ensure that it was "perfect" — that I did nothing that would offend, upset, or bother her — proved to me that we just didn't work. And I thought: when a relationship does not work, each party has the right to exit. It will hurt, but we will get over it, and we will both be better off in the end. The thing is: the pain hasn't gone away. I still miss her. I still dream about her. And lately I have come to think that part of the problem lies in how I broke things off: unilaterally. I took matters into my own hands, as though there were no rules governing how you break up with someone.

"All's fair in love and war" dates to 1850, when the ethics of warfare were very different than they are today. Two world wars generated explicit international agreements as to behaviors prohibited in wartime; we now reject wars of conquest and plunder; we harbor deep suspicions about the glorification of military violence. Have we made similarly substantive revisions in the ethics of love?

"All's fair..." made its debut in the then popular but now

obscure British novel *Frank Fairlegh: Scenes from the Life of a Private Pupil*, by a certain Frank E. Smedley. The scene runs as follows. Frank, on the brink of unilaterally breaking off relations with his love-interest, recoils at opening the seal on a stolen letter — "I cannot avail myself of information obtained in such a manner!" His more pragmatic interlocutor is the one who has the "All's fair..." approach: since the letter promises to reveal her virtue and innocence, he insists that Frank should open it. It is notable that Frank's high-mindedness about invasions of privacy at no point extends to questioning his own breakup plan. He apprehends no moral duty to talk the issue through with the girl.

Today, as in 1850, high-minded people feel free to condone unilateral breakup — in romantic as well as non-romantic love. When people act as I did, exiting a friendship perceived as, on balance, detrimental, we tend to view the decision as sad but not immoral. The reason is clear: we see love as having a certain kind of autonomy from the space of moral judgment. Even the arch-moralizer Kant agreed that you cannot be "morally obligated" to have feelings for someone; and it was for that reason that he interpreted the biblical command to "love thy neighbor" in terms of the rules governing your voluntary treatment of your neighbor. You do not actually have to feel love for them. You cannot legislate yourself into experiencing passion, empathy, or lust.

And this is part of what we love about love: that it affords us an opportunity to lose control, to go a little crazy. But does it really follow from this that a free and clean exit is available? I don't think so: even if it is impossible to moralize one's way into passion, it remains open to us to moralize about passions that are already in place. There are more regulations governing exiting relationships than entering them.

These regulations exist not in spite of but because of the fact that the connections between people are idiosyncratic and passionate. It is precisely because such connections are real and irreplaceable that disconnection is not a trivial matter. Over time, people's lives grow together, such that what happens to one person affects another. When I come to care deeply about you, I can actually feel your pain. And that lateral growth also makes vertical growth possible: with your hand in mine, I become someone who waltzes, paints walls, and drinks Japanese tea that looks and tastes like the forest floor. (Having spent a year abroad in Osaka, she introduced me to tea ceremonies of various kinds.)

You can't waltz by yourself. When I lose you, I also lose the me I became for you. And vice versa. Which is why cutting you off, once we have grown together, is an act of violence. I am not "cutting" anything visible, like your arm or leg, but I am nonetheless cutting away something that is a part of you — me. It is still an amputation. And I am amputating — acting on your life — without your consent. As I see it, cheating on someone is not in any obvious way more wrong than unilaterally cutting off relations from them. These are both ways of taking into your own hands the agreements that bind your life to another person's life; they are acts of psychological violence.

A decade after that breakup, I faced the prospect of divorce. I consulted with friends and family, many of whom advised me not even to discuss our problems with my husband, but simply to quash my concerns until the children were grown. The consensus was that I was morally obligated to stay married for the sake of my children. But even if I could have kept my discontent secret, which was doubtful, I felt that doing so would have been a deep betrayal of the life that I shared with

218

my husband. And once I did, he agreed that divorce was the only option.

The strange thing — or so it seemed to me — was that once we did divorce, those same friends and family pushed me towards "a clean break." I should stop having regular meals with my ex; we should separate our bank accounts; we should reduce our connection to the minimum required for co-parenting our children. One person recounted, somewhat proudly, how he hadn't spoken to his ex since their children graduated from college, decades earlier. Now, a decade after the divorce, the fact that I still share close friendship and many everyday matters of life with my ex is perceived by many as peculiar and in some way wrong, and forgivable only to the extent that it is beneficial for the children.

The parent-child bond is the most striking exception to a blanket "all's fair" permissivism about love. It would take extraordinary circumstances for someone to feel justified in disowning their child, and this makes sense: children depend profoundly on their parents, and moreover they did not consent to enter into this dependence. My view is that a relationship with a friend or a spouse differs from a relationship with one's child in degree, not in kind. My husband and I had come to depend on one another in many ways over seven years of marriage, and those forms of dependence could not simply be ignored or wished or decided away.

As for consent, it is not an alternative to dependence but a mechanism for generating dependence — mostly by way of tacit and gradual and small-scale agreements, but occasionally, as in the case of marriage vows, by way of sudden and large-scale agreements. We don't simply inflict our lives on others; rather, we learn, over time, to coordinate, to synchronize, to co-deliberate. We grow together, bit by bit, by way of

219

agreement and experience: the end result is something too real to be annulled by one party's simply deciding to opt out.

When it comes to moralizing, people tend to take an all-or-nothing approach: either a bond is sacrosanct, entailing a demand of total sacrifice, or everyone is free to "just walk away." When I got divorced, I drank the kool-aid that said I was scarring my children for life. That turned out to be false — they are fine, more than fine, really — but let the record show that I believed it, and went ahead anyway: I was not prepared to completely sacrifice my own happiness for theirs. Nor was it only for their sake that I was reluctant to completely sacrifice the relationship I had with their father. Even if I could have done so, I did not want to just walk away from him. I care about him. I do not want to lose the me I am for him. And I owe him things. No break between us could or should be "clean."

The extremes of total bondage and total freedom strike me as being, somehow, on the wrong scale for human relationships. They are appropriate for creatures much larger than us — or much smaller, perhaps. We humans need to do our living, and our moralizing, in the middle. Often a relationship that doesn't work in one form might work in another form, a renegotiated one. And even if no livable arrangement can be arrived at, such an ending should be the product of the reasoning of all parties involved.

Consider how far we have come from the ethics of *The Iliad*, in which Diomedes is glorified for choking a river with the blood of his enemies. We now understand that moral excellence lies less in using, and more in knowing how not to use, physical force. Humanity has been slower to acknowledge the reality of psychological injury and trauma, and correspondingly slower to see the rules governing violence in that domain. I propose that one of those rules is that you are not allowed to "just walk away."

Obviously I am not saying you can never break up, or get divorced. What I am saying is that all is not fair when it comes to these endings; you cannot simply cut people off; you are not free to leave at any time. If your life is entwined with someone, then a new arrangement between the two of you must be the product of an agreement you can both live with. Also, you must be open, forever, to revising that agreement if and when the other person offers reasons for doing so.

Those requirements are robustly ethical. In my break-up letter to my friend, I made the usual excuses, arguing that the relationship was in some way "toxic"; that this was the best course for both of us; that the break "had to" happen. Whether or not those claims are true, enforcing them on her without her consent was wrong. It was like shoving words in her mouth and forcing her to say them. Instead of deliberating together with her about how to move forwards, I took matters into my own hands: I tore out a part of her life, and a part of mine, violently, just because that violence seemed to me to be in my interest. If that kind of behavior is not wrong, what is?

Which is not to say that it is wrong in absolutely every instance. Just as there are extraordinary cases in which physical violence is called for, so, too, with psychological violence. Some relationships really are toxic; sometimes a unilateral break is the only form of self-defense available to a person subjected to the predations of another. But if you think about how often people call their exes "jerks" or "bad people" or "evil" and how infrequently we otherwise accept this as a characterization of adults we personally know, you will see that we have reason to be suspicious of our own breakup behaviors. We vilify the other to vindicate the shortcut of force.

Romance Without Love, Love Without Romance

And yet the tendency to cheat our way into justification — to make all seem fair when all is not fair — is really a cause for optimism. It is women, more than men, who see the need to vilify, and that makes us some sort of moral vanguard. If you think of your exes as a string of losers and villains, you are, in effect, conceding that that is what they would have to be in order for you to have been permitted to treat them as you have treated them. (But think about your friends' exes, and those of your friends' friends: how many losers and villains can there be?)

It is important to remember that the scope and the stringency of breakup rules are proportional to the depth of connection achieved. If we ignore this, we are apt to caricature the ethics of breakup as mandating contractual arrangements for turning down a second date. If there is nothing there yet — no bond, connection, no fund of shared experience, no grown-togetherness — then moralism is indeed misplaced. There is no symmetry between entry and exit.

THE ROMANTIC EMPIRICIST

Aristotle is likely to strike you as unromantic, especially if you come to him after Plato. In dialogue after dialogue, Plato confronts us with the bottomlessly destructive but transformative power of erotic attachment. Plato is familiar with what a person is capable of doing for the merest glimpse of his beloved, and it terrifies him, and he is riveted by his own terror. By contrast, "tame" is not a tame enough word for Aristotle's discussion of love in the *Nicomachean Ethics*. It is a long discussion — two whole books, a fifth of the entire work — and some of the topics discussed are: what beneficiaries feel for their benefactors, how lifelong friends share thoughts and speeches, the affection of business partnerships. No sex. No passion. No motorcycle rides in the rain. It's true that there are no motorcycles in Plato either, but that is only because they weren't invented yet. *Nicomachean Ethics* rewritten for the third millennium would still be decidedly free of walks on the wild side.

So Aristotle is not a romantic about interpersonal attachments — but that is not the only place romanticism can take root. What about other areas? Poetry is a classic one. Aristotle's aesthetic theory inaugurated a whole tradition of detached, icy-cold, arm's-length analysis. Maybe he is right that tragedies give rise to cathartic experiences, but I doubt anyone has ever had one of those while reading the *Poetics*. Religion? Aristotle's god is Thought Thinking Itself, a god who didn't make the universe and doesn't care whether we live or die. Social Justice? Aristotle is no utopian, and he is unmoved by the plight of the worst off. Aristotle does not romanticize nature either, or wax poetic about ecosystems or sunsets. Unlike other scientists, he does not see the totality of the natural world as a "thing" to be appreciated or even theorized. When he does speak of it, he does so in a maximally unromantic way, as providing a set of tools for humans or environments for animals.

In fact Aristotle rarely uses the word "nature" the way we do: instead of speaking of "nature" as the sub-lunar totality inhabited by lions, caterpillars, dolphins, and the like, he uses the word to refer to each of those inhabitants, severally rather than jointly. He calls them "natural things" or describes each one as having its own proprietary "nature." With this observation, we draw nearer to the fire of the passion that burns in Aristotle. There is one subject that quickens his heart: animals, more specifically body parts. It is not in his *Politics*,

223

Ethics, Poetics, Physics, or *Metaphysics* that we find Starry-Eyed Aristotle. If you want a lyrical Aristotle, you have to read his *Parts of Animals.*

Where else in the corpus do you find him talking about glimpses of beloveds:

> Just as the briefest glimpse of someone we love is more enjoyable than a precise and steady vision of other things, even great ones, so too the most glancing contact with celestial bodies yields more pleasure than we can get from all this earthly stuff around us. For the planets are the noblest of all.

Now this passage demotes animals ("all this earthly stuff around us") by contrast with stars and planets. But if you have read your share of romance novels, you will recognize the trope of the contrastive set-up: "Her face was plain, nothing to remark upon..." Aristotle goes on to say that animals may not be lofty, but they have the inner beauty of what is both near and knowable:

> Even when it comes to those organisms bereft of sensible charms, the nature in them is a kind of artisan who delivers incredible pleasures of the mind to those who, because of their philosophical nature, are able to discern the causes of things.

The word "nature" shows up twice in the Greek of this passage, as in my translation. First, the nature of the thing to be known, for instance a species of tiny crab whose back feet are flattened — almost as if by some artisan! — into the shape of oars to aid them swimming. That "nature" finds its twin in the nature of the knower: a philosopher, on the lookout for the causes of things. Aristotle's famous four causes — formal, final, efficient, material — are the pillars of his scientific worldview, a worldview that stands firmly opposed to Plato's disdain for (what he took to be) the unknowability of the sensible world.

Plato was disturbed by the fact that nothing in the sublunar world stays the same: every object in the office I'm sitting in — the papers, books, desk, carpet — is slowly falling apart, becoming not-itself, transitioning between being and not being. Even a beautiful boy does not stay beautiful for long. Nothing does — except the Form of the Beautiful! And so, just as in Raphael's painting, Plato redirected our attention away from this muddy mess, upward, to the Forms that are always what they are. Relatedly, the forms are simple — unlike someone who is both beautiful and human and seventeen years old and brown-haired. The boy can lose his beauty and stay a boy, whereas the form of the beautiful does not dissolve into a puddle of unrelated qualities. It is beautiful, period. And forever.

Aristotle's big move was to notice a method in what struck Plato as madness. While granting that destruction is one kind of change to which the sublunar realm is subject, Aristotle denied that all changes should be understood on the model of destruction. When animals are generated, alter, grow, and locomote, they change in such a way as to hold themselves together. Their changes exhibit a pattern, an internal logic. The logic is complex: there are patterns that hold across all multiple animals (organs for reproduction, nutrition, locomotion, perception) and then patterns that are specific to a given class of animals (swimming vs. flying) or just one species (see paddle-feet of tiny crabs, above). Each species gives our minds a foothold in the empirical world; they pair the logical nature of our minds with a natural logic of self-transformation.

225

Romance Without Love, Love Without Romance

How do they do this? By being divided into organic parts! "Organic," *organikos*, in Greek means "tool-like": the parts of an animal, like the "oar-feet" of the crab, are the tools that it uses for performing its various functions. The methodology of Aristotle's *Parts of Animals* is to read the diachronic logic of how an animal changes over time into a synchronic logic of organ-parts: the parts of an animal are tools for self-changing. Unlike the (random) set of attributes that any physical object might have, the parts of an animal are "bound together": they are not only undetached, but in fact undetachable. Aristotle explains this special rule for understanding body parts — his famous "homonymy principle" — in yet another poetic passage in the introductory portion of the *Parts of Animals*. He says that a body part — an eye or a hand — cannot be separated from the whole, living body. A severed hand, he says, is no more a hand than the marble hand of a sculpture. It may look like a hand, but part of what it is to be a hand is to be the sort of thing that is used for grasping and pointing. What goes for the hand goes for the body as a whole: a dead body is a body in name only. (Hence the word "body" or "hand" is a mere homonym when used to describe a dead body or a severed hand.)

226

Aristotle makes life an essential rather than an accidental property of the matter that it permeates. The dead body, that is, the non-body, is something that decomposes — it merits Platonic change-cynicism; but a living body is something different altogether, undergoing a very different set of changes. Unlike a Form, an animal is not unified by being simple. Yet it isn't a puddle of properties, either. By virtue of having organic parts that depend both on one another and the presence of life for being what they are, the animal is a unified multiplicity. And this, insists Aristotle, is a thing of beauty that Plato totally missed out on.

Empiricism after Aristotle becomes something "hard-nosed," something to contrast with idealism. The no-nonsense empiricist sees the world as a check on theories concocted in the armchair; his project is that of bringing the high-flying mind down to earth. Aristotle's is not the empiricism of the test but of the quest. Unlike later scientists, Aristotle did not understand the natural world as a testing stone for the "laws" that we try to produce to render it intelligible as a whole. Rather, he saw it as a hunting ground populated by living nuggets of intelligibility. These unified multiplicities are the mind's quarry, which can be sniffed out by the one who discerns causes. Aristotle, you might say, is an Obama-style romantic: animals are the changes we can believe in.

Aristotle anticipates the distaste — he calls it the "childish aversion" — that most people feel for lower animals (bugs, worms, etc.), and tries to win them over to his point of view with an anecdote. He tells the story about the time the philosopher Heraclitus was warming himself in his kitchen. Guests arrived unexpectedly and they were hesitant to join him there. It seemed uncouth to step into such a lowly space as a kitchen. Heraclitus bade them enter by saying: "There are gods here, too." Aristotle presents this as a lesson for how to think about the sublunar world: "in every class of animals there is something to behold in wonder." The animals and animal-parts that disgusted you are, in fact, things of wonder. They are not wonderful because God made them. (He didn't.) Animals have internal principles of change and rest, which is to say: they make themselves, continuously, over and over again. They author their own being. They are not divinely generated. They are, simply, divine.

Like his contemporaries, Aristotle was impressed enough by the regular motions of the planets to classify them as divine. He saw the planets as wonderful, and lofty, and noble. But they are too far away to really love, especially given the possibility of loving the one you're with: *Parts of Animals* adopts the "girl next door" approach, pointing, over and over again, to these whirlwinds of intelligibility, held together through constant change by a pattern all their own: *logical* blood; *systematic* skull-sutures; *distinctive* dung. Slugs, mice, sea-urchins, goats. These things, and their parts, might look ordinary, or boring, or gross, but they are tiny self-creating demiurges, islands of logic, gloriously gory. Is there a heart so hard as to remain unmoved?

ROMANCE

On Wikipedia I never skip past the "personal life" section. So I know that Tove Jansson met her lover using a secret attic passageway, and that they summered together on an island off the coast of Finland. I know that Ingmar Bergman's many marriages included all the mothers of his children — except Liv Ullmann, who might have been his true soulmate. I know that Vladimir Mayakovsky dedicated many of his poems to a woman whose husband sanctioned their love. The Stanford Encyclopedia of philosophy is low on amorous content, except in the case of the John Stuart Mill-Harriet Taylor Mill saga, which it covers in satisfying detail.

I know these things because I care. And I am not alone. The English word "romance" is literally synonymous with the words "excitement," "fascination," and "allure." The sales of romance novels total more than a billion dollars a year, and many non-"romance" novels nonetheless leverage romance as a key plot device; as do a great plurality of pop songs, poems, movies, and so on. It's not hard to guess why: as soon as the slightest suggestion of the possibility of romance surfaces in a narrative, I start willing the characters to get together with a passion that belies the fact that not only I do not know these people, they are not even real. And yet if I could push them into one another's arms, I would.

For all our interest in romance, we don't seem to theorize about it very much. Friendship, attachment, relationships, commitment, all those put-you-to-sleep topics are well-covered in analytic philosophy, but there is no philosophical account of the agonizing process by which lovers reveal themselves to one another and learn that they belong — or do not belong — together. There is no philosophy of all the topics covered in the pop songs: the longing for a soulmate, the heartbreak of rejection, the insecurity of the getting-to-know you phase, the joy of romantic union, the pain of missing one's beloved. My sense is that philosophers view the word "romance" with some embarrassment, and the result is that we lack a theory of it.

Nor can we claim to have mastered the practice: for all the books written on how to get someone to marry or sleep with you, I don't think anyone would even pretend to write a how-to guide on falling in love. There are online lists of tips on how to keep passion in your marriage, to be sure, but following them is about as romantic as online dating. Romance commands our rapt attention and draws our interest magnetically, but we do not have, or even seem to seek, the most basic understanding of how it works, or how to bring it about. We are obsessively inept at romance.

A friend once told me of a girl she grew up with in Russia who, as a child, was terrified at the prospect of falling in love: she thought that after falling in love you die. Raised on a steady diet of fairy tales, this insightful girl saw past the "happily ever after" tagline to the fact that in story after story, after the prince and the princess finally overcome all their trials to be united in marriage, the next thing that happens is: nothing. After you fall in love, the story of your life is over.

Growing up means learning all the ways people rebel against "happily ever after." Affairs, for instance. And yet that is but a new way to fall off the cliff of romance: whether the unfaithful husband opts, in the end, to stay with his wife, or leave her for the new woman, as soon as he resolves this dilemma, the romance is once again completed.

And there is this question: Instead of having an affair, why not pursue romance within your marriage? The answer to it lies in the moralistic tone with which it is usually posed. If something as wholesomely innocuous as marital affection lent itself easily to romance, well, a sign of that would be that those lists of tips would be actually useful for some of us, and unnecessary for most of us. Marital romance is close to a contradiction in terms, which is why it is often a response to external obstacles: children, challenges, tragedies — even affairs.

One cannot avoid sympathy for the rage of the long-suffering wife whose quest for more connection with her ever distant husband ends in the discovery that he sought this connection in the arms of another. And yet her husband's unavailability may have been precisely what made him a possible object of romantic striving for her in the first place. Romance is a tricky thing to want. And this cannot be written off as a problem only for "bad marriages."

Even fans of marriage such as myself — I've done it twice — must acknowledge that it has a world-class PR team. Think about what a coup it was for marriage to win over the gays, rather than allowing them to build a competing institution to which many of the straights might eventually defect. And then

to spin this as a victory for gays rather than for marriage —
"ok, fine, if you absolutely insist, we'll let you in" — is the mark
of master manipulators.

And so when someone claims that lifelong romance is
simply a matter of being willing to work at it — as though
anyone has ever been unwilling to do this kind of "work"! —
I am inclined to dismiss this as moralistic scolding; and I am
equally suspicious of the reassurance that time somehow
automatically, quietly, imperceptibly deepens the marital
connection. I am struck by the contrast between how much
pressure one is under to claim to love their spouse more deeply
with each passing year, and how little clarity there is about
what "deepening" even means in this context. ("Imperceptibly," indeed.)

The fact that romantic yearnings stubbornly resist
incorporation leads some to simply dismiss their validity:
"all anyone can really want, at the end of the day, is a partner
who provides solid, reliable, warm, affectionate companion-
ship." Sorry, Team Marriage. I cannot agree, all the beauties of
conjugal life notwithstanding. The simple truth is that many
people evidently want more romance than a marriage, even a
good one, can offer them. And no one seems to know why.   231

When we were falling in love, I introduced my (not yet)
husband to this Magnetic Fields song, and he explained its
meaning to me:

> You are a splendid butterfly
> It is your wings that make you beautiful
> And I could make you fly away
> But I could never make you stay
> You said you were in love with me
> Both of us know that that's impossible

Romance Without Love, Love Without Romance

And I could make you rue the day
But I could never make you stay
Not for all the tea in China
Not if I could sing like a bird
Not for all North Carolina
Not for all my little words
Not if I could write for you
The sweetest song you ever heard
It doesn't matter what I'll do
Not for all my little words
Now that you've made me want to die
You tell me that you're unboyfriendable
And I could make you pay and pay
But I could never make you stay

He said the message of this song is that you cannot make anyone love you and you cannot make yourself love anyone. No words, no theories, no commands, no machinations afford a person romantic control, because there is no such thing as romantic control.

One thing I have noticed about times of heightened romance is that life seems to become story-like: little details, such as discussing the song in the car, stand out, and other details, such as where we were driving to, fade into the background. Events take on symbolic meaning, and some of them become pivotal or climactic. Even those who had the (romantic) misfortune of meeting by means of online dating will find ways to tell that story in such a way that makes its result a surprise. Romance, like humor, must always be surprising. Just as everyone is a comedian to their own baby, everyone is a novelist of their own romances.

If romance lends to real life the shape and feel of a

narrative, it is also true that fictional narratives become more lifelike when romance enters the picture. In a book or a movie, the emergence of a romantic storyline corresponds to an awakening of attention and interest in the audience — as though, finally, the events were somehow happening to us. Just about every genre of serialized TV show — from comedic sitcoms to detective shows to soap operas — uses the prospect of romantic union between the characters to keep us interested.

There is a connection between the fact that the romance of others can seem so intimately relevant to us, and the fact that we approach our own romances through a kind of aesthetic haze. If something very important and earth-shatteringly good can be happening to me, even though I am not in charge of it, and do not even understand it, then the significance of events is not a matter of my controlling them. Romance does not address me as a knower, or as a doer, but as a powerless appreciator waiting breathlessly to see what the butterfly does next. And once I have been relegated to the position of spectator with respect to my own life, I can take that same approach to the lives of others. If I can see myself as a character in a story and still care, why should I not be able to care about other characters in stories?

Romance fictionalizes life; romance vivifies fiction.

233

ETHICAL SELF-BLINDNESS

When you get what you wanted, that doesn't necessarily satisfy you. Sometimes we don't know what will make us happy; sometimes we don't want the right things. Call this condition "ethical self-blindness."

I borrow the term "self-blind" from the philosopher

Sydney Shoemaker, who introduced it to describe a hypothetical condition of introspective failure. A self-blind person in Shoemaker's sense is someone who cannot "look within" to discover what she believes or desires, though she can make inferences about her mental states by observing what she is inclined to say or do. Such a person has the same access to her own beliefs and desires as she has to those of other people. Shoemaker raises this possibility only to dismiss it: he thinks that we cannot actually imagine a human being who constitutionally lacks inner sense.

Unlike Schoemaker's self-blindness, ethical self-blindness is a term meant to refer to a condition that is not only possible, but actual and commonplace. It is all around us. Someone with ethical self-blindness lacks a certain kind of first-personal expertise—not that which pertains to identifying the psychological contents of her own mind, but that which pertains to picking out the items that conduce to her welfare, her happiness, her good.

Ethical self-blindness is, in fact, our original condition: children need parenting because they do not know what is good for them. Children are not self-blind in Shoemaker's sense, of course—quite the contrary—their sense of what they want is often especially powerful and intense. When I was about eleven years old, what I wanted more than anything was a small rubbery doll, shaped like a worm, that glowed in the dark. It was called a "glow worm." My mother spent a long time—in my memory it was eons—resisting my pleas. She couldn't understand why I would want such a stupid toy, especially since I never played with dolls. Eventually, however, she gave in and bought me one; they only cost a few dollars.

As soon as I got it, I took a pair of scissors and cut it into about ten pieces. My mother looked on, horrified. (I was after

234

the magic of the glow-in-the-dark material, and the fact that it took the shape of a cutesy worm was incidental to my purposes. I knew that if I revealed my plan from the outset, I would never get one.) My objective was to put a piece of glow into each of the pockets of my dresses, and then I would never be in total darkness. This did not pan out—the material glowed much less than I thought it would, and it had to be "charged" by being held up to the light before it would glow for even a short time. The reality of owning a dismembered worm doll came did not measure up to my dream of having pockets filled with light.

And why did I dream of this in the first place? I wasn't even afraid of the dark! Every parent is familiar with the phenomenon of handing a child the gift he has been begging for and seeing it neglected in minutes. The dreams of children are wild, passionate, and misguided. And so we need our parents to make decisions for us—about what to eat, when to sleep, how to spend our time ("I'm bored!"). At a certain point this rankles, and we begin to rebelliously insist on choosing for ourselves.

Unfortunately, however, the leap from the orbit of parental authority does not itself cure one's ethical self-blindness. Peer pressure enters as a stopgap, and replacing the authority of parents with that of friends does not always represent much progress. How does a person learn to want the things that really do make her happy? My suggestion is that she does it by learning to induce self-blindness in the other sense—not the ethical one, but the kind that Shoemaker dismissed as a philosophical fiction.

One thing that filled me with frustration as a child was the fairy-tale trope of wishing oneself into misery. Over and over again, we find the same slip twixt the cup and the lip — you get to marry the princess, but she's a jerk; you get to live forever,

Romance Without Love, Love Without Romance

but as a grasshopper; everything you touch turns to gold, including your relatives. I hated these stories, and felt sure that I would not make the same mistakes as the idiotic fairy tale people all those wishes were wasted on. It might appear that wishes inevitably conduce to happiness: the wisher has no aim but to benefit herself, and the wish gives her unlimited resources for doing so. What could go wrong? The answer is: ethical self-blindness. Stories about wishing gone awry are trying to inform children that they do not know what is good for them, and it is almost definitive of childhood to want to shut one's ears to this particular message.

The alternative to wish is *work*: exercising agency in guiding your goal to realization, thereby steering it out of the way of countless bad options, transforming it in ways that are responsive to what the world has to offer, and thus ending up with something you are actually happy with. Consider the trope of the evil genie who will give you the hamburger you so fervently desire...but he will sadistically make sure that it is encased in a block of lucite, or made from human flesh, or the size of a grain of sand. Since wishing means delegating the filling out of the details to another, there are always loopholes for the genie to exploit. Wishes have a schematic, underspecified, almost cartoonlike character, and this is what makes the mental images associated with wishes so vividly introspectively accessible. Since I am content to leave out most of the details in my wishes, it is easy for me generate the mental image that represents exactly what I want. For example: pockets filled with light. The wishing mind has perfect Shoemakerian self-insight.

The working mind, by contrast, must itself chart the path between the goal and whatever concrete option out in the world comes closest to satisfying it. Over the course of this journey, its conception of what is wanted is never fixed, but always shifting. The working mind is a mind in motion, learning to accommodate to reality: hunger, some specific food, ending up at the grocery store, cooking, eating; or choosing a paper topic, finding a thesis, outline, writing, revising, rewriting.

When we go to a restaurant, we short-circuit the food acquisition process along wish-like lines: hunger to plate. The same happens when we buy a term paper online: topic to paper. The difference, of course, is that in the first case the cooking was merely instrumental, whereas the thinking that was supposed to take one from topic to paper was the entire point of the exercise. I have found, over many years assigning papers, that even when they are honestly produced, shortcuts of one kind or another abound in them: summary in place of analysis; a profusion of weak arguments instead of developing one strong one; failure to proof-read. My pet peeve is when students treat a literary text as a source to be mined for examples of one's independently chosen thesis, rather than allowing the thesis to emerge organically from careful reading. The student's aim is, first and foremost, to get the paper done; she will do almost anything to avoid thinking.

Why do people find thinking so unpleasant? My proposal is this: thinking (up new things) entails alienating yourself from the thoughts that (already) occupy your mind. Thinking puts a damper on introspection.

A lot of what we call "distraction" is simply having a fixed, immediately available mental content stand as alternative to the vague, fuzzy, provisional, work-in-progress character of whatever the working mind was working on. Distractions are in the wish family, as are cravings, which likewise involve an insistent introspective attention to schematically defined object of desire.

The working mind is bereft of such vivid, perfect access to its own contents. We speak of focusing on goals, but this does not mean holding some fixed, wish-like conception of the goal—rather we mean constantly playing with the interface between goal and world. The malleability of such thinking prevents me from ever being able to say, "this is precisely what I want."

The struggles we face to achieve self-control and resist immediate gratification are struggles to endure alienation from the contents of our own minds. It is not an accident that the children who prevailed in the marshmallow test were prone to close their eyes, or to turn their backs to the marshmallow, or to say our loud, "there is no marshmallow." Strength of will involves inducing a kind of self-blindness—not the ethical kind, but the Shoemakerian kind. Shoemaker is right that introspective failure cannot be the natural default for any human mind, but it can become second nature. It is desirable to cultivate some degree of self-blindness in oneself, because thought is the enemy of thinking.

When we find ourselves succumbing to distraction or the cravings of the moment; when we choose wishful fantasizing over meaningful work; when we take shortcuts that leave us disappointed in ourselves, we are inclined to think of this behavior as childish. Adults are continuously engaged in an effort to sideline our *idées fixes*, so as to be open to re-alignment with reality. I watch my child, immersed in imaginative play, and I see him "open a door" where I know there is none. He sees what he wants to see, I see what is there. His mind is sharply introspectively available to him; I hold mine at a distance from myself, the better to employ it for thinking. Or at least: much of the time, I do this. It is easy to forget that adults, too, are capable of dreams that are wild, passionate, and misguided.

In the domain of love, romance, and eros, we encounter a characteristically adult form of unrealism: hyper-attunement to the contents of our own minds and desires, and a corresponding inclination to privilege fantasy over reality. If we say that love is "blind," we may use the term in the ethical sense—love drives us into the arms of our own misery and not the Shoemakerian one. Nothing could be more introspectively available to someone than her feelings of heartbreak or lust or jealousy. It is when their contents are most adult that the operations of our minds most perfectly resemble those of children.

Why does romantic rejection hurt and sting as much as it does? Because we have some image of ourselves, some beautiful picture of how happy we could be if only we could have that one thing—which is to say, that one person—that we want. And then that very person snatches away our dream of pockets filled with light, and leaves us with nothing but a dismembered worm doll.

MITCHELL ABIDOR

The Beliefs of Cyclones

Don't we shudder when we think that in a time of
popular emotion all it takes is a word, just one word
imprudently spoken without hatred by an honest man,
to provoke so horrible a murder?

EUGÈNE SUE, *THE WANDERING JEW*

The most illuminating book ever written about social media was published in 1895. It is called *La Psychologie des foules* — or, in the English translation that appeared a year later, *The Crowd: A Study of the Popular Mind*. The book is a work of social science that reads like the work of a seer.

"A crowd in the process of formation does not always imply the simultaneous presence of several individuals in one place. Thousands of separated individuals can, at a given moment, under the influence of certain violent emotions.... acquire the characteristic of a psychological crowd. Some chance event uniting them then suffices for their behavior to take on the special form of the acts of crowds." The author of those sentences was Gustave Le Bon, and he was a kind of political Jules Verne or H.G. Wells. He foresaw many things — for example, that education is no impediment to participation in the crowd mind: "From the time they are part of a crowd, the ignorant and the learned become equally incapable of observation." As he acidly noted, "a gathering of scholars and artists, by the sole fact that they are gathered together, does not render judgments on general subjects markedly different from those of an assembly of bricklayers or grocers." And he foresaw, without an inkling of the enabling technology, the entire phenomenon of social media-induced conspiracy theories. QAnon, Pizzagate, criminal murders that are turned into political assassinations, the lie of a stolen presidential election, all the proliferating garbage of our twisted era — the wildfire spread of ideas with no value and no basis in fact — all these dark characteristics of our society are illuminated by what Le Bon intuited and described.

I turned to Le Bon because I needed him. Some time ago I wrote a piece for the *New York Times* criticizing the anti-Biden stances taken by the Democratic Socialists of America and other progressives. My son, wiser in the ways of the web than me, assured me that the objects of my criticism would not take it lightly, and that he was preparing to defend me. I shrugged it off. After all, these were my comrades. My son was right, of course. Within minutes of the article's appearance I was being battered on Twitter. This was not simply a matter of the shelter provided by anonymity or the ease with which one can retweet or "like" a negative tweet and bury its subject in invective. There was more at play here, I thought. The venom was spreading with a baffling and sickening rapidity. It was as if the act of reading a tweet caused an uncontrollable desire

The Beliefs of Cyclones

to spread it further. The fury of one person set off the fury of another, like a virus passing through the population, and there was no herd immunity. There was only a herd.

The malice reached frightening proportions, and looking to understand the spread of this rage, its speed and its virulence, I turned back to Le Bon's book. In the century after his book was published he was reviled and mocked — as he is more recently in *So You've Been Publicly Shamed,* Jon Ronson's entertaining book on Twitter mobs — but on reading him again I discovered that when we remove our ideological blinkers (no easy task!) he has far more to say about historical and current developments than his outsider status would lead one to believe.

Le Bon was born Nogent-le-Rorou, in France, in 1841 and died in the Parisian suburb of Marnes-la-Coquette in 1931. He wrote on a dizzying array of subjects. He studied medicine but never practiced it, so we find among his publications a treatise on illnesses of the genitourinary organs, a volume charmingly titled *Apparent Deaths and Premature Burials,* and a collection of slides for a conference on anatomy and histology. He was also the author of volumes on smoking, on Annamite — or ancient Indochinese — archaeology, on travels to Nepal, on equestrianism and its principles. But politics and society were the heart of his work, and the only part of lasting interest.

Le Bon was very much a conservative of his time and place, with a profoundly pessimistic vision of the lifespan of civilizations in the spirit of Gobineau and the later Spengler. Which is to say, there is much in Le Bon to dislike. Hatred of socialism and democracy, of women's rights and universal education, feature prominently in his writings. His stress on the concept of "nationality" and race, and his contempt for non-white races, are not at all hidden. All this explains his banishment to the sidelines of modern social thought. But Le Bon expresses a big idea that we must not ignore. His central and lasting intuition was that once a person becomes a member of a crowd, he ceases to exist as an individual. He is as if "hypnotized" and is "no longer conscious of his acts." With the fading of the conscious personality as he joins the crowd, the unconscious personality predominates, "orient[ed] through suggestion and the contagion of feelings and ideas in the same direction" as those around him. "Isolated, he was perhaps a cultivated individual; in a crowd he becomes someone driven by instincts, consequently a barbarian." Any act becomes possible.

Le Bon's ominous vision of the crowd was strongly influenced by two events he lived through: the Paris Commune of 1871 and the Boulangist movement of the late 1880s. The Paris Commune, the first working-class government in history, was established at the end of the Franco-Prussian War in 1871, in which Le Bon had served as head of the army's ambulance corps, receiving the Légion d'Honneur for his services. The onerous conditions imposed on Parisians by the victorious Prussians, and the newly formed Second Republic's attempt to seize cannons paid for by the workers of Montmartre, led to an uprising that established a democratically elected government in Paris in opposition to the official French government in Versailles. A person with Le Bon's politics could not but look askance on this rebellion, particularly the acts of destruction carried out by supporters of the Commune in its dying days, with the Tuileries, the Louvre, and the Hotel de Ville set aflame and hostages executed in response to the killing of captured communards. The crowd that he witnessed on the streets of Paris did not look to him like men and women fighting for their rights. What he saw was strictly and solely a destructive force.

A later experience of the behavior of the crowd, which he incorporated into his theories, was the short-lived Boulangist movement, which followed the Commune by almost two decades. Boulangism was a diffuse movement that marched behind General Georges Boulanger, a popular figure in the army who was elected to the French Chamber of Deputies in 1887. Behind a vague program that appealed to both the right and the left, to Jews and to anti-Semites, the movement grew by leaps and bounds, until in January 1889 a mass political hysteria swept the country and Boulanger was implored to seize power through a coup d'état. The general refused to do so, the movement faded quickly, and Boulanger fled to Belgium, where he committed suicide on the grave of his mistress in 1891. "What a place in history he would have assumed," Le Bon wrote, "had his character been strong enough to even slightly support his legend." The dangers of the crowd were not, for Le Bon, only a matter of history or theory, but also of lived reality. He was witnessing the birth of what came to be called mass politics.

French history was full of examples that he used to support his theories. The bloodiest events of the French Revolution, which of course Le Bon despised, such as the September Massacres of 1792, when prisoners of the Revolution were slaughtered in prisons all over Paris based on ground-less rumors, were the result of a murderous madness that converted ordinary individuals into a blood-lusting crowd. "The crimes of crowds generally have a powerful suggestion as their motive," he observed, "and the individuals who took part are afterwards persuaded that they obeyed an obligation."

Both the vicious and the disinterested acts of legislators, whom he also considered a type of crowd, along with juries; and criminal crowds, which he defined as the mobs that carried out the Saint Bartholomew's Day Massacre, the killings on the day the Bastille was seized, and the Paris Commune; and voters — all are the result of the crowd mentality. Again citing the French Revolution, he pointed out that among the "most ferocious members of the Convention could be found inoffensive bourgeois who in ordinary circumstances would have been peaceful notaries or virtuous magistrates." Under the influence of events, however, and gathered as a crowd, "they did not hesitate to approve the most ferocious proposals.... And, contrary to their own interests, renounced their inviolability and decimated themselves." The surrender of the privileges of the nobility on August 4, 1789 "would certainly never have been accepted by any of its members in isolation."

It is especially discouraging to think of legislatures, which are supposed to deliberate rationally and decently, as another variety of the herd. Yet even in our own legislatures, in times much less turbulent than revolutionary France but turbulent enough, we have evidence of the truth of Le Bon's observation 245 that "all mental constitutions contain possibilities of character that can manifest themselves when the environment changes abruptly." After September 11, swept along by a mass tide, Congress quickly and almost unanimously passed a Patriot Act that few if any had read. And what was Congress during the Trump years if not a majority gone berserk? And with Trump's defeat, does it not now retain a considerable number of the berserk? As Le Bon said, "The individual in a crowd is a grain of sand among other grains of sand, which the wind blows where it will."

The Beliefs of Cyclones

Though there are sometimes leaderless crowds, as the Black Lives Matter protests demonstrated, crowds generally hunger for leaders, and Le Bon speculated on the qualities of a successful one. Boulangism was a perfect example of the crowd and its leader in action, since people voted for, marched for, and offered power to someone who was the object of almost religious devotion. "One cannot fully understand... certain historical events... unless one has taken into account the religious form the convictions of crowds end up taking." Boulanger — and history certainly provides no shortage of examples of such courageous or opportunistic figures — was proof for Le Bon that for the crowd "one must be a god for them or nothing." Even though modern crowds have turned their backs on the words "divinity and religion," Le Bon shrewdly noted that the Boulangist movement showed "with what ease the religious instincts are ready to be reborn." The devotion of Trump crowds, where people lined up for hours before the rally was to begin decked out in Trump-themed attire while risking exposure to a deadly virus, bears out Le Bon's observations. As a black preacher named Jesse Lee Patterson said of Trump in Tulsa, "He is God." In words that prefigure the personality cults of Trump, Bolsonaro, Modi, and other populist authoritarians, as well as the totalitarian idolatries that preceded them, Le Bon remarks that "the power to remedy all injustices, all evils was attributed to him, and thousands of people would have given their lives for him."

The success of the countless falsehoods and the impover-ished language of authoritarian leaders past and present are explained by Le Bon, who observed, "Pure and simple affirmation, freed of any reasoning or proof, constitutes a sure method to have an idea penetrate the mind of the crowd. The more concise, and free of proof and demonstration, it is, the more authority it has. [This affirmation] nevertheless only acquires real influence on condition that it is constantly repeated and, insofar as possible, in the same terms." Repetition is indeed one of the primary techniques of demagoguery, notably on social media. The horror of this degradation of speech is expressed with great beauty by Yeats in his poem "The Leaders of Crowds":

> They must to keep their certainty accuse
> All that are different of a base intent;
> Pull down established honour; hawk for news
> Whatever their loose fantasy invent
> And murmur it with bated breath, as though
> The abounding gutter had been Helicon
> Or calumny a song...

The crowd, in its fanatical belief in its leader and his bromides, has a crude epistemology. "Having no doubts about what it believes to be truth or error and possessing a clear idea of its strength," Le Bon writes, "the crowd is as authoritarian as it is intolerant." And he adds, in cautionary words that apply also to digital life, "An individual can accept contradiction and discussion; a crowd, never." The futility of arguing with members of any crowd is obvious, for in the psychology of crowds what is clear is "the impotence of reason upon them. The ideas capable of influencing crowds are not rational ideas but feelings expressed in the form of ideas." Or, more poetically, "One no more argues the beliefs of crowds than of cyclones." What confers its ferocity upon the cyclone is the triumph of emotion over thought. Ideas do not at bottom matter to crowds. "People who seem to be fighting for ideas are really fighting for feelings from which the ideas are derived,"

The Beliefs of Cyclones

he wrote in a later book on the nature of opinions and beliefs.

And there is another characteristic feature of the crowd for Le Bon: it guarantees social fragmentation, the descent into schism and sectarianism — into what we call polarization. "The tables of the law are no longer the same for all the tribes of Israel." People come to prefer "ready-made opinions," which are shorthand for entire identities. "One moment of conversation with an individual suffices for one to know what he reads, his usual occupations, and the environment in which he lives." Political and social debates consist in the playing-out of these identity packages. "The mere fact of being a monarchist inevitably led.... to certain definite ideas, and the fact of being a republican conferred ideas that were precisely the opposite. A monarchist knew for certain that man did not descend from monkeys, and a republican knew just as certainly that he did." This made discussion worthless, for "to debate rationally a mystical or affective belief serves only to exalt it."

Dissolve now to the Ellipse in Washington, D.C. on January 6, 2021. The events of that day, with its echoes of the March on Rome, the Beer Hall Putsch, and, most appositely, the anti-parliamentary far-right riot of February 6, 1934 in front of the National Assembly in Paris, took Trump supporters' vision of their leader as a deific figure to its highest (or lowest) level and, almost point by point, bore out nearly all of Le Bon's theses on the nature of the crowd, which, on that date, was truly "as authoritarian as it [was] intolerant." Impervious to reason, they celebrated absurd and provably false claims of electoral victory as unimpeachable truth because they issued from the mouth of their god, whose departure meant the ruin of the republic. And because they were called upon to do so by their deity, they marched on the Capitol to destroy the republic in order to save it. Every act carried out by the putschists at the

Capitol stands as evidence of the mass mind at work, of its infectious nature, of its religious devotion, of its submissiveness to its leader.

Le Bon's theories were the fruit of observation, eschewing statistical analysis or any attempt to ground his observations in scientific theories. His ideas would be elaborated upon by others, who filled in the lacunae in Le Bon's work, and thereby established the subject of group psychology and the "group mind." Intended as sociological and psychological description, Le Bon's ideas were used also prescriptively: Mussolini read him closely, as did Goebbels and perhaps even Hitler. Certainly Le Bon's most famous student on the subject of group psychology was Sigmund Freud. But there were many students — for example, Freud's nephew Edward Bernays, the father of American public relations, who made full use of Le Bon's analysis of the crowd in order to bend it to advertisers' needs. His book *Propaganda*, which appeared in 1928, is not only an application of Le Bon's ideas to modern capitalism but also an essential text for understanding modern America.

The crowd, of course, was not a modern invention, and Le Bon was not the first to regard it as a psychological phenomenon. In 1852, the English lawyer Charles Mackay published a popular two-volume work called *Memoirs of Extraordinary Popular Delusions and the Madness of Crowds*. The work is an entertaining trip through mass fads and manias, from the Tulip Craze to the South Sea Bubble to mesmerism and all the way back to the Crusades. So widespread is mass delusion that Mackay asserted that his two volumes could barely touch on the subject, that even "fifty would scarcely suffice to detail their history." "Religious matters," he added, "have been purposely excluded as incompatible with the limits prescribed to the present work; a mere list of them alone would be sufficient to occupy a volume." McKay explained his controlling assumption in his preface: "Men, it has been well said, think in herds; it will be seen that they go mad in herds, while they only recover their senses slowly, and one by one." He noted that money was often at the heart of the delusions he chronicled, but he was not much interested in the complicated questions of causality: he was writing a book aimed at a wide audience, a "miscellany" more than a history, and certainly not a theoretical treatise.

This was certainly not the case with Gabriel Tarde, an early and once-influential sociologist and social psychologist whose work has in recent decades enjoyed a bit of a comeback in France. In 1890 he published *The Laws of Imitation*, his most renowned work, in which he argued that the engine of social psychology is imitation. Tarde defined it as an "imprint of inter-spiritual photography, willed or not, passive or active. If we observe that wherever there is any form of social relationship between two living beings there is, in this sense, imitation." For Tarde, imitation or counter-imitation, "doing exactly like or exactly the contrary of a model," were at the heart of man's actions in society. In the preface to the second edition of his book, published in 1895, the same year as Le Bon's classic, he addressed the matter of working-class militancy in these terms: "There is no demonstration that goes about recruiting demonstrators that fails to provoke the formation of a group of counter-demonstrators."

Since he gave counter-imitation a role coequal with imitation, Tarde saw something positive in the herd mentality. "Every strong assertion, at the same time that it drags along middling and sheep-like sprits, somewhere gives rise to a diametrically opposed negation of a nearly equal force in a mind born rebellious, which does not mean born inventive." There was no such thing as an original position: everything social was action and reaction, as in chemistry, with positive and negative consequences. Tarde regularly used the term "contagion," now in vogue among many social scientists, to describe the work of imitation and its force, which he applied to art, to hunger and thirst, even to the spread of alcoholism. Le Bon would learn from and modify Tarde's vision. Though Le Bon's ideas stressed the psychological aspects of the crowd mentality, the source of the psychological functions that moved the crowd were left largely unelucidated. "Contagion is a phenomenon easy to take note of, but as yet unexplained and which must be connected to phenomena of a hypnotic order," he wrote. Unconscious drives motivate the crowd, he insisted, but what kind of drives?

The story of this idea leads now to Vienna, Berggasse 19, where Freud, enormously impressed with Le Bon's work, set to deepen his analysis, and in 1921 published *Group Psychology and the Analysis of the Ego*. Freud accepted Le Bon's premise "that an individual in a group is subjected through its influence to what is often a profound alteration in his mental activity." He agreed that man's intellectual ability is reduced when in a crowd and his emotions are intensified "in the direction of an approximation to the other individuals in the group." Freud's brief treatise sought to provide a psychological explanation for this mental change, moving the discussion beyond the barebones explanation of the "unconscious mind."

Freud insisted, not surprisingly, that the concept of the libido provides the key to understanding group psychology. "Love relationships (or, to use a more neutral expression, emotional ties) also constitute the essence of the group mind."

The Beliefs of Cyclones

If the group is held together by some force, "to what power could this feat be better ascribed than to Eros, who holds together everything in the world?" If an individual surrenders his self and becomes the plaything of suggestion provided by the crowd, "it gives one the impression that he does it because he feels the need of being in harmony with them rather than in opposition to them — so that perhaps after all he does it *'ihnen zuliebe'*." This idea that it is love that holds the crowd together makes the crowd seem like a community. But the consequences of this shared warmth are not heartening. Given the basic qualities of the crowd, "the weakness of intellectual ability, the lack of emotional restraint, the incapacity for moderation and delay, the inclination to exceed every limit in the expression of emotion and to work it off completely in the form of action," Freud endorses Le Bon's notion that its mental activity regresses to "an earlier stage such as we are not surprised to find among savages or children."

Freud's acceptance and elaboration of Le Bon's description of the nature of the crowd provided him also with an opportunity to apply his wildly speculative theories on leadership. In *Group Psychology and The Analysis of The Ego* he reverts to his theories in *Totem and Taboo*, which he admits are only a hypothesis. To get to the crux of the matter of leadership of a crowd, indeed of leadership *tout court*, he proposes that the primitive form of human society was the horde, and that this has "left indestructible traces upon the history of human descent." Not only is the group the "revival" of this primal horde, but in the same way that each individual bears within him primitive man, "so the primal horde may arise once more out of any random crowd." This sense of atavism must have been confirmed for him by the mass politics of his day.

Leaders, too, are a product of this primitive state,

according to Freud, for the primal "father" was totally free, "and his will needed no reinforcement from others." Narcissism was the constitutive element of his being, as "he loved no one but himself, or other people only insofar as they served his needs." This is an analytical step forward from Le Bon's simplistic psychological analysis of leaders, which claimed that they were "recruited among those neurotics, those hotheads, the half-mad who live on the edge of madness." The historical confirmation of Freud's formula hardly needs stressing. "The leader of the group is still the dreaded primal father," Freud continued. "The group still wishes to be governed by unrestricted force; it has an extreme passion for authority; in Le Bon's phrase, it has a thirst for obedience. The primal father is the group ideal, which governs the ego in the place of the ego ideal." The crowd, in other words, performs upon each of its members a kind of inner usurpation, in which the self and its struggle for autonomy is replaced by a collective that demands conformity.

In 1951, on the other side of the greatest catastrophe of group psychology in history, Theodor Adorno wrote an essay called "Freudian Theory and Fascist Propaganda." In it, he examined Freud's work on mass psychology in light of his own studies of the authoritarian personality and the rise of fascism. It was intended as an analysis of American fascists, figures such as Father Coughlin and Gerald L.K. Smith, setting them alongside the experience of fascism in Germany. Adorno's update of Freud's update of Le Bon further complicates the story. Adorno is not entirely won over by Le Bon, praising Freud for his "dynamic interpretation" of Le Bon's descriptive text and for his critique of the "magic words" used by Le Bon, which he dismissed for being treated "as though they were keys for some startling phenomena." Freud is also credited with being free of "the traditional contempt for the masses which is the *thema probandum* of most of the older psychologists." Adorno, after all, admired — even as he also feared — the revolutionary masses as much as he reviled the reactionary masses. His idiosyncratic form of leftist thought led him to work with Max Horkheimer on a proposed New Communist Manifesto, but he was later also the victim of vicious attacks by left-wing students, who would write on his classroom blackboard: "If Adorno is left in peace, capitalism will never cease." Adorno knew the misdeeds of the crowd in both its right- and left-wing forms.

Adorno refused to accept that "archaic, pre-individual instincts survive" in "the children of a liberal, competitive, and individualistic society, and conditioned to maintain themselves as independent society." How then, he wonders, can these same enlightened moderns revert in a crowd to "patterns of behavior which flagrantly contradict their own rational level and the present stage of enlightened technological civilization?" He praises Freud for looking further than simple atavism and explaining the surrender of the individual to the mass as being of a libidinal nature, a surrender to the pleasure principle. Adorno regards Freud's refinement of Le Bon as an important advance, because by crediting the libidinal nature of surrender to the crowd "the traits generally ascribed to masses lose the deceptively primordial and irreducible character reflected by the arbitrary construct of specific mass or herd instincts." In doing so, Freud "does justice to the simple fact that those who become submerged in masses are not primitive men [which was Le Bon's claim] but display primitive attitudes contradictory to their normal rational behavior."

Though there is a certain injustice to Le Bon in this, who went no further than the concepts available to him in his time, this notion of the crowd as a contradiction provides an important link in the causal chain of crowd formation and action. What Adorno adds to Freud applies to most political crowds in thrall to a leader: he relates Freud's vision of a leader's hold, derived from the idealization of the leader, to a "narcissistic libido overflow." Explicating Freud, Adorno sees the leader as a paternal figure, but takes this further, seeing him as "a means of satisfying our narcissism."

Adorno's application of Freud's psychological construction of the leader, though based on Hitler, fits another, later, and significantly less diabolical American leader to a startling degree, and is Adorno's great addition to the study of the crowd: "The leader has to himself appear to be absolutely narcissistic." The leader has no need for learned study in order to become adept at crowd manipulation. (Adorno dismisses the standard claim that Hitler studied Le Bon, granting him at best cursory readings of popularizations of the work, while Goebbels, a failed intellectual, was not likely to have mastered modern depth psychology.) Instead, the authoritarian leader has a gift: he "can guess the wants and needs of those susceptible to his propaganda because he resembles them psychologically, and is distinguished from them by a capacity to express without inhibitions what is latent in them... The leaders are general oral character types, with a compulsion to speak incessantly and to fool others...Language itself, devoid of its rational significance, functions in a magical way and furthers those archaic regressions which reduce individuals to members of crowds." Words do not signify, they signal; and the crowd awaits the signal.

The vision of the philosopher Gunther Anders, Adorno's

contemporary and fellow exile from Hitler's Germany, was far more pessimistic than that of Adorno and was formed in opposition to Le Bon. For Anders, modern life rendered Le Bon's ideas "obsolete." As he pointedly observed in 1956 in his (still untranslated) masterpiece *The Obsolescence of Man*, "leading the masses in the style of Hitler is no longer necessary." Anders asserted that it was now the case that it is not just in the crowd that the individual loses his identity: "The erasure of the personality and the degradation of intelligence are completed before man even leaves his house....All submit separately to the process of 'conditioning,' which functions every bit as well in the cages in which individuals are now confined, despite their solitude, despite their millions of solitudes." For Anders, physical and social circumstances are no longer a necessary condition for massification. "If one wants to depersonalize man (and even see to it that he be proud to not have a personality) there is no longer any need to drown him in the river of the masses or to seal him in the cement of the mass." Demagogues and crowds are replaced by a cultural conditioning, facilitated by technology, that passes for being "fun, since it hides from its victim the sacrifice it demands from him; since it leaves the illusion of a private life, or at least a private space, it acts with total discretion." An insidious ideology that demobilizes the intelligence, spread by television and radio, are the modern methods for the negation of the individual's personality. "The erasure, the degradation of man as man are all the more successful in that they appear to continue to guarantee personal freedom and the rights of the individual."

Very much a thinker of the 1950s in this regard, Anders seems to dismiss even the possibility of the resurgence of the crowd guided by the psychological states first laid out by Le Bon. It has now been replaced by an atomized, decerebrated mass. But still to come was a further complication, a further twist, in our own time: this atomized mass now coexists in a new variety of the crowd mind. The monads traverse a digital ether to form a herd. They link, and link up, and link in. Physical apartness has been resolved in a new version of nearness, with no loss of inflammation. In this crowd they are apart and they are together, thinking and amplifying the same thoughts.

There is a tension in Max Weber's writings on leaders and crowds. His description of the crowd in *Economy and Society*, published posthumously in 1922, does not stray far from Le Bon, whom he cites only once. He accepts that "it is well-known that the actions of the individual are strongly influenced by the mere fact that he is a member of a crowd confined within a limited space." Following Le Bon, he also proposes that physical proximity is not required for the formation of the crowd — anticipating Anders' argument, he importantly notes that a crowd can exist in a dispersed state, "influenced simultaneously or successively by a source of influence operating similarly on all individuals, as by means of the press." And eventually by means of more than the press: when Weber made his far-seeing observation, Silicon Valley was just an agricultural paradise known as the Valley of Heart's Delight.

But Weber does not follow Le Bon to the end. Though accepting that "some types of reaction are only made possible by the mere fact that the individual acts as part of the crowd," he adds that "others become more difficult under these conditions." Certain emotions, such as "gaiety, anger, enthusiasm, despair, and passions of all sorts" would not arise "if the individual were alone." Yet Weber has a sturdier sense of the individual's ability to withstand the seductions of the mass. "But for [these emotions] to happen there need not, at least in many cases, be any meaningful relationship between the behavior of the individual and the fact that he is a member of a crowd." It is possible not to be swept away by the crowd, though Weber does not elaborate on the means of resistance.

Weber's later and famous description of the "charismatic" leader has only a distant relationship to Le Bon's deific leader. His charismatic leader has instead a "vocation" for politics. For Weber, the leader "is held to have an 'inner calling' to lead, and people accept his rule not because of customs or laws but because they believe in him." The peoples' devotion is directed at the leader, "disciples and followers and party members are devoted to *him* as a person, his personal qualities." Weber describes charismatic political rule as resembling that of "a nonhereditary warlord, a ruler elected by the people, or nowadays a great demagogue or leader of political parties." That is a diverse range of political types and political systems; but in Weber's hands, charisma is less toxic and less archaic, and is compatible with democracy. Yet Weber was perhaps too optimistic about the constructive uses of charisma — perhaps too certain that this leader will live for his cause, and that he does so "if he is more than a vain and narrow-minded upstart." As history has since shown, a charismatic leader guided by vanity, narrow-mindedness, and narcissism can be just as powerful and dominant as one motivated by altruism. In fact, they are more the rule than the exception.

Weber does, however, issue a stern warning. He accepts that vanity is an "occupational hazard" of politics, that a "lust for power" is necessary for any politician — a "normal attribute." "The sin of his calling," he continues, "begins when the politician's lust for power is no longer grounded in objective reality and instead simply intoxicates the politician personally." But how to secure a society's commitment to "objective reality"? We are wrestling with this perplexity now. Le Bon's jaundiced vision at least accounts for the prevalence of this ill, since for Le Bon the objective reality of which Weber speaks counts for little in the world created by the interaction between the leader and his crowd.

On July 15, 1927, when the newspapers in Vienna announced a verdict of not guilty in the trial of a group of men accused of killing a number of workers, crowds gathered spontaneously around the city and then converged on the Palace of Justice and set it aflame. The police fired on the crowd and ninety people were killed. Elias Canetti, the polyglot Bulgarian Jewish writer then living in Vienna, was in that crowd, and its actions that day would have lasting effects on his intellectual life. He wrote decades later that it "may have been the most crucial day of my life after my father's death." This event would be the motivating force behind a thirty-year process that would result in his renowned study of the crowd and the crowd mind, *Crowds and Power*, which appeared in 1960.

His description in his memoirs of his experience on that day could have come straight from the pages of Le Bon. "I became a part of the crowd, I fully dissolved in it, I did not feel the slightest resistance to what the crowd was doing." Reading about an event like the storming of the Bastille was henceforth superfluous for him: he had lived it almost a century and a half later and half a continent away. *Crowds and*

259

Power is five hundred dense pages on crowds around the world and throughout history, with excursions to Australia, to American Indian lands, to the settlements of Maori tribesmen. As the fine Hungarian critic László F. Földenyí wrote in an essay about the book, for Canetti "a crowd does not simply mean that many people have gathered together; rather that life within the crowd is inseparable from existence itself. The crowd is the *condition humaine*."

No larger claim for the crowd was ever made. Though Canetti bases his work on studies by sociologists and anthropologists, he ignores Le Bon, Weber, and Freud. The core of his book is made up of his own conclusions and statements drawn from eccentric readings of his sources. These are often brilliant, and often too brilliant: they disintegrate quickly under scrutiny. And there is a certain slipperiness in Canetti's methodology. The book begins with a section titled "The Fear of Being Touched," which includes the statement that "it is only in a crowd that man can free himself of this fear of being touched." This observation, presented with no source, can in fact be found in Freud's *Group Psychology and the Analysis of the Ego* in almost the same terms, with Freud even quoting the source of his observation: "According to Schopenhauer's famous simile of the freezing porcupines, no one can tolerate a too intimate approach to his neighbor. .... But the whole of this intolerance vanishes, temporarily or permanently, as the result of the formation of a group, and in a group."

To be sure, Canetti's description of the four key attributes of the crowd are straightforward: "The crowd always wants to grow... Within the crowd there is equality. The crowd loves density...The crowd needs direction." But these attributes, described just pages into the book, all of them rather obvious, give way to a typology of crowds that is absurdly broad and farfetched. There are "invisible crowds," "baiting crowds" "flight crowds," "prohibition crowds," "reversal crowds," "feast crowds." Crowds of the living and crowds of the dead; crowds of men and crowds of women; crowds at theaters and crowds at sporting events and crowds of warriors. And when Canetti is through with his taxonomy of crowds, he presents a taxonomy of packs. His classificatory promiscuity is in stark contrast to Le Bon, who insisted that "the fact that many individuals accidentally find themselves side by side does not confer up in them the characteristics of an organized crowd."

And finally, in his intellectually self-congratulatory way, he goes off the rails. In his section on crowd symbols, for example, Canetti introduces "collective units which do not consist of men, but which are still felt to be crowds." Corn, forests, rain, wind, sand, fire and the sea are included under this heading. Who has ever considered corn to be a crowd? Who has ever gone to the beach to romp in the crowd, or to have crowd kicked in their face? About the sea: "Put your hand into water, lift it out and watch the drops slipping singly and impotently down it. The pity you feel for them is as though they were human beings, hopelessly separated." Has anyone ever felt pity for drops of sea water? "Men readily see their own equality before death in the image of corn." How readily, exactly?

Such pseudo-brilliant nonsense is relatively harmless, but not all of Canetti's leaps of fancy are so innocent. For Canetti, inflation served as a model for the fate of the Jews under Nazism, their treatment an echo of the experience of inflation in the Weimar Republic. "First they were attacked as wicked and dangerous, as enemies; then they were more and more depreciated; then, there not being enough in Germany itself, those in the conquered territories were gathered in; and

The Beliefs of Cyclones

finally they were treated literally as vermin, to be destroyed with impunity by the million." Germans would perhaps not have been brought to participate in this genocide "had they not been through an inflation during which the Mark fell to a billionth of its former value." Returning to the matter of crowds, Canetti concludes that "it was this inflation, as a crowd experience, which they shifted on to the Jews." Numbers, numbers, numbers: has the faith in quantification ever been more perverse? Canetti can be as inhumane as the crowd ever was.

Which brings us to our own golden age of quantification and its contribution to the theory of the crowd. In its neglect of its predecessor, *Crowds and Power* was a retort to *The Psychology of Crowds*. We may consider it representative of the high end of the anti-Le Bon tradition of thinking about mobs. But James Surowiecki's *The Wisdom of Crowds,* a bestseller fifteen years ago, its very title a shot across Le Bon's bow, is quite something else. We know this to be the case because, unlike Canetti, he establishes his vision as being in opposition to Le Bon's in his introduction. For Surowiecki, "Le Bon had things exactly backward. If you put together a big enough and diverse enough group of people and ask them to 'make decisions affecting matters of general interest,' that group's decisions will, over time, be intellectually [superior] to the isolated individual, no matter how smart or well-informed he is."

The phenomenon to which Surowiecki refers is sometimes called "many-mindedness," or the view that the more minds that are applied to a problem, the more likely (and justifiable) its solution will be. Never mind that a consensus of many minds can still be disastrously wrong. *The Wisdom of Crowds* provides a large number of case studies that, in its author's opinion, prove that crowds differ from Le Bon's negative portrayal of them. The crowd is instead a mild, useful, even beatific presence in our lives. Its primary expression is data. We are presented with edifying tales of stock market investors, football coaches, NASA decision makers, scientific researchers, nineteenth-century builders of plank roads, and so on -- everything but the spontaneous psychological crowd, the momentous mobs of history, that worried Le Bon and the others. Surowiecki is not worried. This is a book that could only have been written before Trumpism and the mainstreaming of the alt-right, though the long history of crowds and their consequences provides ample enough not to have required the contemporary experience of an event like Charlottesville. How can anyone even remotely familiar with that history speak of the crowd's "wisdom"?

Like Canetti, Surowiecki treats almost any assembly of human beings as a crowd, and deploys his expanded definition as a weapon against Le Bon. Worse, he attributes decision-making to the crowd. If by decision-making we mean some kind of rational deliberation and reasoned exchange of views, this is the very antithesis of what a crowd does. Marketers know this, of course, which is why they welcome such books: the manipulability of masses of people is their business. They quiver to learn of the "tipping point" at which people will start buying chinos or cellphones. What Bernays called "propaganda," we call advertising. But all this benign behavior — all this shopping — has nothing to do with social and political action, where the stakes are higher and evil may play a part. The crowd at the guillotine is not like the crowd at the Apple store.

The Beliefs of Cyclones

In one case there is an overlap between Surowiecki and Le Bon: the case of juries. Surowiecki mocks his predecessor's claim that juries deliver verdicts "of which each individual juror would disapprove." Yet in the chapter in which he discusses juries, he admits that decades of experimental studies have demonstrated that their deliberations are not, as one would imagine, "a recipe for rationality and moderation." Are juries crowds? Anyone who has seen *Twelve Angry Men* knows that the answer is yes and no. Where there is persuasion, there is demagoguery. But the likelihood of genuine persuasion is greater in a room of twelve than in a town square of thousands. Surowiecki ignores the hard cases, the dangerous cases. He prefers to find wisdom in groups of ants, starlings, and monkeys, as if cooperation is the most significant attribute of a crowd. But cooperation is value-neutral; what matters is its purpose. And what is the decision-making capacity of an ant? (As Charlie Kaufman points out in his novel *Antkind*, even if ants are wise as a group, they are pretty stupid as individuals). *The Wisdom of Crowds* is written for and about a comfortable materialistic society in which the most salient choices are consumer choices. By concentrating on decisions made at this safe level, Surowiecki does not refute Le Bon, he merely avoids the issues that Le Bon raises, and all the mass unwisdom that made Le Bon and the others desperately concerned to understand the crowd.

Gustave Le Bon thought that civilization was on the verge of collapse, a "worm-eaten edifice supported by nothing that will not collapse at the first storm." He warned that "what formed a people, a unit, a bloc, ends up becoming an agglomeration of individuals lacking cohesion and which, for a time, artificially maintains traditions and institutions." The "race," as he called it, though in context this meant the French nation,

264

"is no longer anything but dust made up of isolated individuals and becomes again what it was at its beginning: a crowd." His suggestion that there is a relation between the isolation of the individual and the ecstasy of the crowd was profound. I would like to believe that his pessimism was wrong, but the social and political civilization that remains standing resembles the nightmare world that he described in too many ways for us to be smug about its perdurability, or to assume that the fate he described has been avoided once and for all.

The Beliefs of Cyclones

PETER PHILLIPS

Josquin's Secrets

"A certain famous man said that Josquin produced more motets after his death than during his life." So joked the German music publisher Georg Forster in 1540, nineteen years after the death of Josquin des Prez, the most celebrated composer the world had known. He had lived and died admired and respected, then as now. But loved? With reservations then, and with greater but different reservations now. The course of his extraordinary career and reputation, in this the five-hundredth anniversary year of his death, needs some unpacking.

Josquin died on August 27, 1521. Since then he has been called the first musical superstar, and his influence likened to that of Beethoven; and, like Beethoven, he became the standard by which every subsequent composer in his tradition was judged, directly influencing most of them. So why is he not the household name that Palestrina and Tallis are? (There *are* such households.) Having just presided over a nine-disc set of Josquin's eighteen mass settings with the Tallis Scholars, and having studied and recorded his music all my working life, I will attempt to provide an answer to this riddle. His music is sufficiently difficult to sing that modern choirs do well to think twice about trying it. Josquin was a composer who never settled down to an easily identifiable style. Like Tallis, but unlike Palestrina, he was interested in experimenting with everything that came his way, inventing new sonorities and methods as he went. This has deprived him of the kind of easy brand-like recognition which helps modern audiences feel at ease with composers from the more (and even less) distant past. Concertgoers have heard his name, but they do not know anything by him, which puts him in the rather unglamorous company of composers such as Telemann, Corelli, Dunstable, and Hindemith.

At his death, certainly, there was no doubt about his status. Some of the most prominent thinkers of the time praised him. Luther, an experienced singer, wrote "Josquin is master of the notes, which must express what he desires; on the other hand, other composers must do what the notes dictate." And his reputation endured: in 1567 the Florentine diplomat, philologist, mathematician, and humanist Cosimo Bartoli declared "Josquin may be said to have been, in music, a prodigy of nature, as our Michelangelo has been in architecture, painting, and sculpture; for, as there has not thus far been anybody who in his compositions approaches Josquin, so Michelangelo, among all those who have been active in the arts, is still alone and without peer." His name, if not his music, continued to be cited in the intervening centuries, put on a pedestal to bring a proper sense of tradition to contemporary musicians. By far the most remarkable instance of this was his inclusion on a list drawn up in 1863 of composers to be petrified on the frieze of the Albert Memorial in London. This is the more remarkable in that the English musical establishment in those years seemed to have little interest in foreign composers from the distant past, preferring to wrap themselves in their own Byrd and Tallis. And yet there he is, sandwiched by a committee of mid-nineteenth century English gentlemen, between Grétry and Rossini, with Palestrina, Monteverdi, and Tallis nearby.

Such widespread admiration brought its own troubles. For at least fifty years after Josquin's death, minor composers and hopeful anthologists liked to claim that he had had a hand in their work, hence Forster's words quoted above. The New Grove Dictionary of Music and Musicians lists 315 works by Josquin, of which 136 are classified as being of doubtful authenticity; and this unstable list of compositions is rivalled by the number of composers who claim to have been taught by him, a number which was fueled by one of the most widely read poets of the day, Pierre de Ronsard. In a preface to the *Livre de Meslanges*, a collection of chansons published in 1560, he published a list of all the composers who had been Josquin's pupil, mentioning Richafort, de Sermisy and Mouton, among many others.

It seems more likely that the majority of these were influenced by him rather than actually taught by him, but in the case of Jean Richafort there certainly was a close connection. When Josquin died, a number of these men rallied round to write a succession of funeral motets in his honor, the Renaissance equivalent of a *Festschrift*. The most substantial of these was a six-voice *Requiem in memoriam Josquin des Prez* by Richafort, based on two chansons by Josquin himself; and it remains to this day one of those Renaissance blockbusters waiting to be recognized for the masterpiece that it is. On a lesser scale were the several settings of *Musae Jovis*, the most famous by Nicolas Gombert, whose text includes the words:

Musae Jovis ter maximi
Proles canora, plangite,
Comas cypressus comprimat
Iosquinus ille ille occidit.

Ye Muses, melodious offspring
of thrice-greatest Jupiter, make lamentation.
The cypress draws in its leaves.
The famous Josquin is dead.

So far all the evidence for Josquin's fame has come from men who lived and worked in Flanders, the world into which he was born. But the claim that he was the first musical superstar is based on his travels. In fact he was by no means the first composer to tread the route of fame from the north to the Italian Renaissance courts — Dufay at least had done this before him — but somehow Josquin has managed to steal all the limelight, not just from his contemporaries but also from his predecessors. Somehow he was irresistibly attractive to those several Italian princes who vied with each other in maintaining the most splendid courts. Although Dufay had written the motet *Nuper rosarum flores* that celebrated Brunelleschi's completion of the dome to the Cathedral in Florence, which one might have thought would have put him on those pedestals alongside Josquin, he was soon replaced by the younger man, both in reputation and in cities where Josquin followed him, for example with the Este family in Ferrara and in the Sistine Chapel.

So far as he can be reliably followed, Josquin was born around the year 1455 in the province of Hainaut somewhere near (but not in) the small city of Condé-sur-l'Escaut, to which he moved at a young age. Since Condé is now on the French-Belgian border, it is not certain whether he accounted himself Flemish or French. This distinction seems to have mattered not only to tidy-minded historians, but also to Josquin himself, four days before he died, when making his final will. He seems suddenly to have realized that since he was born in a different jurisdiction from the one where all his property was located, this could be confiscated after his death if he did not register as an *aubain*, a list of illegitimate and foreign residents. By doing this he could legally bequeath his property to his family.

His first professional move was to the city of Cambrai, now in France, where he may have sung as a choirboy in the cathedral; and it was as a singer that he appears in the records of

René of Anjou as a young adult. When Duke René died in 1480, Josquin probably joined the service of King Louis XI in Paris. Louis in turn died in 1483, at which point Josquin's ability to pursue the main chance makes itself clear. By June 1484 he is documented as being in the employment of Cardinal Ascanio Sforza, resident in Milan and a close relative of the reigning duke, Gian Galeazzo Sforza, who had provided the city with "the best-endowed musical establishment in fifteenth-century Europe." In addition to the music that he wrote for the Duke of Milan in the years following 1484 — which probably includes the two great motet cycles and the *Missa Di dadi* —

Josquin's employment in the household of a Cardinal led him to Rome.

From June 1489, and for at least the next five years, he was a singer in the papal choir in the Sistine Chapel. This is known with certainty not only because the account books of those years record every monthly payment made to him, but because of an unusual discovery made in the choir loft, where the singers stood to sing: in 1998, workers restoring the chapel revealed a "JOSQUINJ" carved into the woodwork. It seems very likely that the graffito is by Josquin himself, ironically making it his only surviving autograph. A more speculative conclusion is that it was made on the side of the gallery where the altos stood, suggesting that Josquin himself sang alto. Given the extreme difficulty of some of the parts that he wrote for that voice, this could shed interesting light on what he thought of his own abilities as a singer.

It was in the following decade, between 1494 and 1503, that Josquin's fame really took off. He probably returned to France in these years, but by then he was in touch with Ottaviano Petrucci in Venice, one of the earliest commercial music printers. As a result of being included in Petrucci's first publications Josquin was given, as one scholar writes, "a kind of publicity unknown to any earlier composer." But perhaps Josquin's most celebrated appointment was to the court of Ercole d'Este, Duke of Ferrara, in 1503. Arriving there not long after Lucrezia Borgia, his brief stay — he left again in 1504 to avoid an outbreak of plague, which killed his successor Jacob Obrecht — resulted in a succession of masterpieces which, if any of his music can be described as being popular today, are popular: the *Missa Hercules Dux Ferrariae* and the *Miserere*.

The choice of Josquin to lead the chapel choir in Ferrara provoked some of the most quoted evidence we have of

271

Josquin's standing at that time. Girolamo da Sestola, a singer and courtier, wrote to Duke Ercole (in a letter which shows the kind of one-upmanship that prevailed between the richest Italian courts): "My lord, I believe that there is neither lord nor king who will have a better chapel than yours if your lordship sends for Joschino. Don Alfonso [Ercole's son and heir] wishes to write this to your lordship and so does the entire chapel, and by having Joschino in our chapel I want to place a crown upon this chapel of ours." Yet this glowing recommendation was somewhat offset by a second letter to Duke Ercole from another singer and courtier, Gian d'Artiganova, who provides unique evidence of what sort of person Josquin might have been. In a comparison of Gian Josquin to the composer Heinrich Isaac, who was also from the Low Countries and also very highly regarded at the time (and in my opinion fully the equal of Josquin, though in a quite different compositional style), Gian observed: 'To me [Isaac] seems well suited to serve your lordship, more so than Josquin, because he is of a better disposition among his companions, and he will compose new works more often. It is true that Josquin composes better, but he composes when he wants to, and not when one wants him to, and he is asking 200 ducats in salary while Isaac will come for 120."

From this many commentators have concluded that Josquin was arrogant, unpopular, and his own man at a time when composers were considered to be no more than servants. The very modern emphasis on working when he felt like it, and charging properly for it, is thrown into an interesting perspective by a fact about Josquin's life which has only recently been fully understood: he was independently wealthy. In 1483 he went to Condé to establish his claim to an inheritance left him by an aunt and uncle. Up to that time he had been in the same situation as every other musician — at the beck and call of rich patrons. From then on he could decide what he did and where he went, which may well explain why he left for Italy so soon after receiving the money. This inheritance has led to a further negative judgment about him: that he was worldly to the point of being greedy.

Josquin's ability to pay his own way is another indication of how his life as a professional musician differed from those who had gone before, or who worked alongside him; and it plays well into the modern concept of superstars, who are by definition the antithesis of servants, people who follow their own muse, beholden to nothing but their own genius. This set of circumstances was so unusual for an artist in the early sixteenth century that it is a little hard to believe. But the details of his last seventeen years confirm it. By 1504, and with plague threatening in Ferrara, he decided to go home. He was now about fifty years old: old enough to retire, but young enough to continue traveling if he wished to. He may well have done both, becoming provost of Notre Dame de Condé in 1504 — his almost hometown — where he essentially remained until he died in 1521. He spent these years composing a stream of masterpieces, experimenting with form and content as he liked. When he died he was given the unique privilege of being buried in front of the high altar of the church he had served, leaving a will which stated that his double motet *Pater noster/ Ave Maria* should be sung outside his house on every church procession in perpetuity. He would provide the funding for this from his estate, a field having been bought and rented out expressly for this purpose.

It is only after his death that the written evidence for Josquin's standing becomes abundant. We have seen what observers said about him during his life. But the message from those who would pass their music off as his, years later, is unequivocal. Equally certain, though better motivated, were those composers who took his music and parodied it in their own writing. This may sound to modern ears like plagiarism. But it is important to understand that the Romantic ideal of originality, of unalloyed individual inspiration, is a recent innovation in Western culture, and there was a long and honorable tradition of musicians either learning from accredited masters, or paying tribute to them, by recasting their music in what were effectively new works. These appropriations – as in, for example, a "parody mass" — had nothing to do with artistic theft. And this tradition of borrowing as homage had long legs: Handel famously remade a very ordinary chorus by Alessandro Stradella into the "flies and lice" movement in *Israel in Egypt*, and no one thought the worse of him for it, not least because he so evidently improved on the original. But it was not the purpose of Renaissance composers to improve on their originals, just to nod in appreciation, and to learn, and to move on.

274

Josquin's legacy was a target like no other for this benignly parasitical procedure. Probably the most elaborate example is Palestrina's *Missa Benedicta es caelorum*, based on Josquin's motet of that name. It is an early work by Palestrina, the longest of the 104 masses that he wrote, and obviously an apprentice composition. Its length comes from Palestrina's evident desire to master what he thought of the Flemish approach to phrase structure; and it is a good example, since the end result sounds like Palestrina rather than Josquin, for all that much of it can be found in the original, enlarged. The same can be said of Lassus's *Magnificat* on the same Josquin motet. Even more copied was Josquin's incomparable motet *Praeter rerum seriem*, which spawned parody mass settings by (at least) Matthaeus Le Maistre, George de La Hèle, Cipriano de Rore, and Adrian Willaert; a Magnificat setting by Lassus; many motet parodies by lesser known figures who wanted to share in the glory, such as Sethus Calvisius; and lute intabulations by leading players, such as Sebastian Ochsenkun. The challenge for any composer taking this masterpiece as his model is that it has such a strong character, especially in the opening measures, that it is difficult to think of anything more useful to do than simply quote it. Some did little more than this, though de Rore shows the greatest flair by increasing Josquin's number of contributing voices from six to seven (a feat in itself), and adding new counterpoints over Josquin's searching bass texture at the beginning of every movement. (The writing in this texture strikes me as being so similar to the opening of the Funeral March in Mahler's First Symphony that I am tempted to say that Mahler was also quoting directly. Alas, there is no evidence for this.)

Josquin himself applied the parody technique to the music of his greatest Flemish predecessor and possible teacher, Johannes Ockeghem, with exactly the same intention of flattering him by reference. Whatever his relationship may have been with some of his contemporaries, he was quick to praise Ockeghem, in word and in deed. In his lament on Ockeghem's death, *Nymphes des bois*, Josquin refers to him as his *bon père*, and seems even to invent a style of music outside his normal idiom designed to catch up some of the older man's compositional method. The pacing and the impact of this lament is one of the most perfect in all Josquin's oeuvre, and one of the simplest to perform.

But the references to Ockeghem go well back into Josquin's career — and have the advantage that Ockeghem would have heard them. Josquin's *Missa D'ung aultre amer* is based on Ockeghem's three-voice (soprano, tenor, bass) *chanson* of the same name. This mass provides a good example of Josquin's style of parody, since much of what he was doing can be clearly heard in what is quite uncomplicated music. The tenor from the *chanson* is quoted in its original form (with slight embellishment) once in each of Josquin's movements, except in the Credo where it comes twice. More evidently Ockeghem's soprano part — the most audible voice — is quoted straight in the *Kyrie,* the *Sanctus,* and in the second half of *Tu solus qui facis,* a motet which replaced the *Benedictus,* where it is accompanied by the *chanson's* tenor part. And if you sing the original words, rather than those of the mass, at the points where Ockeghem's melodies are quoted exactly, you have as close a parody as is possible. But even in this embrace Josquin was not merely copying: he was too proud just to quote without adding. In the motet Ockeghem's melodies are given new counterpoints (now in four vocal parts); and, just to thicken the sauce, in the *Sanctus* and the *Agnus Dei* the quotations from the *chanson* in Josquin's soprano and bass parts are combined in his alto with the relevant chants of the appointed Ordinary Mass Cycle XVIII — a piece of technical showmanship which Josquin alone could pull off so effortlessly.

What frame of mind Josquin was really in when he set himself to imitate and quote and try to outdo his contemporaries we shall never know. How much bloody-mindedness was involved? It is assumed that the Ockeghem quotations were done out of genuine admiration. It is also assumed that his swallowing of an entire motet by Antoine Brumel in the third *Agnus Dei* of his *Missa Mater patris* was done for the same reason, to be sung as a lament to Brumel, who had died in 1512. One wonders how Brumel would have reacted to Josquin taking a perfectly satisfactory three-voice motet (*Mater patris*), keeping every note of it unchanged, but embedding it inside two extra voices of his own, and so making a five-part movement to conclude his mass-setting. Again, the technical prowess involved was astonishing, probably well outside Brumel's competence. Would Brumel have been flattered or annoyed at such blatant one-upmanship? Perhaps even this fell within the acceptable boundaries of parodying — and Brumel might have decided to notice only the flattery.

The same basic question could be asked about the two great mass-settings which Josquin based on the melody of the *chanson* known as *L'homme armé*. Here he was unquestionably showing off. Parody involved taking a polyphonic model by a named composer, but paraphrase, which is what Josquin was doing in these two settings, involved taking a tune, a single line of melody, usually chant and therefore anonymous, and working it into an original polyphonic web. In this form there was no question of paying homage, just of playing around with clever contrapuntal techniques. *L'homme armé* was the most famous secular melody of the day, paraphrased over forty times by Renaissance and Baroque composers, ranging from Robert Morton in the 1460s to Giacomo Carissimi in the mid-1600s. Modern composers have also taken it up, including Peter Maxwell Davies, Mark Alburger, and Karl Jenkins. Its origins are obscure, but the armed man may have been a reference to a Turkish soldier, or to a native solider armed to fight the Turks.

As he knew very well, Josquin was joining a well-established tradition, which he set out to make his own. He did this by writing one mass in the oldest compositional methods still current — the *Missa L'homme armé super voces musicales* — in order to show his older colleagues that he had mastered everything that they were doing; and then he wrote one in the most up-to-date methods he could find or invent — the *Missa L'homme armé sexti toni*. Taken together they make a perfect resumé of the styles available to a composer in the last decades of the fifteenth century.

These styles can be summarized as follows. The old-fashioned version concentrates on the traditional Flemish virtues of quoting the melody strictly — it appears almost entirely unembellished in the tenor — and on writing the most complex of contrapuntal tricks with it and around it. These tricks read like a manual to advanced mathematics, which is no coincidence, since music was linked to arithmetic, geometry, and astronomy in the quadrivium, one of the school curricula, all based in numbers. High-points in Josquin's use of numbers in this mass include stating the melody in augmented note-values against itself in original note-values; quoting the melody backwards; and writing a three-voice proportion canon, which involves starting all the voices together, all singing the main melody, but singing it at different speeds. This is surely the *pièce de résistance*, and it had an extra resonance for Josquin in that Ockeghem wrote a whole mass — his *Missa Prolationem* — on this extraordinary principle.

In the super-modern *Missa L'homme armé sexti toni*, Josquin did his best to include opposites. Where *Super voces musicales* quoted the famous melody unaltered for the most part in the same voice, in *Sexti toni* it is found broken into often unrecognizable fragments, dispersed among all four voices. Where *Super voces musicales* maintained a solid four-voice texture much of the time, *Sexti toni* is filled with duets, and its vocal texture kept light and informal through the use of sequences and imitation. Where *Super voces musicales* had canons which impress by their learning, *Sexti toni* has canons which give the impression of being easy-going, especially the one in the sublime six-voice *Agnus III*, which has proved to be the most talked-about movement in all these eighteen masses. *Sexti toni* is like a fantasia on the theme of the armed man; *Super voces musicales* more like a through-composed exercise on a theme given by a demanding tutor.

Another way that composers of a mathematical disposition could pay homage was to quote the name of the person to be praised in musical notation. This was done by reference to the *gematria*, whereby letters become numbers: A = 1, B = 2, and so on. In the more old-fashioned *Missa L'homme armé super voces musicales*, it seems as though Josquin was invoking the name of Ockeghem, which requires sixty-four notes to spell out in music. The potential for slippage in this system is obvious, providing happy hunting grounds for scholars today, but by extending the melody to sixty-four notes by virtue of a cadential flourish, Josquin does seem to have managed this virtuosic reference. Of course, the most direct way to fête someone was to name the composer in so many letters in the text, which was the standard method used in funeral laments, as we have seen. Less direct and least practiced was as an acrostic, where the naming could be concealed without disappearing into mathematical formulae. It was unusual for a composer to name himself in any of these methods, but Josquin managed it in the first part of the splendid motet *Illibata dei virgo*, to a text that he presumably wrote. To convey his message, he cleverly began each of the lines of the motet with one of the letters of his name, so that reading down it said IOSQVIN DES PREZ.

One final clue about Josquin's character is given in the main source for almost all of his masses — Petrucci's publications. Josquin seems to have enjoyed putting his singers on their mettle by writing clever riddles in Latin at the start of some of the movements, rather than writing out the whole part. It is not always clear where these remarks originated, since none of them has come down to us in Josquin's handwriting, but it seems unlikely that any scribe could have invented them unaided, and to do this at all was extremely unusual. On several occasions Petrucci quoted the riddle, but then decided to print the solution anyway, in case the singers could not work out what was meant (and he might not sell so many copies). An example of this comes in the *Credo* of the early *Missa Une mousse de Biscaye*, a movement in which the tenors only ever sing the melody taken from the model, in long notes. This was so straightforward that Josquin must have decided that there was no need to write this part out. But at one point in the score these tenors are required to sing the melody upside down (inversion being a standard compositional trick), about which they would have needed some warning. Rather than write out the whole tenor line of a substantial movement just for this subsection, Josquin wrote, in Latin: "Singer, if you wish to perform this well, do it inversely." Before publication Petrucci got cold feet and wrote out the whole part anyway, excusing himself with the words: "Singers that are not yet grown up should perform it as it stands here."

Perhaps Josquin was just being playful, in the first instance at other people's expense, though the cleverness could rebound on him when nobody was able to unravel what he meant. In Petrucci's print, all the early movements of the *Missa Di dadi,* the "Dice Mass," are preceded by images of dice. (Holy rollers, indeed.) These were designed to tell the tenors, whose part we imagine Josquin once again did not think it necessary to write out, the factor by which the note values of their part in the parody *chanson* should be multiplied in the mass. For example, the *Kyrie* is preceded by a pair of dice showing two and one, which tells the singers that the note-lengths in the *chanson* need to be doubled, in order to fit with Josquin's other three voice-parts. In the *Gloria* the dice read four and one requiring the notes of the *chanson* to be quadrupled in length. Before sections of the *Credo* the dice indicate six to one. In the *Sanctus* it is five to one. Unfortunately, although this works in the *Kyrie* and *Gloria*, it breaks down in the *Credo*; and in the *Sanctus* one finds that the initial five to one stipulation suggested by the dice does not work across all the notes of the original, only the longer ones, a major setback if not corrected. Petrucci, as ever disinclined to publish something that could not be sung, wrote out a resolution of all the tenor parts, thus rendering the dice redundant.

Yet even Petrucci could not save the riddle of the second *Agnus* in the *Missa Hercules dux Ferrariae* from centuries of confusion. Once again Josquin decided to take a short-cut, this time with a three-voice canon, and not write out all the parts, since all three would be singing the same melody, though not at the same time. Instead he wrote out the melody once with the three necessary clefs grouped together at the beginning on one stave, leaving the singers to sort out for themselves when to come in. True to form, Petrucci printed a resolution, but he got it wrong; and it was not until 1960 that the correct reading was worked out, Petrucci's version having been sung and recorded as the true score up to that time.

From the start of my interest in Renaissance polyphony many decades ago, I recognized that Josquin would be the toughest nut to crack. It wasn't just that he was not "sexy": neither was Palestrina, but for the opposite reason — he was too smooth, too predictable, too perfect. I could see that Josquin's secular music was likely to be the easiest way in, since in his *chansons* he was content to write melodies that were both beautiful and relatively easy to sing. His motets, by contrast, have long been thought the best of him, since in those he was free to choose his own texts — by the middle of his career no one could tell him otherwise, so unlike the fate of Heinrich Isaac — and he reacted with unfailing imagination to resonant words. The opening of *Praeter rerum seriem* is one such example. The opening words mean: "Beyond the normal course of events, a virgin mother gives birth to God as man." They cannot be word-painted, so instead Josquin creates an atmosphere.

Yet I prefer abstraction — something, after all, in which every true Flemish composer of that period was adept. Their training was in the God-defining power of numbers in harmony, with little understanding as yet of "romantic" word-setting: if the power of the words was to be expressed outside mathematical formulae, it was to be done through atmosphere. Knowing how delicate Josquin could be in his *chansons* and his motets, it was the more rugged exterior of the masses that attracted me. Maybe inside a tough shell we would find a new kind of beauty. Maybe, despite everything, the magically controlled atmosphere I am always seeking in polyphony was going to be found most tellingly in these eighteen mass settings — a set in Josquin's mind, in that they provided a canvas for variations on a theme. To underline this unity in diversity, he decided to keep to four voices more or less throughout the set, which was not what he chose to do invariably in any other form, sacred or secular, preferring five and six.

On top of this I realized that Josquin had striven to create individual sound-worlds in all these settings: the tools were the same — same texts, same four voices — but they were all different in effect, and I wanted to put my finger on those differences. The comparison with Beethoven and his symphonies — same basic outline of movements, same basic scoring, but separate sound-worlds in every case — acquired a new relevance. This wondrous ability to conjure up different atmospheres with the same resources put them both in a very special category of composer, at the opposite end of the spectrum from composers who found their sound early and then spent their careers moving into it, such as Mozart on the one hand and Palestrina on the other.

If you add to all this the fact that Josquin's experiments are almost without exception difficult for modern singers to sing, you come to understand why Josquin is so little known now. Everything I have described about his music pushes him away from an easy modern acceptance. We cannot hear the mathematics play out in the music without a guide and a score, and sometimes not even then, nor does the average singer today relish parts that can span over two octaves — they are not trained to do it. (The two-octave tenor part in *L'homme armé super voces musicales* was reckoned by Petrucci to be such a stretch that he gave it three different clefs in the course of his edition, one clef normally being enough.) The modern choral voice-ranges of soprano, alto, tenor and bass had not formed fully by Josquin's time: all his masses are essentially scored for low soprano/alto, higher tenor, lower tenor, and baritone. This cluster of all the voices around and below middle C is not normal for choirs today, since it excludes at least half their members and requires an abundance of tenors, always the part shortest on talent.

In the end, finding those different sound-worlds in performance was not as difficult as it might seem, since, as musicians like to put it, it's all in the dots. Once we mastered the idea that singers in Josquin's time would have been performing in small chapels (not usually great cathedrals for polyphony), and would have had no notion of the kind of voice-production required by opera, we could relax with those unwelcome high and low notes all in the same part, singing gently as if to ourselves. True, the modern symphony hall does not always allow such subtlety of delivery — we have to project the difficult notes as well as the easy ones there as elsewhere, mic-less; but we found with practice that we could still adopt the principles of small-room delivery even in great halls. If we sang with a good blend and good tuning, the sound that we made travelled naturally without distortion. And then we were free to relish Josquin's genius, his tricks and his sonorities, the eighteen different ways he approached the *Benedictus*, or the *Osanna*, or the *Et incarnatus est*.

It is significant that Josquin probably stopped writing mass settings in the last period of his life. He never set out to chart the development of his own style through these settings. He simply used them to shoot off in random directions as the whim took him through many decades, as Bartok did with the string quartet. This makes it difficult to put a chronology on them. The *Missa Pange lingua* seems "mature" and the *Missa Une mousse de Biscaye* seems "youthful," but even if that is right, there is a great deal in between. Over the years of studying and performing his music, I came to derive a particular pleasure from how he began to obsess over one note in a span of music. The best example of this is in the last passage of the *Credo* in the *Missa Faysant regretz,* where he worries beyond reason the note D. It makes for the most thrilling music to come from that period.

And yet there is nothing academic or pedantic or snobbish about Josquin's extraordinary complications. It is true that he liked teasing, obfuscating, and putting up barriers; and the graceful side of his difficult personality has to be searched for. But nowhere is he as austere as, say, Bach in *The Art of the Fugue.* Josquin's maddening complexity issues in ravishing beauty. The arcanely inspired sounds are completely seductive. What the ear hears surpasses what the mind knows.

Rosalind

Back when I was a man pretending to be a woman
pretending to be a man
I found myself able to summon

a range of emotions that ran
the gamut from common to not-so-common.
The checkout person at H Mart trying to scan

my fish sauce puts me in mind of a Roman
housewife trying to coax an eel into a copper pan.
The lamb with cumin

hails from Afghanistan.
"*Nomen est omen*," said Plautus. "*Nomen est omen*."
Plautus itself means "plodder" or "Kick the Can

Down the Road." Such was the acumen
of the 9th Legion they devised a plan
to introduce a diet of offal boiled in a sheep's rumen

to the already sluggardly Picts. In 82 AD the lifespan
of a sheep was almost as long as that of a human.
Things were rarely simpler, though, than

back when I was a man pretending to be a woman
pretending to be a man
who now found himself pretending to be a woman.

Chipmunk

Ain't that God's own truth?
Just one more flame-streaked roadster
fresh from the spray-booth.

Viral

1

Any one of these masked avengers
might be moonlighting as another Captain Rock,
might set out not only to censure
but incinerate a rich farmer dreading his knock

at midnight, a cowpuncher, a calf-drencher,
a dweeb journalist, a helmetless jock
courting death by misadventure,
a negotiator trying to break the deadlock

between boss and union, a prominent backbencher
imagining he's standing for re-election
when he's making a speech from the dock,

a career civil servant both inured and indentured
to a twice daily intravenous injection
of horse piss and poppycock.

2

Any one of them might be an insurance underwriter
taking the tube from Maida Vale,
an architect pulling an all-nighter
while she works to scale,

a private investigator flicking a cigarette lighter
and putting another nail
in his coffin, a developer of an antibody titer,
a Muddy Waters failing to curtail

a Lightnin' Hopkins, a bishop adjusting his mitre,
a baker proffering a baker's dozen
of cakes and ale,

a professional flautist, an amateur fire-fighter,
a migrant worker who met your forty-second cousin
at the blading of the kale.

3
Any one of these masked avengers
might be moonlighting as Atticus Finch,
might be reliant on the kindness of strangers,
a blue man of the Minch

crossed with a ginger, a money exchanger
feeling the pinch,
a lumberjack, a barista, a Texas Ranger
tightening the cinch

on any one of these masked avengers
moonlighting as a butterfly nun, a lab technician,
a boxer prolonging a clinch

rather than putting themself in danger,
a restorer of Tintoretto or Titian
taking on the world square inch by square inch.

A Bull

Every day putting a fresh spin
on how he maintains that shit-eating grin
despite his notoriously thin skin.
The quagmire of what-might-have-been.

Every day shouldering an invisible tray.
Hello, hello. Olé, Olé.
His musing on how best to waylay
a hiker passing through a field of Galloways.

Every day aiming to swat
the single fly that keeps tying and untying a knot
before taking another potshot.
Rolling through the Krishna Valley like a juggernaut.

Every day trying to err
on the side of standing firm. Foursquare.
The singlemindedness of a Berber
about to take out a French Legionnaire.

Every day surviving by dint
of three of his four hooves being knapped flint.
Hanging out the bloody bandage of his, hint hint,
barber's pole. His stick of peppermint.

Every day his hoofprints in the sand-strewn park
have enclosed so much in quotation marks.
Not even Job or Abraham, hark hark,
is a patch on our patriarch.

Every day the holy show
of leather dyed robin egg blue by Tiffany & Co.
Areas strictly off-limits? Strictly no-go?
The wilds of Connaught. The stockyards of Chicago.

Every day rising at 5 am,
determined to stem
the flow of misinformation from the well at Zem-Zem.
His dangle-straw from a crib in Bethlehem.

Every day fighting shy
of the possibility his eye
is a shellac-gouge from an old hi-fi.
His helmet appropriated from a samurai.

Every day the mob
threatening a hatchet job.
Their hobbling across concrete. Hobnob. Hobnob.
Their sidelong glances at his thingmabob.

Every day the urge to rut
at odds with his yen for whole grain calf nuts.
The "my-my" and "tut-tut"
of that bevy of cattle at their scuttlebutt.

Every day his own cow's lick
even more at odds with his almighty mick.
How come his second cousin, the dik-dik,
gets to trip the light fantastic?

Every day taking a bow
before settling back to plow
the rowdy-dow-dow
of a Filipino swamp-buffalo, or carabao.

Every day plotting how to get even even with the get
who's trolling him on the internet.
Under the vapor trails of the jet set
the solidity of his silhouette.

Every day his image picked out in tin
to signify there being room at the Inn.
Bottoms up. Chin-chin.
The gulping of milk punch from a pannikin.

Every day cruising the main drag
in anticipation of raising his own red flag
to the plaza's rag-tag
bunch of scamps and scallywags.

Every day forced to cram
for some big exam.
The difference between *quondam* and *quamdam*.
The origins of the dithyramb.

Every day a razor. Every night a strop.
Rush tickets for *Carmen* at the Met cost $25 a pop.
Get a move on, would you? Chop chop.
A world in which so much "art" is agitprop.

Every day taking a hit
from some little shit
armed with the latest version of lit crit.
The fly still looping the loop in his Messerschmidt.

Every day, it would seem, rekindling a flame
against the culture of shame
and its interminable blame game.
Every day countering a counterclaim.

Every day forced to pit
himself against Holy Writ
and the nitwit
for whom the Lascaux paintings are counterfeit.

Every day having to whisk
away the versifiers averse to risk.
The ignominy of being supplanted, tsk tsk,
by a ram on an Egyptian obelisk.

Every day lying down with the lamb.
What-might-have-been? More water over the dam.
Having to meet the future head-on. Wham-bam.
His muzzle a spermicide-slick diaphragm.

Every day the thrill
of balancing a natural proclivity and an acquired skill
after a walk-on part in *Cattle Drive* with Chill Wills.
His tongue turquoise-teal from chlorophyll.

Every day learning not to pin
his hopes on there being grain in the bin.
The situation supposedly win-win
when he mounts an upholstered Holstein mannikin.

Every day the likelihood of a snub
from a warble grub
even as he rises above the hubbub.
Every day the flash-freezing of his syllabub.

Every day busting sod
whilst straddling a divining rod.
His permanent disdain for the god squad
by whom he was once overawed.

Every day contending with the holier than thou
attitude associated with the sacred cow,
"kowtow" and "powwow"
being terms he's now obliged to disavow.

Every day cutting some slack
to the youths leaping over his back
in Knossos. His dream of trading endless ack-ack
for a week on the Concord and Merrimack.

Every day starting to dig
with his one obsidian hoof through the rigs.
A lily-pad where a bigwig
flies in and out in some sort of whirligig.

Every day muddling through
thanks to his tried and true
ability to rise above the general to-do
by thinking of it all as déjà-vu.

Every day chewing gum
like a Teddy Boy in a bombed-out slum.
As for his success in rising above the humdrum?
For a moment only. Only a modicum.

Every day striking a blow
against a more-or-less invisible foe.
A life lived in slo-mo
ever since a chute opened at the rodeo.

Every day creating a stink
against being pushed to the brink
by the powers that be (nod nod, wink wink)
with their newspeak and doublethink.

Every day those massive chords on the synth
as he's rabble-roused from his plinth.
His taking everything to the nth
degree despite being consigned to a labyrinth.

Every livelong
day making of his hide a parish-encircling thong.
His panko-encrusted balls a delicacy in Hong Kong.
Subsisting on a diet of mashed kurrajong.

Every day waiting for someone to deign
to give him free rein.
That shit-eating grin. How it's maintained?
Running rings around a mill that crushes sugarcane.

Every day trying to weigh
in the scales those who still flay
the burnt offering and those who naysay
such exaltation of the everyday.

Every day making a dry run
for either his moment in the sun
or an air-injection captive bolt stun gun.
The china shop of his skeleton.

DAVID THOMSON

Stealing Kisses

There was a pounding in my dream. Could it be the surging chant of the Crystals' killer line, *"And then he kissed me"*? It seemed to me I was about to have the wild gaze and wilder hair of Natalie Wood or Harpo Marx descend on me. But as I awoke I realized that the eager head was Lassie come home.

Kissing can be pretty nice, you used to hear. Between the ages of ten and thirteen, in the dark, kiss-kiss scenes went from being squirm-making to *I can't get enough of this*. There were teenagers in the back row at the Regal and the Astoria who seemed to be going further still. What a time!

Where has that habit gone? Was it waning at the movies

well before Covid? Had "sincere" love stories turned comical, shoved aside by deadpan ironies for kids to sneer at? There was a time when filmgoers wept over love stories. Past the age of fifty, you may recall the collisional rapture of two faces and the overflow of mouths. Did waves peak in oral caves? Tongues winding in the dark. The binge streaming with saliva. Are you beginning to be thrilled or nostalgic in our protocols of distancing? Or does such sensual language feel awkward now? Foreplay rhapsodies from 1959 are generally as dead as *On the Beach or Ben-Hur*. In that same year, *Some Like it Hot* served up sex as a buffet of custard and blancmange, but the sweets tasted sour to warn us that the old association with love was demented. Hot could be very cold.

Still, I love the metamorphosis from Harpo to Lassie, and every station on that line. Even if we've forgotten the other creature's name, we only have to close our eyes and inhale to regain the hesitation and its wondering — will the other mouth be open to us? Real kisses depend on risk.

So here's a cue. I won't tell you yet where it comes from, except to say it seems more or less modern, though that could tell you how old-fashioned I am: "The voice fell low, sank into her breast and stretched the tight bodice over her heart as she came up close. He felt the young lips, her body sighing in relief against the arm growing stronger to hold her. There were now no more plans than if [X] had arbitrarily made some indissoluble mixture, with atoms joined and inseparable; you could throw it all out but never again could they fit back into atomic scale. As he held her and tasted her, and as she curved in further and further toward him, with her own lips, new to herself, drowned and engulfed in love, yet solaced and triumphant, he was thankful to have an existence at all, if only as a reflection in her wet eyes. 'My God,' he gasped, 'you're fun to kiss.'"

Are you having fun, or imagining it? As I re-read this book during the pandemic time, I felt not just the fun but also the falling. Isn't this [X] slipping into love, or into his adolescent scheme of that condition? And I felt yes, that's what it can be like, even if the scene is confined to his point of view. He decides; he makes the move; he tastes her. She is there, no doubt: she curves in towards him; she has and uses her own lips. It's possible that she detects "fun," too, but we don't quite know that as we brim with his feelings.

I'm not yet saying where the passage comes from. But I feel its behavioral accuracy. Then as I read it over more slowly, I am unsure whether it deserves to be regarded as Serious Literature or romantic pot-boiler. In the age of movie, so many novels turned randy. A bodice is mentioned, and though it isn't ripped you can feel it yielding. Or does that depend on the reader being male, or as "turned on" as I suspect the author was while writing it?

The passage comes from a novel, and it does reproduce the awe and the urgency of a man in that situation. But it reminds me of how the movies used to do such scenes. The man is there, aroused , though literary propriety does not allow him a physical tumescence or require that he start to undress her and get to the matter of what was called "sex" for so long. Is he watching himself doing it, as in a movie? Had that cultural weight gathered by the time the passage was written? Maybe today she would undress him, a decisiveness that would once have been as shocking as nakedness on screen.

You see, there was a time when going to the pictures was finding an impossible window to gaze on provocative strangers or other available views that you might be granted. You would stand before a prairie that could be your ranch, or a suave bedroom for amorous splendor; you might buzz a

299

frisky auto down the highway, or land a single-engine aircraft on a rocky south American plateau. Or you might shift forward, more from desire's magnetism than real motion, and collapse into the arms of Alain Delon or Doris Day. It cost a quarter to behold Colbert or Lombard in and out of Travis Banton gowns on Park Avenue. The cusp between absurd luxury and common poverty was as taunting as the one between your plain-faced envy and the sated narcissism of a movie star. The medium sighed, all the time: *"Don't you want us?"* Can you believe how that innocent longing subdued Depression or war?

The continent of old movies shines with all its absurd hopes. Isn't that the special thing with humans – it can work with love and death – that wondering means the most? And so we swim against the current that says you could have him or her, or both of them, or you might die tonight.

I am looking out on the historic sea of movies, doing my best to be a visionary or a helmsman. At the end of last summer, there were urgings to believe that Christopher Nolan's *Tenet* was the film event that would rescue theatrical cinema, a spectacle to draw millions of us back into the dark, no matter that it might be infectious still. In that spirit I wondered about *Tenet*, the film on which Nolan was able to spend some $200 million, with a palindromic title for a world in which our disasters could shrink back to zero. It had a romance arrangement that was only schematic, in which the technology of reversing time was a truer object of lust than the adjacency of John David Washington and Elizabeth Debicki. What turned Nolan on were the special effects, the culture that has eclipsed the chance of humans being specially affected. This was so unpromising I started imagining another movie to rival it.

Mine is called *Kiss Me* .... (The ellipsis is crucial; it gets at the precious hesitation in the act and its air of danger.) I need to admit at the outset that my project is not just risky, or insane; it may even be deemed anti-social, unwholesome, incorrect, and fit to be banned. Are you alarmed, or are we always eager to be stirred up by the prospect of a movie that could be kept away from us? Censorship and denunciation are the Santa Ana winds on the embers of desire.

My starting point is simply that this has been a time of not touching, not kissing. Millions of us have felt constrained: we are cautious about kissing grandchildren, let alone yielding to the passing possibility of a stranger. Please don't be horrified at this risky opportunism — but don't rule out the chance that in your happy marriage or your settled relationship, you *might* be open to the moment of kissing that stranger, or better, being kissed by him or her, that one, coming down the stairs, or squeezing past in the corridor. I know, you shouldn't do this illicit thing, but surely that doesn't mean you stop thinking about it in the stairwell or the corridor. The cinema was always constructed as an uneasy place of delicious wondering. Even in the forbidden summer of covid, it has occurred to some of us to approach that person in the corridor and hazard a kiss. Of course, this would be horrendously perilous and irresponsible — but those are brinks where we have always waited.

So in my *Kiss Me* ... I propose a series of brief meetings, with a glance and maybe a few words, and the dark promise of a first kiss. With this extra: there is a CUT before any kiss can be consummated. And the frustrated faces are the treasury of actors who have done kissing scenes in the last hundred years. You want examples? Think of Rudolph Valentino putting his arm and uneasy authority around Angie Dickinson; or Louise Brooks prepared to lure George Clooney out of a snooze with a cool-hand gotcha; or Jeanne Moreau getting into Nabokovian chat with Cary Grant, as they offer each other the wary eyes they always kept as they contemplated doing it; or Katharine Hepburn ready to grab Lupita Nyong'o; or the Julia Roberts from *Pretty Woman* frolicking in a Beverly Wilshire tub with the monster from *Alien*; or that youthful Julia (Miss Vivian, the hooker magicked into a social princess) being aroused by the more celebrated Julia from *Notting Hill*. For far too long in the thundery build-up of narcissism we have swallowed the nonsense that stars cannot play with themselves. They *only* reflect on themselves. (Nicole Kidman wooing her mirror could be a blockbuster.)

Please don't turn naïve on me. Don't widen your eyes and ask, *For heaven's sake, how can we or they do this?* They can do anything they can imagine. Cinema is the playground of fantasists ready to give up the ghost of fact. In our lifetime, photographic naturalism (think of it as fidelity) has been swept aside by the seething promiscuity of technological command, so that imagery of Gary Cooper in *Desire* in 1936 could be put side-by-side, arm in arm, or mouth to mouth, with the Kristen Stewart in *Personal Shopper* in 2016. Do you want to see that?

Please don't act confounded. This is no more than the fulfilment of the infinite library of the plain, charmingly humble screen that has been prepared to whore away, night after night, with any and every fresh movie you put up on the whiteness.

I plan to let my *Kiss Me …* run several hours, enough for a bingeable evening, and since you're in the habit of four hours a night now you have no pretext for dismay or inconvenience. What do you have left now but wondering in the all night long?

I foresee a montage rhythm, with scene after scene, stars lined up for their close-up and the moment (as if it was a vaccine), always leading to the CUT that leaves us sighing, *oh this time, please, let those mouths mingle.* There will be no story, just the motif of people attempting to be expressed, to be riding on desire into love – to put their lips together and blow. The audience can come and go in their home theater. If you miss something — if a friend says you really had to see James Dean with Garbo, together yet in rivalry over being alone — well, you can go to rewind if you want, or just add one more legendary extra to the anthology of every screen coupling in one hundred and twenty five years of movies. The medium may have kissed more people than it killed. And perhaps you will fall in love with desire again, which seems to me the pressing hope that *Tenet* ignored.

You deserve a pause, and a clue. That passage that I offered above was published in 1934, though its kiss had occurred over ten years earlier — at night, in the mountains. Put aside the generosity of this clue (and the fits of frustration it may stimulate — desire needs denial as Dracula thirsts for blood). I want to suggest that the dating of this incident in 1934 is instructive. It's not that kissing hadn't been going on a while, but its special dreamy currency had been freed by movies. Suppose that in the mid 1930s a new chance at middle-class love bloomed in the smoky light of cinemas.

Imagine a great swell of newcomers: essentially poor people but educated to read and to question old norms, able to believe there might be fresh ways of running society so that nobodies could be in love. This was the enormous increase in

303

population after about 1850, the one that has never stopped; and these are the people who recognized the photograph and the movies as a breathtaking horizon of desire. It could be Lauren Bacall urging Bogart that kissing is better when the other person helps: 19 telling 45 that she'll do anything. Her insolent talk ushered in fantasy gratification, so it might be hard for real companions to stay kissed for decades in the habit known as fidelity. We were kissing strangers and we have never given up on that gamble.

You will not find reliable social statistics on this collective promiscuity, but dreams thrive without stats. It may seem innocent to a point of infancy now, but consider how far in the first age of cinema the technology of voyeurism colluded with fantasy situations not just to educate us in how to kiss (no minor thing) but in grasping how the initiation could be a prelude to happiness.

In the blink of an "open sesame" millions of people learned to behold glamorous strangers possessed by a new code of "beauty" or attraction, and to explore the vicarious state of romance. These screened figures could not take off all their clothes. They could not do "it," whatever it was; and we need to be respectful of the uncertainty in the early years of movie about how "it" worked. But the restrained, illicit privilege of cinema encouraged the voyeuristic imagination. And it established that this vector was not only a Peeping Tom but a Madeleine (or a Judy) holding her breath to see how far sympathy would go.

The rapture was there in silent pictures, but its fullest commitment came with sound. Albeit in a hush or a suspension, kissing registers aurally. You can film and record a kiss so that the couple feels removed from our observation. But you can also do it as if from inside the mouth, in a way that allows for breathing, a few swallows, and the undertone of digestion. Tongues need not speak, but they can be as muscular as the shark in *Jaws*.

It is possible to track this progress, from Garbo and John Gilbert, all the way to Jimmy Stewart and Margaret Sullavan or Astaire and Rogers — Fred could kiss the woman with the merest touch. Still, kissing was regarded as a liberty requiring Hays Code rules: not prolonged, not too searching, not too abandoned or exultant. Do you recall — can you forget — Jean Arthur and Joel McCrea on the stoop in *The More the Merrier*? Until, in *Notorious* in 1946, Hitchcock had Cary Grant and Ingrid Bergman act like real people — like themselves even — as lovers who find a secret place and just kiss and smooch for hours on end, chatting sometimes to draw breath, and knowing that the talk is as carnal as the tongues. And Hitchcock taught us to watch — not simply where to look, but how to grasp human nature by spying.

So there was an age — not long, but profound — in which spectators came to feel the possibility of love and the beckoning of an abandon that could not be seen because of censorship. That impediment was vital to the arousal. Thus one could be transported by the way Montgomery Clift and Elizabeth Taylor kissed in *A Place in the Sun* (1951), while knowing the lovely restriction that their embracing could not escape the screen — so he was going to be executed for dispatching or contemplating the murder of an inconvenient prior girlfriend (the whiny Shelley Winters).

The best love stories in those days did not guarantee a happy ending. Desire was a streetcar that hurried past and gave us the anguish of feeling left behind. In *From Here to Eternity* (1953), Clift nuzzled Donna Reed (a whore out of the *Ladies Home Journal*) and glimpsed the possibility of peace and bliss instead of being bullied by the Army. In the same film, Burt Lancaster and Deborah Kerr rolled in the surf on a beach in Hawaii, and we agreed that it was the sexiest scene the cinema had ever permitted itself. "Nobody ever kissed me the way you do," she told him. (I had to pretend to be fourteen to get in.)

Those two romances would be cut off by the storylines, allowing Kerr and Reed to meet on the ship taking them back to the states in a wistful realization that their men had been pals. Both screen women were more ladylike than James Jones had intended in his novel. But the romance was set for eternity, forever out of reach.

In the 1950s — a heyday of screen desire — you could feel the pressure building for these beautiful people to do the lovely thing (and the confidence that it was lovely, instead of physiological and elemental). If you were a teenager then, you were so lucky to be alive in the dark. But maybe you were doomed too, imprisoned in the medium of arousal, the cult of desire.

I'm speaking for myself, and my gender choice, and in those 1950s the diagrammatic set-up for screen desire was very restrictive. Cinema was a show for guys — no matter that Clift for one was uncertain about his own sexual status. So I was vulnerable to the few occasions on which I got to kiss someone intensely and one thing led to another. It is hard to claw your way back from desire's brink to what might be normal life. Indeed, it was a key strategy of the movies — and the doom of the culture that made — that normalcy was left seeming drab or unworthy.

The name blanked out in the test quotation above, the [X], is Dick, or Dick Diver, the central character in Scott Fitzgerald's novel *Tender is the Night*. Dick has been in American uniform during the war and then he is a charming psychiatrist, living and working in Europe. The Swiss clinic to which he is attached has a needy patient, Nicole Warren, who was raped by her father. She is sixteen now, and she has noticed Dick and his spiffy uniform. She writes notes to him, half-flirtatious, half-cold and, always childlike. But Fitzgerald makes clear what Dick can hardly admit or forget, that she is very beautiful and sufficiently rich.

Tender Is the Night moves me more than *The Great Gatsby*, even if both dwell on disasters that can attend desire. Even so, *Tender Is the Night* is untidy, not least in the way Nicole is both a presence and an absence. The narrative cannot take its eyes off her, but we never know what she feels or how disturbed she is. She is infatuated with the brilliant young doctor and wants to keep him in attendance. Perhaps she is replacing her father? But we never touch on what that rape did to her, beyond learning that from time to time she cracks up and is the center of "scenes" in bathrooms, fragments of distress heard and seen by alarmed bystanders.

Does Nicole like to be kissed? Is she "turned on"? Do she and Diver have sex there in the Swiss night on the cold grass? Fitzgerald could no more get to that level than Howard Hawks would shoot Bogart and Bacall naked together in bed (though the public was surely thrilled that after *To Have and Have Not* the two became lovers, as if to prove that movie fantasy worked). So we are left uncertain whether Nicole becomes addicted to an older lover who has the veneer of a magic that may care for her disturbed mind, or is simply a rich and spoiled young woman who will engineer the course of tragic events through the blunt agency of her money.

Stealing Kisses

Dick and Nicole marry. This is an inappropriate arrangement misunderstood by onlookers. Dick's professional partner sees that Nicole's money could fund a clinic. Nicole's older sister, "Baby," disapproves, but she decides to bet on the professional proximity of Dick caring for the unpredictable Nicole. The couple have two children, but the "fun to kiss" passage is their climax of desire, and it is over as soon as it has begun.

The moral complacency of Dr. Diver is underlined (rather too forcefully) when, once married, Dick falls in love with a teenage screen actress named Rosemary Hoyt and does eventually have sex with her (described very vaguely, as if Fitzgerald was unsure what happened in such transactions or was shy of spelling it out in a Scribner's novel that might be a big seller). But Rosemary's screen hit is a romance, a silent film called *Daddy's Girl*. There are times when you hardly know whether Fitzgerald is witty and allusive or just lost in the dark.

The Divers have a heady season on the Riviera, making a beach fashionable and focusing an indulgent American tourism that came to be branded as "the lost generation." Dick loses himself in kissing and a party-going lifestyle. But he is on the slide from the start, less a skilled surfer than a man who will drown one day. He dazzles onlookers, but nothing conceals his weakness. When Fitzgerald published the novel, he began it with the Riviera glory and then flashed back several years to the seduction of Nicole. But after the book had disappointed readers, he wondered whether he should have started with the seduction, to clarify the moral compromise. After Fitzgerald's death, the critic Malcolm Cowley supervised a re-arranged structure, stronger and more tragic, so the book is now available in both versions, letting us assess its composition. The charm that Fitzgerald managed so easily has given way to autopsy.

Dick turns alcoholic, prematurely middle-aged, and a liability as a clinician. With the effortless calm of even the wounded rich, Nicole discards him for a stupid but handsome second husband. Dr. Diver goes away; he is last heard of in upstate New Yok, clinging to sparse professional assignments and the women in the vicinity. The book still needs a lot of work, and a better and non-Keatsian title, but *Tender is the Night* is unforgiving on the damage done by a reckless kiss in the era when movies were a slick treatment for just about everyone.

We could guess what was coming by 1960. In *Psycho*, Hitchcock cut Janet Leigh to ribbons when he was not permitted to undress her fully. The sexual revolution had ways of uncovering intimate violence at the movies. In the next decade censorship broke down in landmark works such as *Blow Up, Belle de Jour, Point Blank, Carnal Knowledge, Last Tango in Paris.* An edge of hostility underlay the sexual breakthrough. But even the novelty and the naughtiness of those films was incidental if you could see that a tsunami was coming: *it,* the thing itself, the simulated outrage of pornography, where men and women become slave bodies through the sacrifice of talk, character, and narrative purpose. The cat was out of the bag: the cinema had invited the bourgeoisie to fuck as if it were a new right, free from the encumbrance of love. That required taut bodies, gymnastic agility, and bereft conscience, with the deadpan confidence that emotionally nothing mattered. Fantasists have escaped responsibility. And so it is that our movies these days seldom bother with luxuriant kisses and have given up on poetic desire.

There was another consequence to all the liberated rutting: that movie romance is no more. (The stale and silly "rom com" formula, from which desire has been almost completely banished, is evidence of the decline.) And the demise of romance could mean the demise of cinema itself.

We are left stranded, uncertain what healthy bodies and reckless minds are going to do with family, faith, and aging once the first kiss has taken up residence in our lonely mind — the prison of desire.

CELESTE MARCUS

The Pluralist Heart

"Purity of heart is to will one thing," Kierkegaard famously proclaimed. He was right about purity but wrong to aspire to it. It is a common mistake, made all the more familiar to ordinary people because it is a quality that heroes and fanatics, the characters who spice religious liturgies, history books, novels, poetry, and Netflix often have in common. Even Dante, no stranger to the complications of life and character, endorses it: "One object, and one object only, is rightly to be loved 'with all my mind, with all my soul, and with all my strength.'" Purity is simplifying, and it is romantic, and in an existence as relentlessly variegated as ours it promises a great relief.

And so it is tempting to structure one's life around a single, dominating idea or community, to be fanatically, singularly loyal. But like some of the most irresistible temptations, this one is false. Life will never be simple and people will never be pure. Perhaps it is our very impurity that engenders the myth that purity is a human achievement, the solution to the problem of the difficulty and drabness that are regular features of living. But what if purity, were it even attainable, were instead a human failing? What if diversity, of kinds and of qualities, is an unalterable and enriching characteristic of individual and communal experience? It seems almost platitudinous to point out that the individual lives in many realms and has many loyalties. In a single day she may in one realm be a hero, in another a loser, and often just another body standing in line.

Our various realms are the settings for the various roles we all play. An individual engages different parts of herself in a museum than in a place of worship, and with her friends than with her family, and with her mother than with her husband. Her priorities, the pattern of her attention, even her tone alters depending on which of her contexts she inhabits at a given moment. She is not faking it, she is still herself, but herself is many things. These shifts and developments are not deceitful; complexity is not synonymous with promiscuity. People cannot live fully in any other way, and we are right to seek fullness.

It is in some ways much easier to adopt the Kierkegaardian ideal and devote oneself entirely to a single loyalty. It is easier, but it is not consistent with the mess of human life, which is why such an exclusive commitment breeds dissatisfaction with reality. In extreme cases, for those inclined towards melodrama, the undivided path can become a search for martyrdom. In such cases, the sort that Marianne naively romanticizes in *Sense and Sensibility*, one sacrifices oneself to a love that was never compatible with reality. These loves are not sublime, they are absurd. And while this sort of sacrifice certainly requires courage, so can folly. It is entirely distinct from the heroism of sacrificing one's life for others, for the sake of life, which is the heroism that we rightly admire.

Contrast that type of heroism with Antigone's sacrifice. Against the order of the king and on penalty of death, Antigone buried her brother's corpse so that it would not rot above ground. Upon a first reading of Sophocles' play, she is strikingly noble. Ismene, her sister, acknowledges the integrity of Antigone's devotion, even while Ismene accuses her of being "in love with impossibility" or, as we might say, out of touch with reality. Indeed, Antigone admits outright that she was able to face certain death in service to her brother's memory only because she had no interest in staying alive. "For death is gain to him whose life, like mine, is full of misery." If she had some reason to keep living, she would not have been able to do what she did. Suicide is not a sacrifice for someone who wants to die. Antigone's single-mindedness proved fatal. To appropriate a contemporary platitude, she chose only one lane, and it led to her destruction.

Madame de Stael's intoxicating heroine Corinne suffered from a related contempt for real life. She whipped herself into a long and fatal frenzy in service to a love she knew could never be realized. A perpetual state of excitation was the only kind of loyalty of which she was capable; she could nurture only a single love, and so consumingly that it would kill her. Corinne's intensity, not her love, demanded the highest sacrifice. It was a product of her temperament, and not based on the object of her love, on her lover's qualities. The heat all

The Pluralist Heart

came from her. Reality bored her. She wanted it to be more, or grander, than it was; she could not tolerate the inanities of ordinary existence. "I had learned about life by reading the poets." she confesses. "It is not like that. There is something barren about reality that it is useless to try to change." And so she chose to defy it.

Both these women could not sustain a loyalty tested by commonplace experience. It was not that their hearts were too strong for the quotidian. They were, more accurately, too weak for it. A single, overwhelming love premised upon perpetual excitement is feeble, not powerful. Corrine and Antigone suffered from the same weakness, and it manifested for both in a similar monomania. For both of them, the simplification of self, its attempted transformation into a single thing, was poisonous. One-lane roads are the most dangerous ones.

But it is also quite possible to love many loves poorly, and to dramatize all of them the same way that Corinne dramatized hers. Dissolve to Russia. Anna Karenina loved many people and idealized all of them. And despite nurturing multiple obsessions for different people, she was still dominated by a single loyalty: to her own feverish intensity. Actual human life was not enough, and it was too much, for her. Tolstoy's omniscient narrator knows everything about Anna in each sentence describing her, but he knows only the Anna of the sentence, of the moment, who may not be the Anna who appears a few paragraphs later. Her intensity manifests in part in mutability, in rapid reinvention. She changes constantly and emphatically, in a saga of serial self-simplifications. If she stayed for too long in one place, she would be forced to reckon with the underwhelming horizons of human life. This makes commitment quite complicated for her. When she assures her son that she loves him "best in the world," she believes it as much as he does. ("I know that," Seryozha replied.) Later we discover with mild disgust that Anna's image of Seryozha is dearer to her than the child in front of her: "The son, just like the husband, produced in Anna a feeling akin to disappointment. She had imagined him better than he was in reality. She had to descend to reality to enjoy him as he was." As she is thrust from the orbit of one love to another, Anna's center shifts and with it her heart. When she pledges her loyalty, when she tells them she loves them, her lovers are not wrong to believe her. Anna's sincerity was not false, and there is nothing wrong with shifting centers. Her error was not that she loved many simultaneously, but that she preferred her idea of each one to the flesh-and-blood version. The fantastic intensity of her focus, its magic-making power, was possible for her because it was stimulated by attention that was never submitted to the test of time. Anna, like Corrine, preferred poetry to prose.

Anna's heart, you might say, was a serial monist. To find a way to escape the drudgeries of human life, she sought single intoxicants, one love and loyalty after another. The consequence of her desperate need to idealize was to shrink herself, to lose her sense of reality by photoshopping it, and stripping it of everything unattractive.

She believed that true loyalty must be blind, when the opposite is the case. Every person — and every country and every culture and every religion, for that matter — worth loving is sometimes pathetic, ugly, mean, stupid, and dull. The highest love is love that is not dispelled by lucidity or by criticism. It is the love of an individual capable of evaluating herself and her contexts with some degree of objectivity. Such an individual will not be simplified by love, or worship an "all-consuming" passion. She does not want "all" consumed. She

315

will recognize that she is many things, admirable and not, and so is her lover; and so is her group and her style of life. Inferring from the fact that her own contexts and communities contain both strengths and weaknesses, she will conclude that others too contain strengths and weaknesses. She will discover — not unhappily — that she, and life, is plural. And this recognition of the mottled richness of reality, this plurality of values and moods and experiences and origins, this multiplicity of temperaments and cultures, will make her curious and adventurous. She may begin to wonder about existences and communities unlike her own, and she may decide to study them, and even to join them. She will cross boundaries. She will strengthen herself inwardly by moving outward.

There are philosophers who argued vehemently against the possibility of this sort of migration. Herder declared that "each nationality contains its center of happiness within itself." He believed that to become a person in full, to develop completely, one must be firmly rooted within a particular group which will equip its members with a distinct language, worldview, culture, and history. Once incubated within this culture, it is impossible to uproot and pick a different one. Herder emphasized that every aspect of life is tinctured by one's origins. Thought itself is a product of where one comes from, and ideas grow like cacti in the desert, into and a part of their landscape. This is because language, which he called "the organ of thought," is developed by nations. A people, with all its predilections, inclinations, and prejudices, made it.

Herder did not regard these particularities as parochial or stifling. Or rather, he regarded all of them as parochial and none of them as stifling. Parochialism is not a curse for this kind of pluralism, because parochialism is all there is. We all live in our specificities; but this specificity, this parochialism, the enormous power of one's origins, does not quash the possibility of individual expression. By delving deep into one's inherited resources, by absorbing and being absorbed by one's tradition, Herder believed that a person can hope to gain some relationship with transcendent ideas. We already possess what we need for our highest purposes.

By recognizing the richness in specificity, Herder secured his nationalism against chauvinism, because the specificities are everywhere: all cultures are equally authentic and equally rewarding. Whereas he believed that all cultures are incommensurate from one another, he did not mistake incommensurability for inequality. Herder did not argue for the superiority of any one culture, or that a member of one culture cannot esteem an alien one (though some of his intellectual heirs did). Appreciation for the uniqueness of one's own form of life inculcates an appreciation for other forms of life. Since one judges one's own culture against its own standards, one learns not to judge a different culture according to one's own standards. Membership in a specific group teaches us about membership generally, and so the member of one group who does not respect the particularities of another group is a hypocrite. (In this spirit, we might say also that a cosmopolitan with no love for her own country cannot really love all countries.)

Yet there is something ironic, or worse, about Herder's love of the many. It teaches respect across the borders, but it hardens the borders. It is deeply centripetal, and suspicious of travel. Its celebration of difference ordains that we stay with our own. There are many lanes, but we each take only one

The Pluralist Heart

of them. This thinker who wanted us all to acknowledge the worth of every system did not encourage us to investigate any system but our own. This is a decidedly unadventurous pluralism, which prefers authenticity to curiosity. It precludes the possibility of escape, of seduction, of conversion, even of understanding anything foreign. Differences are universal but there is no universalism. Since we are not poor, none of us, we should make do with our own resources, each of us.

In Herder's view, human life is pluralistic but human experience, individual experience, is not. Surely this is a stunted and inaccurate account. Is the multiplicity of traditions and cultures only something we know about and revere, but do not sample and explore? Of course not. If this were true, any attempt to understand an alien culture, let alone to adopt one, would be impossible. We would all be trapped in our particular idioms, like the punishment at Babel. But the punishment at Babel failed: there are overlaps, there are bridges, there are translations, there are mobilities. Take Herder's view of the genesis of ideas. In truth they do not grow like plants in the desert. They travel. They are refined and developed and applied far away from where they are born. Indeed, their birthplace may be the most trivial fact about them; and this may be true of people, too.

History offers many examples. Consider the American, French, and Haitian revolutions, beginning in 1775, 1789, and 1792, which were like ideological dominos, one following the other despite an ocean of water and cultural and linguistic differences. The idea of political liberty did not belong to any one of these revolutions, because ideas do not belong to anybody. All of these movements borrowed and altered a group of concepts, and changed the way that the previous champions of the concepts understood them. The Haitian

318

revolution naturally inflamed the question of slavery in the United States, underscoring the irony that Americans continued to deprive their own people of the freedoms in the name of which the American revolution had been fought. A concept, no matter where it comes from, can be better honored by strangers than those who earlier articulated it. The same lesson has been reinforced by recent history: the greatest championing of the American kind of freedom occurred not by Americans on American soil, but by the citizens of Hong Kong waving the American flag in their streets in protest against the most powerful and nefarious contemporary enemy of that symbol. The people of Hong Kong recognized themselves not in Donald Trump's America, but in the American heroes of 1776. Likewise, the American revolutionaries of the eighteenth century should have recognized themselves in the early days of the French Revolution, as Haitians did.

Of course not all loyalties are freely chosen; nobody entirely invents herself. Inherited loyalties should not be rejected merely because they are inherited. We do, all of us, in every group, inherit wisdoms. And often one discovers oneself already inside. Family, country, language, culture: these things are not less precious, when they are precious, because they were not freely chosen. But equally precious are the stimulations from outside. Is learning another language leaving one's lane? And if it is, so what? Is it treasonous to conclude that the philosophy of somebody else's ancestors is right, or better for oneself? What culture ever developed without cross-fertilizations from other cultures? Does coming from somewhere demand going nowhere?

Everywhere in human life there are crossings, conversions, and migrations. A convert or an immigrant chooses her loyalties in a way that a born member does not, and so her identity has its own authenticity. Religions have always found converts spiritually glamorous (converts in, not converts out), and Americans, though not recently, have felt the same way about immigrants. A lonely soul — authenticity is no guarantee against loneliness — might wander into a church or a synagogue or a mosque or a classroom or a meeting hall in search of a philosophy or a community, and she might find it there, and good for her.

Taking multiplicity seriously is not easy. In a pluralist society, the individual begins with at least two loyalties: to her square in the quilt and to the quilt itself. (Without the quilt there is no square.) But this is just the beginning of her heart's trajectory. What happens when she is exposed to the other squares? Members of our own pluralist society often dread this possibility. They think that their responsibility as citizens is to ensure that the state secures their square as much freedom and support as possible, and that the society flourishes best when each of its composite parts retreats inwards towards their kin. But this is not pluralism, it is Balkanization. Genuinely pluralistic living is unsettling for the nomadic impulse in all of us. It may quash that impulse or it may encourage it.

Living in multiplicity is made up of unexpected challenges and inescapable influences and conflicting (or at least many) loyalties. Most of the time the unsettledness of living with conflicting loyalties will offer a healthy challenge, oxygen from our different settings, the distance to evaluate our own biases with a modicum of objectivity. But sometimes the freedom and the variety will be grueling. There will inevitably be moments when one will have to choose one loyalty over another. Camus publicly grappled with a challenge of this sort when, in 1957, after the ceremony in which he was awarded the Nobel Prize in literature, he remarked: "People are now planting bombs in the tramways of Algiers. My mother might be on one of those tramways. If that is justice then I prefer my mother." (There are many versions of this story, but I take it from the careful appendix to Alice Kaplan's edition of Camus' *Algerian Chronicles*.) He had many commitments and many identities, and while he rejected none of them he still had to choose; and with fortitude, immediately, without a nervous attempt to justify it with what Bernard Williams would have called "one thought too many," he made his choice. Every person who lives at the nexus of many loyalties will have moments of this kind, if much less melodramatic ones.

Ideas and the other equipment of the spirit are not owned by people. It sounds silly to have to say, but it does bear saying now, that when I am captivated by an element of a foreign culture, so that I study it and reflect its influence in the work that I do, I am not stealing it, because it is much bigger than its provenance. The same is true of someone who is exercised by, and adopts an element of, my ancestral culture. I thank them for their interest. The calculus of gain and loss is the inverse of the one described in the Shakespearean speech: he enriches himself and does not make me poorer. No one was ever impoverished by being emulated. An idea only grows in influence and sophistication when it travels. If something is true in Chinese, it is also true in Arabic. If a concept was first expressed in English, does that mean non-English speakers can never understand it? Is democracy "Western," and if it is "Western," as the post-colonial critics say it is, then are non-Western democrats guilty of cultural appropriation? It is nothing but an expression of respect when a people translates a foreign literature into their language; there are many cultures that date a revolution in their literature to the first translations of Shakespeare into their to native tongues. Was Langston Hughes out of his lane when he wrote sonnets? And readers of all genders continue to learn from Flaubert and Tolstoy what it is like to be a woman.

It is the solemn duty of every citizen, particularly those of a multicultural and multiethnic society, to leave her lane, temporarily or even permanently if she wishes. Nobody can understand the world, or respect what is not familiar to her, while confined to her own lane. This is the lasting imperative of the pluralist heart.

LEON WIESELTIER

Where Are the Americans?

They are begging us, you see, in their wordless way,
To do something, to speak on their behalf
Or at least not to close the door again.

DEREK MAHON

In foreign policy, the remedial efforts of the new administration, the post-Caligula administration may come down to this: the position of the United States in the world must be restored, *but not too much*. Sometimes, when people speak of all the damage that Biden must undo, they talk about giving us a fresh start by getting us back to zero. But zero is zero; and nobody in their right mind, in the terrifying social and economic crisis in which we have been living, would propose zero, a return to 2016, as the proper objective of domestic policy. In social and economic policy we must be ambitious, monumental, transformative, and finally translate the humaneness that we profess into laws and programs and institutions; we must assist and even rescue the weak and wounded millions in our midst. But the Rooseveltian moment is to be confined to our shores. Abroad, I fear, we will rescue nobody. We will be only national humanitarians. We are resolved to "repair our repaired alliances," as we should — but this leaves the larger question of what we are to accomplish with our alliances, what we and our allies are to do in the world together. We are similarly resolved to "restore American leadership," but we are also haunted by the prospect of genuine American leadership, grand leadership, leadership with power as well as politesse, unpopular but persuasive leadership, not least because we have distorted the modern history of American leadership into an ugly story, a sordid and simple tale of imperialism and exploitation, which is a calumny that will cripple us for the conflicts that are on their way, and are already here.

One of the reasons that a return to 2016 will not suffice to recuperate our foreign policy is that the wayward course of the United States, its choice to abdicate global preeminence and to withdraw from decisive historical action, did not begin in 2016. We have been living contentedly in our shrunken version, in an increasingly Hobbesian world, in this springtime for Hitlers, for a dozen years. When historians record the history of American foreign policy in this century, they will be struck by the continuities between the Obama administration and the Trump administration, and thereby discomfit (I hope) many people. There are some differences, of course. Obama's diplomatic diffidence was sold suavely, like everything he sells: an emotionally exquisite realism, a tender-hearted hard-heartedness, Brent Scowcroft's policies with Elie Wiesel's words. It was not, as in the case of Trump, animated by anything as coarse and candidly indifferent as

America First, but in practice the callousness was the same. In the Obama era, no country, no ally, no democratic rebellion or dissident movement, no cleansed or genocidally attacked population, could count on America. (There was another difference: Trump, a swindler who hated to be swindled, at least got China right. The good news is that Biden appears to have noticed.) In 2016, in a radio interview, David Remnick, a wholly owned subsidiary of Obama, remarked to Ben Rhodes, another wholly owned subsidiary of Obama, that the president was "asking the American people to accept a tragic view of foreign policy and its limitations, and of life itself." And he added, unforgettably: "Sometimes a catastrophe is what we have to accept." What sagacity! But which catastrophes are the acceptable ones? So many atrocities, so little time. It takes a special kind of smugness, and politics, to be stoical about the sufferings of other people.

Insofar as the new Biden foreign policy apparatus is the old Obama foreign policy apparatus — are they now the Blob? — there is reason to worry that their former leader's aversion to conflict, and his soulful patience with the anguish of others, will live on in a busy cosmopolitanism that mistakes itself for a robust internationalism — a genial, worldly, multi-lingual era of good feelings and recovered sanities that will still offer no serious impediment to the designs of rivals and villains. We will soon see how far the return of truth to government will reverse the isolationist foreign policy that was developed during government's recent adventures with falsehood. Returning from Trump to Obama will not suffice. They knew the truth in the Obama White House, they knew the facts, but it set nobody free.

Those who are pleased by the reduction of America's position in the world like to say that America should lead

325

not by power but by example. It is a clever argument, in that it imposes no obligations upon us other than to be ourselves, which is always the laziest imperative of all. Unfortunately for those who recommend this historical leisure, this self-congratulatory lethargy, the City on the Hill is presently in ruins. Who on earth would want to be us now? I exaggerate, of course: we never were Weimar America, and we sent our orange strongman packing, and our Constitution held; but we are miserable. Even in the good times, there was nothing terribly helpful, it was even a little insulting, to say to the wretched of the earth, be like us. The only way any of them could be like us was to fight their own fights, in their own communities and in their own cultures, for the opening of their societies, ideally with the expectation that the United States would be there to assist them in their struggle for their particular inflection of the universal value of freedom. There was also another way in which they could be like us: they could come here and join their democratic and economic appetites with ours, which is why we should regard immigration as the definitive way of taking America's promise seriously; but on immigration, too, we lost our footing years ago, and are a haven no more.

How can we lead by example if we are not exceptional? But it is the people who despise the idea of American exceptionalism who insist that our example is our only claim to global authority. Their implication is that until we have justice at home, we cannot take an interest in justice abroad. We may as well inform the Uighurs and the Syrians and the Rohingya and the astonishing citizens of Hong Kong that they must wait forever. The worst example of such reasoning — it is one of the most outrageous sentences I have ever read — was Simone Weil's observation that as long as France had colonies it had no moral authority to fight Hitler. As if ethical action is the duty only of saints. But the struggle for justice, at home and abroad, is always the work of sinners, whose introspection is supposed to catalyze, not paralyze, them. No, there is only one way to win the friendship of people beyond our borders, and it is to help people beyond our borders. We can be big in the world by doing good in the world. Lacking bigness or goodness, we (and not only we) are doomed.

I will be accused, at the very least, of a lack of irony. Don't I know about the innocent blood spilled in the just wars? What about the interventions that went wrong? What about the infringements of sovereignty, that most hallowed of Westphalian principles? And the cocky way I am using that word "good" — good according to whom? These are fine and urgent questions. Naivete is especially unpardonable in discussions of power. Idealists have a special obligation to attend to considerations of costs and benefits; otherwise, as the Latin adage about doing justice warns, the world may perish for their stubbornness. Moreover, the rhetoric of political virtue, of enlightenment and liberation and democracy, was long ago appropriated by modernity's monsters: they, too, use moral language, words like "good."

But there are no perfect Westphalians: interests of state have regularly over-ruled the inviolability of states, often for shabby reasons. There is something grotesque about living with immoral and amoral transgressions against the state system but drawing the line at the moral ones. All these historical and philosophical complications persuade me only that we should be intellectually scrupulous, not that we should be practically feckless. The shoals of relativism, the taunts of epistemology, the consistencies of pacifism, pale before the sufferings of individuals and peoples. Their pain is overwhelmingly actual. Its facticity is almost stupefying. I have been reading a beautiful old essay by Ignazio Silone called "The Choice of Comrades," where I find this: "It is a matter of personal honor to keep faith with those who are being persecuted for their love of freedom and justice. This keeping faith is a better rule than any abstract program or formula. In this age of ours, it is the real touchstone." Pretty unsophisticated, no?

It is now a terrible anniversary. It has been ten years since the beginning of the first great disgrace of the twenty-first century. I am referring to the Syrian catastrophe. Except for the dead and the raped and the tortured and the exiled, except for the refugees and the survivors, the dust seems to have settled for everyone else, and so it seems time for Americans to do what Americans do best: move on. Anyway, what can we do? The democratic rebellion in Syria that began in Dara'a in April, 2011 was defeated. It was successfully transformed into an ethnic and religious conflict, the direst kind of contemporary war, by the tyrant Bashar al-Assad, who proceeded to destroy his own country and bomb his own people and, when his weakness was showing, deliver his state to the aggressions of the Iranians and their Hezbollah allies under the protection of the Russians, who rushed in where America feared to tread. This was a moral and strategic (look again at the map) failure of staggering proportions. It was a genocide and an invasion and a conquest. We chose to stand idly by, feeling bad and watching it. And the effects of our passivity were not confined to the borders of the ravaged land. As a consequence of the West having done nothing, so that the murderers met no resistance from outside, no force that could obstruct them, the stability of Lebanon and Jordan has been threatened, Turkey has embarked on a dark path, Russia has become a semi-demi-hemi-superpower, Iran has become a regional hegemon, the position of the United States in the world has plummeted, and fascists are coming to power in Europe. Not bad for nothing.

There are primal historical scenes that leave an indelible imprint upon one's sense of the world — one's expectations of it and one's obligations in it. When I was growing up, there were two such primal scenes, and they generated antithetical views of history and politics. The first was World War II, the second was Vietnam. All I needed to know about an individual was his or her primal scene, and the rest was easily filled in. There was post-war and there was anti-war. People who were postwar, who were imprinted by the effects of American power against fascism in Europe and Asia, and by the testimonies of the victims of totalitarianism who regarded American soldiers as saviors, had a large and admiring view of America's role in the world, and a verified confidence that American power could be used justly and for justice. Post-war was not pro-war, but it was prepared to use American force in the name of certain values and certain interests — and did, with good, bad, and mixed results. Vietnam, the subsequent primal scene, was supposed to have shattered that confidence, and anti-war people deplored American intentions and interventions, which they viewed as cynical projections of power for power's sake, and for money's sake too, and as nothing other than imperialism. These different outlooks were to some extent generationally determined, but not entirely; they were applied not only to the uses of American military power but also more generally to the level of American activism around the world and to the level of American preeminence in the world; and they may be described, if labels be needed, as liberalism and progressivism. (Biden is a post-war become an anti-war, I think.)

Now there are two new primal scenes, from which two corollaries of historical and strategic understanding similarly flow. The first is Iraq, the second is Syria. Iraq is Vietnam's successor in the foreign policy of progressives, the transgression from which there is no recovery, the obscene noun that silences all talk of American action. As Obama remarks in his memoir, "of course, I considered the invasion [of Iraq] to be as big a strategic blunder as the slide into Vietnam had been decades earlier." Iraq was the reason that we did not go into Syria. The poor Syrians had the misfortune of being exterminated after 2003. Their horrors came too late, when the United States was sunk in historical memory. I am not suggesting, of course, that American forgetfulness would have been preferable; only that the infamous lessons of Iraq are not as obvious as every person on every street corner in Washington seems to think.

I should confess immediately that I supported the Iraq war. I believed, on what I (and almost everybody except Scott Ritter) regarded as good authority, that Saddam Hussein possessed chemical and biological weapons, and since he had already used chemical weapons against the Kurds in Halabja in 1988, the question of his willingness to employ weapons of mass destruction was not a theoretical one. The use of such weapons, I continue to believe, and the threat of their use, constitutes a global moral emergency. When I realized that the assumption behind the invasion was wrong, that the dictator in Baghdad was bluffing his way to his own destruction, I promptly retracted my support, but I did so in a way that did not please the anti-wars. I wrote that the United States had been taken by its leaders into a major war on the basis of a mistake or a lie, and that this was a great historical scandal — but I expressed no regret about the overthrow of Saddam, and I continued to hope, not without evidence, that democratic progress could be made in the political openings that we — perhaps not by right, but in fact — were creating and supporting. I ardently hoped to see democracy in an Arab country. I was not surprised by the sectarian strife that was released by the collapse of the dictatorship, but this was a problem that Iraq, and other Muslim countries, would sooner or later have to face. In heterogeneous societies, tyranny is, among other things, a stop-gap measure, a deferment of the inevitable confrontation with the political challenges of difference and disharmony.

I certainly did not come away from the partial debacle in Iraq with the conviction that the United States was henceforth disqualified from international interventions. There were a number of reasons for this. For a start, there is no single event that explains everything, that is all we will ever need to know. Paradigms, and primal scenes too, enslave our thinking, and historical analogies are never precise. (During the Trump years, for example, we never had our Reichstag fire.) Those who forget history are sometimes condemned to repeat it and sometimes not; and those who remember history will know that it never slows down or stops, it offers no ellipses or time-outs, there is no interregnum between crisis and crisis in which we may calmly reflect and attend conferences before we act again. If ever we needed a respite from history, it was in 1945; but events in Europe and elsewhere did not allow it. (The isolationism of the 1930s, and America's unconscionably slow start in the defense of England and the other democracies, was owed to a similar exhaustion, and to vivid memories of a recent war.) It makes no sense, at least to me, to say that we could have halted the genocide and the occupation of Syria if only we had not intervened in Iraq. The relentlessness of history, and the eruption of evil, is always inconvenient. We are never adequately prepared for it, intellectually and materially, but there it is. If we should have intervened in Syria, we should have intervened in Syria.

There were many, of course, who did not agree that an intervention in Syria would have been justified. Obama never said so explicitly, but my obsessive study of his foreign policy led me to the conclusion that it was his belief that the United States has no right to make itself in any way responsible, directly or indirectly, for a significant change in another country. (In accordance with the anti-war account of American foreign policy, however, there were three exceptions to this quietism, three countries about which American guilt demanded American action: Vietnam, Cuba, and Iran.) There are many objections, historical and philosophical, that can be made to such a view. This debate must still be engaged. The Obama people, who in the Trump years swanned around like disappointed interventionists, argued that there was nothing, *nothing*, that we could have done in Syria, and eventually some of them bizarrely had algorithms made to settle the matter. But the important point is that we tried it their way, and it failed. Whereas we do not know what the outcome of American intervention in Syria would have been, we do know what the outcome of American non-intervention in Syria has been. Was sitting on our hands really worth it? We were disgusting. In the Obama years I had the honor of many visits from many Syrian friends who wanted to talk with me on their way to an appointment at the White House. I advised them all the same thing: tell the officials what you know about the situation on the ground, be useful to them, speak as eloquently as you can, appeal to

American ideals and American interests, and expect nothing.

If Iraq is now one primal scene, Syria is now the other. Syria is the cautionary tale about the stupendous consequences of inaction. Here is another heresy: I have no doubt that the costs of American action in Iraq have been much less than the costs of American inaction in Syria. Governments and peoples everywhere were watching. The governments learned that they can do whatever they wish to their peoples, and the peoples learned that America will not try hard, or at all, to stop their governments. The governments also learned that they could send their troops across borders with impunity, in campaigns of aggression that seize territory and disrupt states, as Iran did in Syria and elsewhere, and Russia did in Ukraine, and China is likely to do in Taiwan and the South China Sea. It is true that we do not have the power to determine the policies of other countries, but we do have the power to inhibit them and complicate them and thwart them. We have the power, *if we want it*. Anyway, we know all about the limits of American power: it is the foreign policy cliché of our era, our diplomatic catechism. The question before us is which limits to accept, and why. A limit is not a fate. In domestic policy, certainly, we are correctly enjoined to "go big," and never mind the warnings about what the economy will bear.

But how does the dispatch of American troops to another country differ from the Russian dispatch of troops to another country? Are our actions acceptable because they are ours? Of course not. All interventions are not the same. We have sometimes abused our power abroad, and we have experienced legal and political and cultural reckonings with those abuses. What makes the difference, plainly, is the purpose. When, in the first Gulf War, we and our allies expelled Iraq's troops from Kuwait, we were upholding international law and coming to the assistance of an invaded country — but when James Baker, who was asked about the reasons for the war, said "jobs, jobs, jobs," he put a bit of a dent in its legitimacy. There is a commonly held view that an American presence is no longer welcome in the Muslim world after Iraq. I do not speak or read Arabic, and my evidence is journalistic and anecdotal, but I wonder. It cannot have been lost on many Muslims that most of America's military campaigns in recent decades were designed partly or wholly to assist Muslims — in Bosnia, in Kosovo, in Kuwait, in Afghanistan, in Libya, even in Iraq. (The Libyan campaign, though, was a model of how anti-interventionists intervene: the objective of the mission almost immediately became to end the mission, and we hastily left Libya to its hell.) Syrians, certainly, were desperate for American intervention; and the one night in ten years that I saw my Syrian friends happy was the night that Trump fired fifty-nine cruise missiles at a Syrian air base in retaliation for the Syrian regime's sarin attack on the village of Khan Sheykhoun. When I asked H.R. McMaster whether the American operation represented a new policy of engagement or a Tweet with missiles, I angered him; but alas, it was a Tweet with missiles.

People who need help usually welcome help. They do not ask to see the ideological credentials of those who have come to save their lives. The credentials game is the sanctimonious pastime of those who are not in need of rescue — the American left, for example, which had nothing at all to offer the Syrians, or the Ukrainians. The journals of the American left have established a strange intellectual ritual about human-rights emergencies: they report on them in plangent detail and then deplore any suggestion that we might actually do something to alleviate them. They deify dissidents and their hearts break for the women and the children, and then the ideological prohibitions kick in. In this planet of horrors nothing horrifies them more than the prospect of an American soldier somewhere. It suits many Americans to believe that for the rest of the world we are still the ugly Americans, since the subject of intervention is moot if we are not wanted.

We certainly should not go anywhere as conquerors or occupiers, but there may be justifications for an American military presence that have nothing to do with conquest or occupation. We must always be respectful of the "local dynamics," though there will be occasions when the "local dynamics" are precisely what bring us to a faraway place. But when there is an earthquake in Haiti or a nuclear accident in Japan or an invasion in Ukraine or a genocide in the Balkans or a plague in Liberia, the broken countries generally, and correctly, look to us. We are not the cops of the world, but we do not turn our backs, at least not always. Right now we are hardly in danger of doing too much. This has been a golden age of too little. Soon, if we do not recover our sense of our historical role, the imperiled of the world, and the prudent, will start looking to China. (They will discover the original meaning of attached strings.) During the Obama years, when friends would return from trips abroad and offer reports over drinks, a pattern began to emerge from their observations. Wherever they went, to Europe, the Middle East, South Asia, Japan, or Latin America, in meetings with officials and journalists and politicians and bankers, they were asked the same question — a question there was no need to ask during the Trump years because its answer was repulsively self-evident. The question that hounded them everywhere was, Where are the Americans?

"O to be discussing this *face à face* (or *mano a mano*, in this case) outside Kramer books with a stiff drink. Our last conversation there was really memorable." So wrote a cherished friend not long ago, a man of strong intellect and immense learning, a steadfast liberal. He was right: we needed a long and rigorous conversation. The situation called for a café. We had been corresponding about the question of interventionism, about Syria and Iraq, about what the new administration's foreign policy should be. We disagreed. Our moral and philosophical premises were the same, but he was shaken by my stubborn confidence that American force could still be used in service to those premises. "Are you not at all chastened by the damage such confidence has caused over the past two decades?" In fact I believe that the "damage" is not remotely the whole story, that the results have been decidedly mixed; and in this vale of tears I cannot scant mixed results. "We *and* the Syrians," my friend wrote, not at all complacently or triumphantly, "are paying the price for the Iraq folly." As a factual matter, he was right.

And then he expressed another objection, an exceedingly interesting one. "This is not a moral disagreement," he explained. "What I object to is the reflex to transform political problems into moments of moral self-revelation and self-definition — Malraux moments. 'Here I stand" — yes, yes, I know, but sometimes you need to stand over there and pipe down." About not piping down, I plead guilty as charged, though I fail to see why the other side should not also stifle its ringing certainties. But in these debates I do not really mind the noise: the stakes justify some heat, which hopefully will be generated by some light. "For Zion's sake I will not hold my peace," the prophet Isaiah proclaimed. Elsewhere in his letter my friend had indeed impugned me for speaking not liberally but prophetically. And Isaiah's proclamation may indeed be described as a Malraux moment.

I understood what my friend meant by this notion. André Malraux was many things, but one of them was a grand self-mythologizer who, from the 1920s to the 1940s, valiantly but also narcissistically, hopped from world-historical crisis to world-historical crisis — China, Cambodia, Spain, Nazi-occupied France — an intellectual who dreamed of being a man of action, turning his participation in those cataclysms into an epic of self-description, and into novels. If he was a hero, it was not least in his own eyes. I had noticed long ago, in others as well as in myself, the grandiloquence that sometimes results from high moral arguments, the way that impassioned participation in a war of ideas can be confused with another variety of historical participation, the inflation of the self that comes from a certain intensity of commitment. (In 2002, during the debates about al-Qaeda and Iraq, Christopher Hitchens, with whom I stood shoulder to shoulder at least on these questions, declared: "You want to be a martyr? I'm here to help." I remember thinking that his self-conception had crossed the line.) The prophetic feeling is a nice feeling, especially in a land where prophets pay no price.

"Liberalism," my friend continued, "should teach an art, or at least see the need for an art, of discerning when a fundamental moral issue is at stake and when it is not." This is liberalism as a mentality, not as a doctrine. At the café I would have retorted that if intervention to stop a genocide, or to assist a democratic rebellion, is not a fundamental moral issue, I don't know what is. But his charge of Malrauxism stays with me. He is on to something. Foreign policy must not be a form of self-expression. It must not be, as Americans like to say, about us. When we act abroad, it should not be to confirm a flattering picture of ourselves, or to furnish a sensation of our own rectitude. This is in part because statecraft should be a profoundly empirical activity, based on a sober evaluation of threats and opportunities — on an analytical disinterestedness without which our promotion of our values and our pursuit of our interests may become a menace to the world. The delusions of statesmen have murdered many millions of people.

Yet my friend's warning against Malrauxism provoked me to another conclusion, which he will find perverse in the context of his prescriptions for caution. It is this: that there are circumstances in which our foreign policy, if it is not to be about us, must be about others. I do not mean only that diplomacy and strategy are always to some extent reactive, in that we do not have the capacity to determine all by ourselves, in our own time, based on our own preferences and our own moods, whether a crisis represents, say, a "new cold war." There is always the not insignificant factor of the behavior of other states, inside and outside their borders. When I say that our foreign policy must sometimes be about others, I mean also something more radical, more swift, more humanistic, more exercised by peoples than by governments: that there are times when we must take action because of the needs of others.

The needs of others: we must agree to be distracted and quickened by their plight. They cannot be neglected because we are still discussing humility and hubris. We must be prepared to pause, to look up from the ordinary practices of international relations, for the purpose of support and rescue. People who are not citizens of a country sometimes have a legitimate claim on its power. In the case of refugees, for example, Kant recognized a "cosmopolitan right" that he called "universal hospitality," which was eventually codified in the Refugee Convention of 1951. "We are concerned here not with philanthropy," he sternly wrote, "but with right." In this instance, the rights of strangers impose an obligation upon us. Do people who are being tortured, raped, thrown into concentration camps, and slaughtered so as to erase their identity from the face of the earth — do they have a right to demand that we come to their assistance and even liberate them? Maybe not, but it should not matter. They have a claim on our sympathy, and sympathy is cynical, vain, with no relation to conscience, unless one acts upon it. (There are many kinds and degrees of action: Iraq is hardly the model.)

By what right do we help them? It is the wrong question. The right one is, by what right do we abandon them? On certain occasions humanitarian intervention will coincide with our interests, and there is of course the long-term reward of gaining the friendship of the people we help; but sometimes we should use our power only because it is the right thing to do. We had no interests that would have been served by intervening against the genocide in Rwanda, except for our interest in being able to look at ourselves in the mirror.

There are hard-boiled types who will scoff at all this, and dismiss it as altruistic, and mock it as not the way of the world. Well, so much the worse for the world. The world is the problem, not the solution. There is no shame in altruism, and when it practiced by a state, by a strong state, by a great power, it may even modify international norms. It is certainly not inconsistent with the toughness that will be demanded of our leaders by the Great Game that has already begun to define this century. And it is certainly not the whole of foreign policy, though the less sentimental problem of world order will also require a new American emboldenment. The opposite of America First is not America Second. It is America in full, unafraid of history's pace, unembarrassed by its enthusiasm for democracy and human rights, larger than its mistakes and its crimes, comfortable with the assertion of its power in its own defense and in the defense of others, inspired by the memory of its magnitude, repelled by the rumors of its decline. Only we can bring us down and only we can lift us up, and not only us. "We fell victims to our faith in mankind," wrote Alexander Donat, a survivor of the ghettos and the concentration camps, "our belief that humanity had set limits to the degradation and prosecution of one's fellow man." There are already too many people in too many places who fell victim to their faith in America.

341

CONTRIBUTORS

GILLES KEPEL is the Middle East and Mediterranean Chair Professor at the Ecole Normale Supérieure in Paris and the author most recently of *Terror in France: the Rise of Jihad in the West* and *Away from Chaos: The Middle-East and the Challenge to the West*. This essay was translated by Henry Randolph.

INGRID ROWLAND is the author, among other books, of *From Pompeii: The Afterlife of a Roman Town*. She teaches at Notre Dame.

VLADIMIR KARA-MURZA is a Russian opposition politician and writer. He chairs the Boris Nemtsov Foundation for Freedom and serves as vice president at the Free Russia Foundation.

PAUL STARR is a professor of sociology and public affairs at Princeton University, and the author, most recently, of *Entrenchment: Wealth, Power and the Constitution of Democratic Societies*.

HENRI COLE is an American poet. *Blizzard*, his latest collection of poetry, was published last year.

BECCA ROTHFELD is a PhD candidate in philosophy at Harvard and a contributing editor at *The Point*.

ENRIQUE KRAUZE is a Mexican essayist, producer, and publisher. He is the author of many books and the founder of the magazine *Letras Libres*. This essay was translated by Thomas Bunstead.

WILLIAM DERESIEWICZ is the author of *Excellent Sheep* and, most recently, *The Death of the Artist*.

BENJAMIN MOSER is the author, among other books, of *Why This World: A Biography of Clarice Lispector* and *Sontag: Her Life and Work*.

CHAIM NACHMAN BIALIK, who was born in 1873 and died in 1934, was one of the giants of modern Hebrew poetry and one of the founders of modern Jewish culture. This translation is dedicated to Allan Nadler.

DAVID NIRENBERG is the Dean of the Divinity School of the University of Chicago.

AGNES CALLARD is a professor of philosophy at the University of Chicago.

MITCHELL ABIDOR is a writer and translator, most recently of Victor Serge's *Notebooks 1936-1947*.

PETER PHILLIPS is a choral conductor, a musicologist, and the founder of The Tallis Scholars.

PAUL MULDOON is an Irish poet. His most recent book is *Frolic and Detour*.

DAVID THOMSON's new books *A Light in the Darkness: A History of Movie Directors* and *Disaster Mon Amour* will be published this year.

CELESTE MARCUS is the managing editor of Liberties.

LEON WIESELTIER is the editor of Liberties.

Liberties — A Journal of Culture and Politics is available by annual subscription and by individual purchase from bookstores and online booksellers.

Annual subscriptions, which offer a discount from the individual cover price, can be ordered from libertiesjournal.com. Gift subscriptions are also available.

In addition to the regular subscription discount price, special discounts are available for: active military; faculty, students, and education administrators; government employees; and, those working in the not-for-profit sector at libertiesjournal.com.

Liberties — A Journal of Culture and Politics is distributed to booksellers in the United States by Publishers Group West; in Canada by Publishers Group Canada; and, internationally by Ingram Publisher Services International.

Liberties, a Journal of Culture and Politics, is published quarterly in Fall, Winter, Spring, and Summer by Liberties Journal Foundation.

ISBN 978-1-7357187-2-9
ISSN 2692-3904

The insignia that appears throughout *Liberties* is derived from details in Botticelli's drawings for Dante's *Divine Comedy*, which were executed between 1480 and 1495.

ERRATA:
In the last issue of Liberties, on page 64, "Peter Serkin" should have been "Rudolf Serkin." We apologize for the error.